SHOOTING OURSELVES IN THE FOOT

SHOOTING OURSELVES IN THE FOOT

—

Bernard J. O'Keefe

BOSTON

HOUGHTON MIFFLIN COMPANY

1985

Library of Congress Cataloging in Publication Data

O'Keefe, Bernard J.
Shooting ourselves in the foot.
1. United States — Economic conditions. 2. United States — Industries — History. 3. United States — Politics and government — 19th century. 4. United States — Politics and government — 20th century. 5. Competition, International. I. Title.
HC103.O44   1985   330.973′092   85-7651
ISBN 0-395-38511-3

Printed in the United States of America

V 10 9 8 7 6 5 4 3 2 1

Contents

SHOOTING OURSELVES IN THE FOOT

—

1

The Ming Mentality

THE CHINESE write funny. Instead of using alphabets like sensible people do, they draw pictures like they didn't know how to write. Some of these pictures are simple, but very descriptive. The Chinese designation for the mother country is 中, Chung (kuo), which means the Middle Country, or, more broadly, the Center of the Universe. The Chinese have always been centrally oriented, with their eastern agricultural lowlands bordered by the arid Siberian steppes and the inhospitable Tibetan mountain ranges. Their early cultural development roughly kept pace with the cultures in the other great river-valley civilizations of Egypt, Babylonia, and the Indus Valley, forging ahead in some aspects, like pottery manufacture, falling behind in others, like the use of bronze.

It was not artisanship, but philosophy that made China unique among nations. Historically, the country had its quota of rulers and warlords, with successions of individual emperors extending into dynasties lasting hundreds of years. The first

1

great philosopher, Confucius, was born about twenty-five hundred years ago, during the Chou dynasty. Confucius taught no religion, preached of no God, promised no afterlife; he spoke of the dignity of the individual and the necessity to work together for society and good government. He emphasized education, rules of conduct, public service, and respect for authority. The Confucian concept led to the emergence of a civil service that was perpetuated independently of the emperors who came and went over the ages. A couple of centuries later, Taoism, a second philosophy, emerged, partly as a reaction to the organized concepts of Confucianism. The ideal Taoist is a person who avoids conventional social obligations and leads a simple, spontaneous, and contemplative life close to nature.

The Chinese philosopher prospered. He had it made. He could go several ways. As a Confucianist, he could go to work for the government; there, he could develop the martial arts of map making and wall building, the agricultural techniques of reaping and irrigation, the scribal skills of record keeping, or the legal intricacies of rule making. (If he aspired to be a comedian, he had available an infinite number of one-liners beginning: "Confucius say . . .") As a Taoist, he could become a poet, a painter, a pottery maker, or practice the priestly arts of the many coexisting religions. Remarkably tolerant, the two philosophies coalesced about twenty-two hundred years ago, during the Ch'in dynasty, whence the Occidental name China.

From then on there developed the artistically tolerant but bureaucratic type of government that was to characterize the history of the middle country. Weights and measures were standardized. Roads and canals were built. The several great walls, built by successive emperors to keep the nomads out and to keep the farmers in, were connected into a single Great

Wall of China, the only artifact of man's ingenuity that can be recognized from outer space. Gunpowder was invented. Paper making was developed. As the Western nations sank into the murk of the Dark Ages, the continuity of the middle country's Confucian civil service maintained the momentum of technical and artistic progress during the first millennium of the Christian era and absorbed without turmoil the conflicting tenets of the great religions that filtered across her borders, from Buddhism to Christianity to Islam.

While the West alternately battled and slumbered, the middle country artisans improved the techniques of printing and paper making to retain the cumulative knowledge of the successive emperors; they interwove the skills of poetry and painting and calligraphy into an art form unsurpassed to this day; they developed distinctive schools of architecture, theater, and music; they perfected the touch of the potter into delicate, colorful ceramics, culminating in the translucence of fine white porcelain; they finished the Great Canal; they built the first astronomical clock. The country was truly the world's center of art, science, and culture.

During that millennium occasional merchants and missionaries wandered across the mountains or the steppes, returning with elaborate tales of the wonders and the mysteries of the Eastern Kingdom of Cathay, but there was no reciprocal travel; the philosophers of the middle kingdom had no more interest or curiosity about the barbarians of the West than the sages of ancient Greece would have had about the Bantu or the Bushmen of darkest Africa.

At the beginning of the thirteenth century, the relative tranquillity of the dynastic successions was shattered. A group of nomadic tribes from Manchuria, Mongolia, and Siberia was forged by a Mongol who was to be known as Genghis Khan into an efficient fighting machine not seen since the early days of the Roman Empire. This ruthless, ambitious military genius conquered northern Asia before turning his hordes south, west, and east to India, eastern Europe, and China. He conquered Russia, Persia, much of Arabia, and reached the gates of Constantinople before turning east to overthrow the Ch'in dynasty in 1215. His son laid waste a large part of Hungary and Poland and threatened the civilization of western Europe. His grandson, the Kublai Khan, completed the conquest of China and founded the Yüan dynasty, which ruled the middle kingdom for a hundred years.

Although the Mongols were considered ruthless barbarians by the conquered countries, they proved quite tolerant to all religions and nationalities once the conquest was complete. Under Kublai Khan, travel was opened up throughout the empire, freeing the exchange of merchandise and ideas between East and West, leading to the fabulous wanderings of Marco Polo and his relatives. East-West trade flourished by land and sea.

The Mongols were good soldiers but not very good administrators. They were unable to organize a loyal civil service, and their finances were in constant disarray. Secret societies grew up to expel the hated barbarians, and through a series of revolts, the last Mongol emperor was overthrown in 1382.

The Chinese character for the sun is 日 . The character for the moon is 月 . The two combined, 明 , are pronounced ming, signifying brilliance, brightness, or enlightenment. The new dynasty chose that name, Ming, the brilliant, enlightened dynasty, the center of civilization and knowledge.

Once in power, the new rulers expelled from their midst all elements of the despised barbarian Mongols, slamming down for centuries to come an Iron Curtain on the land routes between East and West, keeping open only the seaports they could control. But the Mings, like the hundreds of mandarins who preceded them, had a mentality of superiority that could not be suppressed. They were the center of the universe, and all the world must know it. Under controlled conditions, they allowed delegations from less enlightened nations to visit their centers of civilization so that these nations might sip of the cup of knowledge and bring back to their less fortunate rulers the rudiments of culture and technology. The Japanese sent two official delegations — as the Japanese are wont to do — to absorb the Chinese ideographs and impose them on a language of an entirely different background. As a result, the Japanese language is a hodgepodge of Chinese Kanji and native syllabic alphabets. It is still possible to distinguish the periods at which the particular Chinese characters were borrowed. Others came to pay homage or bring tribute or seek protection or military assistance.

As the Ming emperors, isolated and freed from the taint and dominance of the Mongols and the West, prospered, they became more aloof, more secluded, more removed from the people and the civil service, more dependent on the small group of advisers who constituted the palace guard. The insiders chafed at the isolation, anxious to demonstrate to the world the glories of the empire. The third Ming emperor, Yung Lo, was persuaded to send out naval expeditions that carried messages of his grandeur into all the surrounding seas. These expeditions, from 1405 to 1433, the vastest until then seen on our planet, enlisted some thirty-seven thousand in their crews, in flotillas as large as 317 ships. They roamed the western Pacific; they covered the Indian Ocean; they explored the Straits of Hormuz; they cruised the west coast of Africa. They had the technical capacity to circle the African continent and sail to Europe as well, but they didn't — there was nothing there to interest them. All this while Prince Henry of Portugal was just getting his feet wet and Columbus had not been born.

These flotillas sought no tribute, brought back no slaves, committed no atrocities. On the contrary, they brought gifts, handed out gold and silver, gave technical assistance when requested. It was a medieval Marshall Plan, one to seek peace and gain approval, not by exacting tribute but by distributing largess to the backward and the less fortunate. They did not stoop to conquer.

Suddenly a new emperor, one more attuned to the messages of the civil servants and the bureaucracy, came into power. They persuaded him to look inward, not outward — that the infrastructure and the environment were more important than exploration. They persuaded him that the middle country culture and technology were superior, requiring no outside influence. They persuaded him that the quality of life, not progress, was the ideal. They persuaded him that the arts and the humanities were the overriding national priority, that the pursuit of the sciences was beneath his dignity. Most important, they persuaded him to redirect his resources to the administrators of the capital city, who would oversee this cultural redirection. There was, of course, no need for civil servants on sailing ships.

In 1433 the Iron Curtain clanged down on the sailing ships as it had previously on land voyages; the flotilla was called home. A series of imperial edicts followed, imposing increasingly savage punishments on Chinese who ventured abroad. Within a few years "there was not an inch of planking on the sea." The Great Withdrawal had begun.

Chinese reclusiveness was an old story, symbolized by the isolation of the Great Wall. There had always been a feeling of self-sufficiency, of superiority. But the Ming emperors developed it to its quintessence. They were the Sons of Heaven, the Enlightened, supreme rulers and superiors over all people on earth. The monopoly mentality, the mandarin mentality, became a unique Ming mentality, a national arrogance that disparaged all cultures and concepts but their own.

To their credit, they also developed magnificent works of art, but art is not a social structure that can stand alone; rather, it is an expression of the culture of a society. The outstanding cultural achievement of the period was the accumulation of all knowledge into an encyclopedia of 11,095 chapters, a two-hundred-year task completed by the great philosopher Ku Yen-Wu. This collection of the wisdom of the Ming world is contrasted by Joseph Needham with the renaissance of the humanities and the scientific and economic development in Europe at about the same time.

> Four years before Ku Yen-Wu was born, Galileo had invented his telescope and Kepler was publishing his new laws of the movements of the planets. While Ku reconstructed his archaic pronunciations, Harvey had published his work on the circulation of the blood, and Galileo his two great works on astronomy and the new science. Eleven years before the beginning of the critical study on history, Torricelli had completed his great experiment on the pressure of air. Shortly after, Boyle formulated the law that bears his name. The year before Ku completed his epoch-making philological studies, Newton had worked out his calculus and his analysis of white light. In 1680 Ku wrote his preface to the final texts of his philological works; in 1687, Newton published his *Principia*.*

The middle country maintained its Ming mentality for the three hundred years of the dynasty, continued in concept for

---

*Joseph Needham, *Science and Civilization in China* (New York: Cambridge University Press, 1965).

another three hundred years under the Manchus. The Ming mentality of superiority faded into a malaise, an inability to cope with external and internal pressures. China was a dying star, the brilliance of the early Ming years yellowing in the ineptitude of the Manchu dynasty, reddening under the embarrassment of eighteenth-century foreign exploitation, darkening with the corruptness of Chiang Kai-shek, and finally collapsing into the black hole that was the Cultural Revolution of Mao Tse-tung.

In modern society events move much faster. Its mind-boggling aspect is the compression of time. A journey of a hundred days is compressed into a few hours. The description of a battle that might have taken weeks to write is captured by the television camera in a few seconds. The lowest resolvable unit of time, which might once have been a second, is now a millionth of a second, or maybe a millionth of that. Political and cultural changes that might have taken the centuries of a dynasty now develop in a fraction of a lifetime.

History is yesterday. Tomorrow is a hundred years away. With all our ability to mass communicate, with our capacity to collect information suffocating in its complexity, it is as difficult as ever to analyze our actions and react in time to modify our behavior. It is not easy to remember back to the last president. It is terrifying to realize that the present one, responding to the threat of world annihilation, may have only minutes to instruct the computer. Time has suffered a sort of relativistic compression. The Latin doggerel of childhood runs through my mind: "Tempus fugit, non cum backibus."

We Americans have come suddenly, reluctantly, and late onto the stage of greatness. We didn't ask for it. We weren't prepared for it. A century ago we were an agrarian nation, country bumpkins to the sophisticated Europeans, licking our wounds from a divisive Civil War, looking wide-eyed from afar at the turmoil of the Industrial Revolution. We cut our international teeth on the First World War, stepping in late to "save the world for democracy." Disillusioned, we lapsed back into isolationism and suffered a Great Depression, learning too late that the world had already begun to shrink. We were pressed on either side by tyranny and aggression, slowly coming to the conclusion that our oceanic barriers were quickly drying up, and it took only the spark of Pearl Harbor to release the latent energy that would lead us to world domination in three and one-half years, a blink of an historian's eye.

Like all collective nouns, the word *American* covers a variety of contrasting qualities. We are at once generous and greedy, hospitable and hostile, unassuming and arrogant, visionary and obtuse. Our first forefathers came mostly from the British Isles and northern Europe, not for plunder and suppression as did Spain and Portugal to the south, but for freedom and relief from oppression. Yet the early Thanksgiving paintings show them generously offering to the Indians the grain grown on the farmland wrested from them and the birds shot on the Indians' very hunting fields. As we progressed across the continent, land was ceremoniously claimed in the name of queen, king, prince, deity, or democracy, depending on who was the employer of record, completely oblivious to the prior claims of the existing inhabitants. The Constitution was written by the most enlightened group of men ever attended by slaves; the West was won by adventurers who assumed they owned the place, with generations of moviegoers applauding the pillage of the populace who had the foolhardiness to stand in their way. We conquered a continent without even noticing that other people were already there.

We came to World War II with a cockiness born of misunderstanding. "Goodbye, dear, I'll be back in a year" —

none of us felt it would take that long, not thinking that we had no ships, no planes, no guns. Within two years we had the greatest armada the world had ever seen; another year and a half and it was all over. We were king of the hill.

There were 5 million men and women of the United States under arms in 1945, spread all over the world — most of whom had never been fifty miles from home in 1940. The picture we brought back was one of overwhelming U.S. superiority. From the Pacific we brought back the memory of little yellow men cowering at their temerity to have challenged the Colossus, from the Atlantic the image of trodden people, ally and foe alike, weary of the carnage, thankful for the deliverance. It was an image of children begging for candy, women available for cigarettes or simple sociability.

Inferior people or not, our hearts went out to them. There was no rape nor were there reparations; we set out to rebuild their countries and their lives. It was our finest hour. President Harry Truman's Marshall Plan was probably the most enlightened postwar policy in the history of mankind. It was reminiscent of the early Ming years when the treasure ships set out from the center of the universe to purchase peace through largess. Generous as it was, there was the underlying assumption of omnipotence, of superiority, of the Big Daddy. We developed a Marshall Plan mentality — we would rebuild the world, but on our terms, militarily, ethically, and morally. Rebuild it we did, and we called the shots. We were putting up the dough, so we did it our way.

It was a pretty good way. Within a decade, factories were rebuilt, elementary economies were restored, cities arose from the ashes. Our own civilian production capacity soared, first to meet the pent-up demands of our populace, then to fill the increasing wants of the rest of the world. Steel, copper, rubber, machine tools, automobiles, tractors, refrigerators, radios — the demand was insatiable. We became the new center of the universe, the new middle kingdom. American English became the language of the world in diplomacy, commerce, and communications. When the United Nations was organized, no one questioned that its headquarters should be in New York; Geneva and Paris were passé. When the world monetary system was revised, the meetings were held in the United States, at Bretton Woods, and the dollar was made the linchpin of world currency. Why not? None of the other currencies could buy anything anyhow. When other nations were unable to rebuild and simultaneously defend themselves against Russian expansionism, the United States became the policeman of the world, paying for it all both in dollars and in personnel.

Our institutions and techniques were admired and copied throughout the world. We knew best how to research, develop, invent, produce, sell, distribute; we knew how to plan, manage, finance, market; we knew how to educate, advertise, promote; we knew how to organize, administer, govern, fight. Others, particularly the Japanese and the Germans, flocked to our shores to learn our techniques, copy our methods. What everyone forgot is that we had a monopoly. Since none of our industries or our cities or our institutions had been destroyed, we were automatically the market leader, the efficient producer. We could do nothing wrong. We had solved the secrets of the sun in its thermonuclear fury, maintaining world dominance despite the Soviet threat. We had conquered outer space and put a man on the moon. We were the sun and the moon put together, the shining, brilliant example of excellence. We didn't have to search for excellence. We were it.

We entered our monopoly mentality. We had a monopoly on everything. Why worry about the rest of the world? We would sell to them if they insisted, but on our terms and our conditions. World trade was really a bother, with its silly kilometers and millimeters and liters, its driving on the wrong side of the road, its irritating voltages, which blew up our electric razors, its crazy worthless currencies, the yen and the lira. If the buyer was sensible, wanted to use feet and inches, drive on the right side of the road in miles per hour, use 110 volts, and pay in dollars, we'd sell. Otherwise, forget it. We had the biggest market domestically and nobody could lay a glove on us at home.

Monopolies are seldom self-sustaining. A free market need have no fear of them. Unless they are regulated or protected, they grow fat, slow, and lazy. Competitors nibble at the edges, pick the fattest cherries, introduce new techniques, work harder, sell stronger. Eventually the monopoly fades away in its inefficiency.

It began to happen to us. As the other nations grew stronger and wiser, our monopoly began to wane. First it was photographic equipment and specialty machinery from the engineering skills of the Germans; then a trickle of automobiles from Europe, shoes from Italy, textiles from the Orient. Then it was electronic equipment from Japan — radios, televisions, record players. We told ourselves it didn't matter; foreign goods were of poor quality, tinny, they didn't stand up. We still had the top-of-the-line items, the capital goods, the things that counted. Besides, we were busy with our own affairs. We had wars to fight, the world to police, the quality of life to protect. We were looking at a bigger picture — the affluent society, the postindustrial society, the service economy. It wasn't what you made that was important, it was how you used it.

A generation grew up with constant reminders of the splendor of the emperor's new clothes, of the desirability of an environment in which those clothes could not be sullied, of

the ultimate fairness of a society in which each of us should
have a set as splendid as an emperor's. That generation developed its own mentality, the Ming mentality, a mentality
that envisioned a society in which we would all be emperors,
share and share alike. The argument was simple, generous,
noble, typically American, and, in retrospect, probably deserved a try.

We had developed a magnificent production machine, military and civilian. Let the armed forces police the rest of the
world, and let the main thrust of our society be directed
inward. We could produce enough to satisfy all of our wants;
why shouldn't all of us have what we wanted? Why should
we have poverty, why should we have inequality, why should
we have our environment sullied by smokestacks? If we had
to fight a war at the same time, why not? — as long as we
didn't have to go. We could afford it. Look at the record. We
already had the pie. The problem was how to slice it. With
a strong government commitment and enough civil servants,
went the Ming mentality, we could solve those problems.

Gone was the recollection of the Great Depression. That
was twenty years ago. Gone was the remembrance of the
isolated nation, unarmed and so lacking in spirit that the great
powers of the Axis deigned to declare war on it, unprovoked.
That was before our time.

The sentiments were noble and unassailable, but they ran
into the perversities of human nature. The poorest among us
were already wealthier than 90 percent of the world's inhabitants, a world that was coming closer and closer to compete
with us economically. It was contrary to the great American
tradition that a rising tide lifts all boats, that a larger pie
provides bigger slices for everyone, that more production provides more jobs, that redistribution could provide only a
partial answer. The other problem was that there are, unfor-

tunately, some people in this world who, when they don't have to work, won't. Then the bureaucracy kept getting in the way. The very people assigned to solve the problem soaked up the resources as effectively as any penurious employer. If all the money appropriated for the poor reached them, the poor would be well-to-do. Poverty program appropriations have averaged $25,000 per year per poor family. It is frustrating. The problem remains.

A great deal of progress was made on equal opportunity during the Ming years. The constitution guaranteed that all of us were created with the opportunity to be equal; the courts took the lead in enforcing that guarantee with results that were commendable or laggard, depending on whether you were guarantor or guarantee. Somewhere along the line, that program went off the track. Equality of opportunity became confused with equality of result, especially in education, where the skilled were restrained and made to mix with the mediocre. Quality and equality were equated. (That is an oxymoron, like military intelligence or congressional ethics.) Some of us are stronger, run faster, leap higher, learn easier, and work harder than others. That is an unfortunate fact of life; not even the mightiest Ming monarch can modify it. It is sad that in our compassion for the underprivileged, we can hold back the very sort of citizen who can best improve his or her lot.

So it is with our environment. As the world crowds in together, we must be concerned with the adverse effects of our proximity. But we can't all be Ming emperors, unsullied by the air and water around us. There must be some tradeoffs with the economy. When I was young, a smokestack meant jobs, not pollution. The smokestacks are disappearing, but so are the high-paying jobs that went with them. The poorest environment of all is poverty. The lungs may be clean, but the stomach will be empty.

The world kept crowding in around us. Fulfilling our self-appointed policeman's role, we tried to fight a war in southeast Asia. We ignored the lessons of history, which warned that a land war on that continent was unwinnable; our all-powerful self-delusion drove us on. When we could not win, we blamed it on our own will power, not geography. Reluctant to have it interfere with our Great Society, our Ming mentality chose both guns and butter, unleashing the greatest inflation in our history.

Our magnificent production machine was fueled by the slippery hydrocarbons of petroleum. When, in 1968, we became a net importer of oil, nobody noticed, or if they did, nobody gave a hoot. We controlled the Middle East. We had found the vast oil deposits. We had primary title to them. When the OPEC (Organization of Petroleum Exporting Countries) nations exercised control of their own resources and imposed an embargo, we could not believe that other nations could be so audacious. We castigated our own oil companies — it must be their fault.

Other nations began to challenge our supremacy. France broke off from NATO to handle its own defense. We watched helplessly as the Soviet Union built up its nuclear capability to equal ours. The Arabs raised oil prices to usurious levels; we paid for their oil with arms. Fidel Castro repeatedly spit in our eye. The final ignominy came from the American embassy with the nightly television taunts of the Ayatollah Khomeini's hooligans.

The Ming mentality metamorphosed into a "malaise," a dispirit foreign to the American soul. The voters called for a change, but all was not won. Control of the Great Society's inflation brought about a long recession and an enormous deficit to mortgage our future. The dollar exchange rate went out of whack, and the import trickle rose to a torrent.

We ignored the imports until we realized that they were not only cheaper but of better quality. The high-paying jobs in automobiles, steel, and rubber continued to disappear, the danger covered by a rush of lower-paying service jobs, which lowered the overall unemployment rate. There were pooh-poohs from the postindustrialists, the service economists, who looked toward a future of serving each other high-technology hamburgers, leaving hard goods production to the rest of the world. There were calls for industrial policies, a new euphemism for tariffs and protectionism. There were those who would emulate the Japanese model. But the problem won't go away, even if we learn to eat with chopsticks.

The world continues to shrink. We are in the midst of the economic redistribution that accompanies its constriction. This is an age of information. Wherever that information can be communicated, goods can be produced for distribution anywhere in the world. Three technological revolutions — one complete, one in process, and one just beginning — are accelerating this redistribution at breakneck speed.

The first technological revolution was in transportation. With the development of high-speed jet aircraft, it is now possible to travel quickly and comfortably to any of the developed or undeveloped countries of the world in less than twenty-four hours at reasonable cost.

The second is in information. Inexpensive hand-held calculators and crystal-controlled watches appeared on the market only ten years ago. They were made possible by the invention of the microprocessor and the improvement of solid-state computer memories. Now those computer memories, the general measure for capacity, have improved *256 times,* a figure that staggers the imagination when you consider that in transportation the improvement in speed from the horse and buggy to the jet aircraft was only about two hundred times. We are now in the middle of this computer-led revolution, with perhaps another factor of ten yet to be realized.

The third revolution, communication, is just beginning. We have seen the development of fiber optics for long-line telephone communication and the introduction of cable television into the home; but for the world economy, the big change will come with satellites.

In 1983 a satellite was deployed over southern India which opened up communications with millions of inhabitants of that nation in an area that had had only the most primitive access. These millions of people have an annual income of less than $100 per year. Within the decade, many of these peoples of India will be competing in the international labor market for jobs, just as the Filipinos, the South Koreans, the Sri Lankans, and the Indochinese do today. As the space shuttle program gains momentum, as many as two satellites a month will be deployed, bringing the developed nations into easy communication with hundreds of millions of Indians, Pakistanis, Burmese, and ultimately Chinese. As these nations develop and raise their standards of living, they will become huge markets for the developed nations, but in the meantime they will be competing for jobs all over the world. It's a Catch-22 situation. If their standards of living are not brought closer to ours, they will represent a vast well of discontent.

We in the United States are poorly equipped for such competition. With our Ming mentality, we have become accustomed to the trappings of empire, the concept of Fortress America, with our huge domestic market, our abundant natural resources, the vast expanses of the oceans to serve as buffers to foreign competitors. No more. We have grown lazy, inefficient, and ineffective in our attitudes, our economics, and in our institutions. The evidence of our deterioration is stark. As producer to the world, we had exported more than we imported. In the eighties, that has turned around. In 1982 our international trade deficit, the excess of imports over exports, was $40 billion; in 1983 it was $60 billion; in 1984 it exceeded $100 billion and was climbing.

The proximate cause of our problem is certainly the budget deficit and the strong dollar, but our woes lie much deeper. During the postwar years of world economic dominance, this country, like a benevolent potentate, has tried to be all things to all people. We rebuilt Japan and Germany, now our biggest economic competitors as well as customers. While we perform the task of policeman, those we protect militarily are beating out our brains economically. We have tried to solve all our domestic and international problems with hastily conceived assistance programs, many of which have proved to be counterproductive. In our economy, in our government, in our educational institutions, in our approach to sociological problems, we have set up roadblocks to our institutional efficiency, which are costing us dearly and preventing us from competing effectively in the international marketplace. We are no longer the Mings of old with our mighty armadas. We are still powerful competitors, to be sure, but we will have to battle hard to keep our position in the sun. With metaphors flying like flags from our mastheads, we must keep our economic guns at the ready and our financial powder dry, but most of all, we must keep from shooting ourselves in the foot before we enter the fray.

We are a raucous society, a swashbuckling society, a tumultuous society, and, in many ways, an unconsciously hypocritical society. We have a firm, written, time-tested Constitution, which the courts, acting like the oracles of old, reinterpret almost on a daily basis. We have simple, strict, well-defined delineations of powers among the three sectors of our constitutionally democratic system of government, yet the executive, the legislative, and the judicial branches routinely spar and skirmish at the borders of their territories. We are a society deeply rooted in the heritage of the Judeo-Christian ethic, yet, in the name of the Constitution itself, we seek to expunge all traces of that ethic, from concepts of creation to catechisms to Christmas crèches, as we would scour an operating room to rid it of all traces of infectious bacteria. We have labor union leaders who, piously proclaiming the priorities of the workingman, have priced whole industries out of competition, leading to massive unemployment in the heartland of America.

We have businessmen, thundering against the apostles of protectionism and extolling the virtues of free trade, who simultaneously labor diligently to build up barriers to exclude competitors from their own area of activity. In fact, I have never known a businessman who felt that the concepts of a totally free market applied to him; that's for the other guy.

We have egalitarians in our society, and they serve a useful purpose; we have educators in our society, and they too serve a useful purpose; but now we have spawned a hybrid horde of egalitarian educators who do not understand that egalitarianism and quality education are mutually exclusive.

We have technologists who fervently feel that any restraints on the unfettered application of technological developments are sins against nature, and we have antitechnologists who equally fervently believe that any genie can be put back in the bottle if enough laws are passed.

We have a communications contingent, collectively called the media, who are overwhelmed by the advances in modern communications technology. So much information is transmitted in such a random, chaotic fashion that the citizen seeking to be informed is literally "snowed," to use a technological term, and has great difficulty identifying a tree in the forest or a grain of wheat in the chaff.

All this is good.

In all its raucousness, in all its tumultuousness, in all its unconscious hypocrisy, this society of ours reflects the "invisible hand" of a free democracy in the true Adam Smith tradition. The blessing of this tumultuous society of ours is that it forces change, it forces adaptation, it forces evolution to keep up with the rapidly changing world. Most societies will not — some cannot — adapt to the changing world order. Europe has become a welfare society, sluggish, borrowing from its future, eating its seed corn. Japan is a consensus society, well suited to the single task of emerging from its wartime destruction to a modern industrial state, but already showing confusion as the future grows dimmer and the postwar consensus fades. The developing nations are too tied up with their immediate problems to give much thought to the future.

At the far end of the spectrum is the Soviet Union, a country currently incapable of change. It is locked into an economic philosophy designed 150 years ago by a German, Karl Marx, who lived much of his life in England. Marx himself would have been astounded to find that his theories were rejected by the industrial nations of England and Germany, where they were aimed, and adopted by the Russian agricultural nation to which they were poorly suited. Lenin did not live long enough to adapt the Marxist philosophy; it was left to the tyrant Josef Stalin to cement his own version of it, in blood, onto a helpless Soviet citizenry. There are no more Marxists in Moscow, but the heavy hands of Marx and Lenin and Stalin remain. Only if we can continue to demonstrate the superiority of our system can we hope for the Soviet citizenry to temper their leaders' obstinacy. Only in these United States can there be hope for the model society of the future.

But our society is exceedingly complex. The number of special groups vying with one another for resources in a Darwinian struggle for the sociological survival of the fittest is huge. In Washington alone, twenty-five hundred separate lobbying organizations are listed in the telephone book. (I probably belong to at least a dozen of them.) The future is so uncertain and the guidelines so vague that some lose their sense of direction and begin to work against their own interests in the confusion, like a football player running toward the wrong goal. When that happens, the Adam Smith concept of an open society reverses. Instead of enriching the whole by the struggle for the part, they send society down the wrong path to the detriment of us all.

A cruel example is Vietnam. Three presidents, John F. Kennedy, Lyndon B. Johnson, and Richard M. Nixon, drew us into and kept us in that quagmire because they felt that withdrawal would discredit the honor of the office of the presidency. They did far more damage by staying than they possibly could have done by simple admission of error and subsequent withdrawal. Senator George Aiken of Vermont had a more pragmatic solution at the time: "Declare a great victory and get out," he advised. We need more pragmatists and fewer ideologists.

In this book, I examine those areas in which elements of our society are unwittingly acting in a manner prejudicial to their own interests through ignorance, narrow-mindedness, confusion, malice, or just plain ideological obstinacy. When they do so, they not only damage their own cause, or evade their own responsibility, but they subtract from society instead of adding to it, and so hurt us all. I treat broad and general areas by selecting specific examples of where we are going wrong. I suggest solutions, a few of them ideological, but most simply pragmatic. We have a great society (no caps), but we can have a greater one. Before we can confidently put it forth as the greatest in the world, we shall have to discard our Ming mentality and make a few corrections. Before we can compete effectively in the international fray, we shall have to stop shooting ourselves in the foot.

2

The Snail Darter

THE SNAIL DARTER is a fish about three inches long. Its real name is *Percina imostoma tanasi*. If the snail darter wore a name tag, the name tag would be longer than the fish. It was first discovered in the waters of the Little Tennessee River by Dr. David A. Etnier, a University of Tennessee ichthyologist. As fish go, the snail darter is not particularly distinguished. It is a variety of perch, of which there are hundreds of species. The snail darter family itself contains at least 130 species, 85 to 90 of which are found in Tennessee alone, and 45 of those live in the Tennessee River system. New species of darters are constantly being discovered, at the rate of about one a year. This is a pretty tough task, even for trained ichthyologists, since one species of snail darter tends to look pretty much like another. The problem is compounded by the federal government, which, not appreciating the importance of either snail darters or ichthyologists, continually underfunds the research.

Nor is the snail darter easy to find. It lives on the bottoms

23
•

of fast-flowing rivers and feeds on river-bottom snails. Not a very exciting existence, nor one that would be recommended for a career, even for a fish.

Before we look down our noses too much at fish, we have to remember that since Jonah a number of fish have made it to the big time. In literature, the great white whale in Herman Melville's *Moby-Dick* was on the best-seller list for years; and on the movie screen the man-eating shark came back to clear the beaches over and over again in *Jaws, Jaws II, Jaws III*, and *Jaws to the Nth Power*. But even though the whale and the shark were thousands of times bigger and much more media apparent than the snail darter, neither of them ever made it to the Supreme Court.

The significance of this achievement should not be underestimated. Already the parade of *Jaws* presentations has been relegated to the wee hours of the morning on the higher-numbered UHF channels behind reruns of "Lucy," "M*A*S*H*," and "All in the Family," while the great white whale is entombed between the antiqued covers of the sets of *100 Greatest Books* advertised on the front pages of the airlines' throwaway magazines, destined to stand, forever un-opened, in the self-assembled Sears, Roebuck bookcase in the parlor as testimony to the family erudition.

No such fate for the snail darter, now eternally ensconced in the annals of American jurisprudence. In thousands of law libraries throughout the country, the snail darter lurks deep in the waters of the data pool, contentedly munching its mollusks, waiting to be summoned to the surface by electronic impulse from the clerk who enters the query ***UNITED STATES SUPREME COURT***FISH?*** and is instantly rewarded with the crisp and cogent answer: *S*N*A*I*L *D*A*R*T*E*R*.

The mechanism by which the snail darter came to fame is a piece of congressional legislation known as the Endangered

Species Act. This is a noble, well-intentioned act, originally intended to protect the bald eagle in its habitat and to stamp out illegal traffic in alligator skins. But, like so many pieces of social legislation, it tried to accomplish too much, to satisfy too many constituencies, and to allow too many exceptions. As a result, it was alternately too restrictive and too permissive.

The very origins of the legislation bristle with incongruities. Although its forerunners date back into antiquity, the present act was put together in 1973 by John Dingell, a congressman from Michigan. Representing as he does the auto-making district of Dearborn, Mr. Dingell might have been better advised to concern himself with that most incipient of endangered species, the American gull-winged automobile, but that degree of prescience is rare in the pressure-packed halls of Congress. A tireless, intimidating six-foot-three-inch bundle of energy, he is at once a hunter and a conservationist, a champion of "dirty air," according to his environmentalist opponents, while a proponent of a 22.5-million-acre Alaskan wildlife range, a tireless enemy of the "jack-booted fascists" who espouse gun control, but an ardent champion of the St. Croix lizard, the Morro Bay kangaroo rat, and the New Mexico ridgenose rattlesnake. To cap the incongruities, the act was prepared in Mr. Dingell's office, where the mounted remains of a wild boar, a pronghorn antelope, two caribou, a wood duck, and a rare albino white-tailed deer stared down incredulously at the goings-on.

Administration of the Endangered Species Act has been assigned to the competent but overworked personnel of the Fish and Wildlife Service of the Department of the Interior. All sorts of problems arose in its application. Some thought it too strong, some too weak. Some were overly zealous, using the legislation to list any mammal, bird, fish, or flower that had the slightest prospect of being endangered or threatened; some used it for their own purposes to block public or private developments to which they were opposed.

The sheer complexity of the task was overwhelming. The act attempted to preserve from extinction every animal and plant species, subspecies, and population in the world needing protection — approximately 1.4 million full species of animals and 0.6 million full species of plants, with the numbers increasing by three to five times when subspecies and individual populations are counted. Without doubt, an impossible task.

Nevertheless, the department laid into it with gusto. The tons of paperwork notwithstanding, by the middle of 1978 the department had classified 228 domestic and 457 foreign species, for a total of 685, with an additional 137 animal species and 1850 plant species formally proposed for listing. The lists were fascinating to read, with many "from faraway places with strange-sounding names." Many of the names on the lists were familiar and popular, such as the Columbian white-tailed deer, the southern bald eagle, the Arctic peregrine falcon, and the American alligator. Others made great grist for the media mill; for example, the Hawaiian hoary bat, the California least tern, the Yuma clapper rail, the San Francisco garter snake, the humpback chub, the Moapi dace, the Bib Bend gambusia, and the unarmored threespine stickleback.

The inclusion of some of the species doesn't seem to make much sense. For example, the Australian kangaroo is listed as a threatened species because the Australians are killing them off. There are more than 10 million kangaroos in Australia, where the animal is considered to be a pest. The kangaroo population is reported to be increasing faster than the human population. Since there are only about 14 million people in the country, it is hard to figure out which is threatened, the people or the kangaroos. In any event, I do not understand why we have to spend good taxpayers' money worrying about the Australian kangaroo. Let the Australians worry about it. It's their kangaroo.

Inevitably, as the lists grew longer and the bureaucracy grew stronger, conflict began to develop between land developers and administrators of the act. At first, the conflicts were minor and could be resolved through negotiation. In Mississippi nesting habitats of the endangered whooping crane were salvaged by rerouting an interstate highway, and in Texas a commercial real estate development managed to move forward when the endangered Houston toad showed up in locations other than the suburbs of the city of Houston.

The case of the furbish lousewort almost brought matters to a head. The furbish lousewort is a scraggly-looking plant that most of us would call a weed. (I do not know who Mr. Furbish was, but the lousewort part came from the belief in medieval Europe that a related species transmitted lice to cattle.) A botanist for the Army Corps of Engineers announced in 1977 that the furbish lousewort, supposedly extinct for thirty years, had been rediscovered in a bank of the St. John River in northern Maine. The corps had planned to build a pair of dams on the river — the Dickey-Lincoln project — which would inundate the plant's habitat. Corps officials in Washington advised Congress that the project might not go through if the plant were added to the endangered list.

Not to be intimidated, the Interior Department promptly announced its intention to include the lousewort among the first fourteen plants to be classified as endangered species and receive federal protection. The reaction was a combination of hilarity and outrage. Congressman John Myers, an Indiana Republican who sat on the powerful House Appropriations Committee, complained that if the environmentalists had their way, "A thousand years from now, we may have a United

States of louseworts, and nothing else." Newspaper editorials uniformly condemned the department's obstructionism. In the Office of Endangered Species, which administers the act, staff scientists were beleaguered by telephone calls from reporters and were forbidden to answer questions without special permission.

But the confrontation was not yet to be. It turned out that the citizens of northern Maine had little interest in either the lousewort or the Dickey-Lincoln dams and wanted no part of the whole project, which, after a brief burst of publicity, died a quiet death. The bureaucracies of the Department of the Interior and the Army Corps of Engineers had collided and negated each other, much like a particle and an antiparticle in nature annihilating each other with a brief burst of energy, after which nothing remains.

Enters now the villain of the story, the Tellico Dam. The history begins in the 1930s when President Franklin D. Roosevelt proposed the establishment of the Tennessee Valley Authority (TVA), with the very broad mission to upgrade life in one of America's most impoverished areas, the eastern part of Tennessee along the Tennessee River.

TVA performed that job so well — by harnessing flood-prone rivers, generating cheap electricity, and promoting industrial development — that it became a model for similar developments as far away as India and Egypt. One of the two dozen dams that TVA envisioned in the 1930s was Tellico, a short distance from where the clear, fast-flowing Little Tennessee meets the much larger Tennessee River near Knoxville. Sidetracked by World War II, Tellico was not formally outlined to the Congress until 1965. By that time the Tennessee Valley was no longer one of the nation's most impoverished areas; thanks to TVA and its dams, it had become one of the prosperous areas in the country. The surrounding farmland had increased dramatically in value, and many felt that there were enough dams in the area.

Rich farmers and environmentalists brought suit under the new environmental laws, and congressional opponents cried "pork barrel." But Tennessee was not northern Maine, and the Tennessee Valley Authority was a power in itself. Pork barrel or not, the project prevailed. Congress first appropriated construction funds in 1967. Almost immediately the project was embroiled in a tangle of lawsuits and administrative proceedings. By 1973 the federal district court had given it a clean bill of health under the National Environmental Protection Act, and it was off and running again.

Land was taken, the rich topsoil removed, families relocated, and the inevitable remains of Indian burial grounds transferred. Roads and bridges were built and concrete poured. When the Endangered Species Act was passed in 1973 the Tellico project was about half completed. At about the same time the snail darter was discovered by Professor Etnier. It took a while to get the snail darter listed, but by 1976, with the project almost 80 percent complete, a suit to block construction under the Endangered Species Act was filed by another University of Tennessee professor, Zygmunt Plater, from the law school. Some people thought the suit was a joke because it looked like a name taken from the Endangered Species Act itself. But it was no joke.

When the snail darter was first discovered, opponents of Tellico seized upon the Endangered Species Act to achieve their purpose after having been defeated in the courts under the National Environmental Protection Act. A group of citizens of the area, fronted by a conservation group and some biological scientists, petitioned the secretary of the interior, Cecil Andruss, to list the snail darter as an endangered species. After receiving comments from various parties, including strong objections from both TVA and the state of Tennessee, the secretary formally listed the snail darter. In so acting, he noted that "the snail darter is a living entity which is genetically distinct and reproductively isolated from other species."

This was a long reach, considering the ninety species of darter in Tennessee. The research into the sex life and reproductive system of the elusive little fish to prove this point alone would have taken years to carry out and would have required the attention of a shoal of ichthyological Masters and Johnsons and schools of academic physiologists. More important, Mr. Andruss determined that the snail darter lived only in that portion of the Little Tennessee River which would be completely inundated by the reservoir created by the Tellico Dam's completion. Subsequently, Andruss declared this area to be "the critical habitat" of the snail darter, and that "all federal agencies must take such action as is necessary to ensure that actions authorized, funded, or carried out by them do not result in the destruction or modification of this critical area."

These were strong words, used with the complete knowledge of not only the intent of Congress, clearly stated in repeated appropriations bills, and in the federal district court in clearing the project under all legislation existing at the time of the project's inception, but also of the positions taken by TVA and the state of Tennessee in the performance of their own obligations. Irrespective of the merits of the Tellico Dam project, this was a clear and blatant attempt on the part of a federal appointed official to use a piece of legislation for a purpose for which it had never been intended. The Supreme Court, to its credit, clearly noted this point in its later opinion, stating, "This notice, of course, was pointedly directed at TVA and clearly aimed at halting completion or operation of the dam."

TVA, backpedaling frantically after this unexpected directive, tried diligently to find alternative sites that might sustain the fish. Mr. Andruss, ignoring the biological fragility of his own determinations, stated that it would take five to fifteen years to determine whether the darter could survive in a new location, and that this remedy was unacceptable. Besides, he reasoned in a masterful piece of bureaucratic circumlocution, if the snail darter could live anywhere else, it would already be there. That one was hard to beat.

The Federal District Court of Eastern Tennessee was not impressed. It had lived through all the environmental lawsuits and had cleared the project for construction, so it was not about to change its mind on this transparent action. The court noted that the Endangered Species Act had been passed some seven years after construction on the dam had commenced, and that Congress had continued appropriations for Tellico with full awareness of the snail darter problem. Assessing the various factors the district court concluded:

> At some time a federal project becomes so near completion and so incapable of modification that a court should not apply a statute enacted long after inception to produce an unreasonable result. . . . Where there has been an irreversible and irretrievable commitment of resources by Congress to a project over a span of almost a decade, the Court should proceed with a great deal of circumspection.

To accept the plaintiffs' position, the district court argued, would inexorably lead to the absurd result of requiring a court "to halt impoundment of water behind a fully completed dam if an endangered species were discovered in the river on the day before such impoundment was scheduled to take place. *We cannot conceive that Congress intended such a result.*"

To most people not versed in the ways of the law, and even

to many well versed, the district court's lucid opinion would seem to have settled the matter. The Senate and House Appropriations committees certainly thought so, appropriating the funds for Tellico after noting the district court's opinion. Both houses of Congress must have thought so since they passed the budget without comment. President Jimmy Carter must have thought so, because he signed the bill, effectively reversing the decisions of his secretary of the interior.

Up to this point the story has a certain amount of déja vu about it. It is the kind of story Americans relish and chuckle about over their morning newspapers — a simple, scraggly weed like the furbish lousewort lousing up a vast hydroelectric project such as the Dickey-Lincoln Dam or a three-inch fish nibbling away at the powerful Tennessee Valley Authority. The protagonists were soap opera stereotypes: misty-eyed environmentalists, tongue-twisting ichthyologists, tweedy bird watchers, an albino deer-killing congressman expiating his sins by ardent conservationism, pork barrel politicians, insensitive land developers willing to sacrifice verdant farmland and to submerge ancient Indian burying grounds in the name of senseless progress, a crafty cabinet member twisting the intent of a noble piece of legislation to halt a valuable $100 million public works project, litigious lawyers, and thoughtless legislators ready to stamp out for eternity an endangered aquatic animal whose unique genes and chromosomes, if preserved, might someday prove the key to unlocking the microbiological secrets of cancer and the common cold. It's all there. Name your poison.

And it's all good fun up to a point.

Eventually, the American public expects its responsible institutions to call a halt to such frivolous activities; to exhibit some reasoned judgment backed by experience and mature cogitation; to put the problem into some perspective so that our intellectual resources can be redirected to more serious matters. The case of the snail darter and the Tellico Dam demonstrates an ominous tendency on the part of our most hallowed institutions to depart from these traditions, to lose the ability to distinguish between wheat and chaff, between forest and trees, and, in so doing, to clog up the gears of our judicial, legislative, and executive machinery with trivia, rendering them incapable to deal effectively with the larger issues of our society.

Inevitably, the court decision allowing construction to proceed was appealed. The court of appeals reversed the district court's decision. It held that the degree of the project's completion was irrelevant; that repeated appropriations by Congress were merely "advisory opinions"; and that the only point to be considered was the social and scientific costs of the disappearance of a "unique form of life." No attention was given to whether the form of life was truly unique or whether its probable disappearance had been adequately ascertained.

Most of us nonlawyers are not particularly impressed by appeals courts. They are sort of shadowy institutions with no juries, no witnesses, no press coverage. At worst, they convey the concept of not being very fair, of being agents of the establishment. How often do we follow stories of juries that award tens of millions of dollars to impecunious victims of rapacious insurance companies (which have plenty of money and can well afford it) only to have the award set aside as excessive by some faceless appeals court that no one has ever heard of. At best, they are looked on as legal limbos, way stations along the precarious path of justice, since every piece of litigation worth its salt must eventually find its way to the ultimate tribunal, the Supreme Court.

So the reversal by the appeals court caused little commotion. On the contrary, it was more like the three-rounders on a boxing card, spicing up the audience and giving it a taste of blood in anticipation of the big show to come.

If the appeals court felt that the congressional appropriations were merely "advisory opinions," the Congress was equally disdainful of the court. The appropriations committees stated explicitly in their bill that the court's interpretation was "not the intent of Congress in enacting the Endangered Species Act, [that] funds should be appropriated to allow these projects to be completed and their benefits realized in the public interest, the Endangered Species Act notwithstanding." Both houses of Congress passed the bills by wide margins with that language intact, and the president signed them into law without adverse comment. If that was not the intent of Congress, what was?

Although there was little disagreement in the Congress as to its intent, there was still a substantial disagreement in the courts about the retroactive provisions of the act and about the intent of Congress. Accordingly, the Supreme Court agreed to put the case on its docket for the 1977 term. I have never been able to figure out why the Supreme Court agreed to hear the case at all. If there was anything to it, it was merely a poorly drafted piece of legislation in which the Congress had simply neglected to include provisions for cost-benefit tradeoffs so that some degree of reasonableness could be factored into the analyses. Nor had grandfather clauses been included to protect projects that might be going on-line at the time the act was passed. Such provisions are common and are generally considered marks of good draftsmanship.

It was not as though the Court had time on its hands or lacked more substantive issues to consider. Chief Justice Warren Burger had been roaming the hinterlands, making speeches to any group that would listen to concerns about overcrowding in the courts in general, and the Supreme Court in particular.

Of issues there were many, and several of them were pressing: the one-man, one-vote concept for state and city elections was receiving confusing considerations in the lower courts; school desegregation cases abounded; the Miranda decision on prisoners' rights was increasingly under attack; the unresolved abortion question was an emotional issue throughout the country; and hundreds of prisoners were languishing on death rows in prisons all over the country. Nor was a question of substantive law involved. This was a very narrow issue with little potential applicability to other litigation, even under the same act.

Whatever the reasoning, the Court did decide to take up the case. The snail darter had finally made it to the big time. Beginning with the premise that operation of the Tellico Dam would either eradicate the known population of snail darters or destroy their critical habitat, the Court asked itself two questions: Would the TVA be in violation of the act if it completed and operated the Tellico Dam as planned? If TVA's actions would offend the act, was an injunction the appropriate remedy for the violation? The Court held that both questions must be answered in the affirmative.

Somewhat sheepishly the Court admitted, "It may seem curious to some that the survival of a relatively small number of three-inch fish among all the countless millions of species extant would require the permanent halting of a virtually completed dam for which Congress has expended more than $100 million." They went on to say that "the paradox is not minimized" by the fact that the Congress had continued to appropriate large sums of money for the project even after being apprised of its impact on the survival of the snail darter. These conditions notwithstanding, five members of the Court, Justice William Brennan, Justice Potter Stewart, Justice Byron White, Justice Thurgood Marshall, and Justice John Stevens, joined with Chief Justice Burger in concluding that the explicit provisions of the Endangered Species Act required precisely that result.

The Court argued that "the plain intent of Congress in enacting the statute was to halt and reverse the trend towards species extinction, *whatever the cost*" (my emphasis). It buttressed its arguments with examples showing that the value of all genetic heritage is "incalculable." One of the examples cited was that critical chemicals in the regulation of ovulation in humans were found in a common plant.

Justice Lewis Powell, in his dissent, stated that he could not believe that Congress could have intended to produce this "absurd result," in the words of the district court. He regarded the decision as an extreme example of a literalist construction, not required by the language of the act and adopted without regard for its manifest purpose.

Let us look at the decision in more detail. In the first place, the basic scientific data on which the determination was made was badly flawed. This fish was not a distinct and easily distinguishable species like the American bald eagle. It is one of more than a hundred varieties of darter. Very little is known of the genetics of these little fish. Was the snail darter a distinct species, immutable from any other? It would take many years of research to verify its uniqueness and to state with any degree of certainty that it was any more distinct than a redhaired, blue-eyed human whose characteristics might appear randomly in a family and then not surface again for a couple of generations.

Was the Tellico area the only natural habitat of the fish? Did it not exist anywhere else in the world? Such a determination would again have taken years to verify at a cost of many millions of dollars. The Court should have used a little common sense and taken these factors into consideration.

In its decision, the Court waxed fulsome in its concern for genetic heritage by saying "Who knows, or can say, what potential cures for cancer or other scourges, present or future, may lie locked up in the structure of plants which may yet be undiscovered, much less analyzed?" Nonsense. The Court, in the narrowness of its collective background, exhibited an appalling lack of knowledge of modern microbiology, in which enormous strides in genetics are being made by synthesis of genes and chromosomes whereby the desired characteristics are built up from the basic building blocks of nature, rather than by the outmoded laborious techniques of analysis of existing biological specimens.

The key statement in the decision is the phrase "whatever the cost." This statement is so absurd that it is embarrassing. Some might say that it is a small part of a long decision, and not all that important. But it is repeated several times and is clearly meant to be the key phrase in the decision. The Supreme Court, as the arbiter of last resort, weighs its words carefully. What if this strict construction of intent were applied literally? It would mean that the United States must halt all developments, public and private, to examine whether there might be a potential endangered or threatened animal or plant involved. It would also mean that the Department of the Interior must be funded to step up its investigations of the millions of potential endangered species all over the world, lest one become extinct before we catch up with it.

Certainly this is bad law. The case itself was not important, but the principle involved is crucial to the health of our democracy. The courts are out of touch with our complex technological society. Trained in the narrow discipline of the law, judges at all levels make decisions that fly in the face of reason in our modern world. They make sociological decisions on the basis of outmoded legal procedures. In the snail darter case, they should have been able to send the case down for late information on whether or not the fish was still considered endangered. There was already a good deal of data to the contrary. There should have been a mechanism to communicate with Congress to determine whether they meant to protect this species at all costs, which the Congress did not. Finally, the strict constructionism was not at all necessary. Case law is replete with examples of the courts interpreting the intent of the Congress. The expression "whatever the cost" is in itself an interpretation of the intent of the Congress, since the words appear nowhere in the statute.

It would have been bad enough had only the courts been at fault in this silly situation. But no, the Congress and the executive also played parts in the fiasco. When the Supreme Court affirmed the appellate court's injunction, the project, already shut down for two years, was permanently enjoined from completion, unless the Congress were to take action. It would have been a straightforward matter to correct the statute in a couple of simple ways. First, there should have been provision for cost-benefit analyses. The statement that "the value of this genetic heritage is, quite literally, incalculable" is not an operable one. If the statute had been in force in the 1930s, should the entire TVA project have been shelved? Or the Panama Canal? Should Moses have paused when he got to the Red Sea? Second, there should have been a grandfather clause in the statute giving consideration to projects under way at the time it was enacted. This is necessary to do justice to those who acted in good faith prior to 1973 and to give scientists enough time to make the proper analyses, so as not to list a species as endangered when it is not.

Congress ducked. With all the publicity, the snail darter became a hot potato. Politicians don't like to deal with such things if they can help it. Howard Baker, senior senator from

Tennessee, minority leader, and presidential aspirant, thought he saw a way out. He persuaded Congress to establish a cabinet-level committee to decide if exemptions to the act *should be* granted in the case of irreconcilable conflicts between projects and endangered species.

Unfortunately for Baker, the new committee was masterminded by the same fox who had been minding this chicken coop from the beginning, Secretary of the Interior Cecil Andruss. By now it was becoming obvious that snail darters were a dime a dozen throughout the southeastern United States, so the committee didn't have much leeway under its charter. In a brilliant political stroke, the committee ignored its charter and decided to kill the project on other grounds. Charles Schultze, chairman of the President's Council of Economic Advisors, stated, "We would be inundating $40 million worth of farmland. We would lose important Indian archeological sites, scenic values, and the river in its natural state."

All of this had been gone over before. Never mind that the topsoil had been removed, the farmers relocated, roads and bridges built, the Indian burial grounds transferred. All that would remain would be an unsightly pile of 90 percent concrete. TVA management swallowed its pride and principles after battling for the project for more than twenty years, stating no objection to the committee's conclusions.

Howard Baker did not give up so easily. He said, "If that's all the good the committee can do, to put us right back where we started from, we might as well save the time and expense. I will introduce legislation to abolish the committee and exempt the Tellico Dam from the provisions of the act." He did just that. It took him a while to do it, but he finally prevailed. The House passed the bill the first time, but the Senate killed it. The bill was amended and the House passed it again. This time the Senate, with considerable pressure from Baker, who was soon to be the new Senate majority leader, passed the bill and sent it to the president, who signed it without objection.

The silly saga of the snail darter was settled, once and for all.

The dam was completed forthwith and Tellico Lake began to fill. The Supreme Court went on to other matters. Congress continued to diddle with the Endangered Species Act but made no substantive changes, even though as prestigious an organization as the National Audubon Society had supported the Baker amendment, believing that the act was too rigid to be politically tenable.

The new secretary of the interior had other fish to fry and would have no part of the inedible snail darter. The TVA staff, blithely ignoring its temporary defection, prepared multicolored brochures extolling the virtues of the location for industrial development and wholesome family living. The latest, entitled "Proud of Your Product, Be Proud of Your Location," could almost have written itself.

> Tellico offers the best of both worlds for your company's next plant location: the natural beauty and ease of living afforded by East Tennessee's mountains and lakes as well as important practical assets needed to compete in today's national and international marketplace.
>
> Tellico offers 5,000 acres of controlled, reasonably priced properties combined with major positive service factors in the heart of the Sunbelt. The properties are readily accessible to major highway, rail, water, and air transportation services.

The brochure discreetly neglects to mention that the fishing on the lake is excellent.

The snail darter is doing just fine. Several thousand are

estimated to be thriving in the Hiwassee River, more than there ever had been in the Little Tennessee. It has also been sighted in eastern Tennessee's South Chickamauga Creek, Sequatchie River, Sewee Creek, and Watt's Bar Reservoir, in the Paint Rock River in northern Alabama, and in several rivers in Georgia.

Asked about all this, Dr. Etnier suggested that ichthyologists had "a wrong mental image of the conditions the animal can tolerate." The Little Tennessee was "cool, clear, pristine," yet the fish was found in a polluted creek in Chattanooga. How wrong can you get?

●   ●   ●

One would think that after all that fuss the government would be a bit more careful in the future. Not so. Consider the case of the Westway, a new project to replace the deteriorating West Side Highway in New York City. The project was started in 1971 during the days of Governor Nelson A. Rockefeller and Mayor John V. Lindsay, both environmentalists to the core. The project received some impetus in 1973 when a section of the elevated highway collapsed, causing a number of injuries and severe dislocation to members of the local community.

The Westway was expensive because of its crowded location, but it seemed environmentally innocuous for the New York City scene. It would be only 4.2 miles long, replacing an existing highway between the Battery and Forty-second Street. The plan was not only to improve highway safety and decrease pollution from stalled traffic, but also to spur the development of the run-down West Side and create ninety-three acres of parkland. The project seemed to be a sociological four-bagger.

By 1978 Governor Hugh Carey and Mayor Ed Koch had agreed on a Westway plan that included a state park and some state support. Since the project abutted a navigable waterway, it also came under the watchful eye of the U.S. Army Corps of Engineers. With all that surveillance the project moved slowly, but by 1981 the chief of the Corps of Engineers had issued dredging and fill permits, and it seemed to be on its way.

Included in the project were two hundred acres of landfill, which would not seem great compared to a three-hundred-mile river on one end and one of the world's largest harbors on the other. However, suit was brought against the project on behalf of the striped river bass. Apparently the juvenile bass use a band of the Hudson River, including the Westway fill area, as a place to spend the winter. Federal Judge Thomas P. Griesa, who heard the case, was incensed at both state and federal officials for concealing information about Hudson River fish. He ordered the corps to reconsider its landfill permit. On further analysis it was determined that there was not much information to conceal: as one might expect, it is not very easy to collect information about a particular two-hundred-acre section of a fast-flowing three-hundred-mile-long river, especially when it is contiguous to an area the size of New York Harbor.

The corps is trying valiantly. At present the district chief, Colonel Fletcher H. Griffis, says he has reached only three conclusions.

> That presently available data demonstrate that juvenile striped bass use a band of the Hudson River which includes the West-way fill area; that the Westway fill area is an important over-wintering habitat; and that the Westway fill would destroy a portion of the habitat found within this bank. However, the

probability of Westway actually causing such a catastrophic
impact is unknown at present.

In other words, nobody knows. To try to find out, the state
proposes to spend $8 to $10 million on a study that will take
at least two years to complete and will delay a $2 billion project
for at least that long, at a cost of more than $150 million per
year for the delays. The fish in question do spawn in the
Hudson River, but they range the entire Atlantic seaboard.
No one will ever be able to determine how many other rivers
they spawn in; nor will any study be able to determine if the
modification of one small section of the entire Atlantic seaboard will have any significant effect on the spawning habits
of one particular breed of fish. Too many variables affect the
ecosystem. Storms, changes in rainfall, world temperature
patterns, riverbed erosion, harbor pollution, natural variations
in food supply or in predators, and the lack of baseline data
for comparison are just a few of the factors that are certain to
make the data inconclusive. The whole thing is a waste of
time. It would be ridiculous if it weren't so pathetic.

So what if we lose a few fish? The striped bass is not going
to become extinct by this action. What of the other effects of
delay or of possible cancellation of the project? What of the
effects on highway safety? There have already been serious
accidents. What of air pollution from traffic congestion? What
of the development of a run-down section of the city? What
of the parks for the children to play in and the adults to enjoy?
Couldn't Judge Griesa take these factors into consideration,
or must the judiciary remain strictly constructionist?

There is an adage in legal circles that "bad cases make bad
law." In the computer business it is expressed more succinctly
as GIGO — garbage in, garbage out. Both expressions mean

that if the input to the treatment of a problem is defective, the output will be flawed. So it is with the Endangered Species Act and a number of other pieces of sociological legislation. The intent is superb but the treatment is atrocious.

• • •

The press has a field day with furbish louseworts, snail darters, and striped bass, but I have found no serious analysis of the costs of these fiascos in the literature. The courts are voluminous and pompous in the explanations of their opinions, but seldom seem to test them against the tenets of rationality. Mr. Dooley's cogent analysis that "the Supreme Court reads the newspapers" comes close to the mark. The bureaucracies of the executive branch, concerned about their jobs, waver and bend with every shift of the wind, as did the TVA staff when the cabinet committee voted to cancel the project. So it goes.

The Tellico Dam project makes possible the generation of 200 million kilowatt-hours of electricity a year. Since hydroelectric power is practically all fixed cost, the loss of the generating capacity amounts to over $10 million per year. In the three years that the project was held up, the total cost was about $30 million. In the total U.S. economy $30 million does not amount to much. But our economy no longer has a surplus. In fact, we are in deficit, some $200 billion per year in 1985. That means that the $30 million has to come out of somebody else's hide. It will not be available for the poor, the underprivileged, the sick, the elderly, the uneducated, or for other environmental or sociological programs. The $30 million is only the tiniest snowflake on the top of one of the highest Alps in our economy. The Westway project alone costs $150 million for every year of delay. These two projects are only examples of hundreds of projects in delay or in negotiation all over the country. We can no longer stand this drain on our productive capacity. We must pay for it in a reduced standard of living at home or in loss of jobs to other countries because of reduced competitiveness in the international economy. There is no alternative.

It's time to stop penalizing ourselves with such nonsense. Let's stop shooting ourselves in the foot and put these legitimate concerns in the proper perspective. The snail darter won't care. It was taken off the endangered species list in 1984.

3

—

Vive la Différence

On THE AVERAGE, women
live longer than men. I don't know whether the mere statement would be considered discriminatory, but according to
recent court decisions any business or government agency
which considers that fact in the course of its day-to-day operations can get itself into real trouble. And the number of
businesses and agencies getting themselves into real trouble
is increasing pretty rapidly. At first it was just the Los Angeles
Department of Water and Power, which got caught requiring
women to make larger contributions in order to receive the
same monthly pension benefits as men. The reasoning was
that women lived longer, and on the average would receive
more money. Therefore, they should pay in more. Next came
the Arizona Governing Committee for Tax Deferred Annuity
and Deferred Compensation Plans. The Arizonans used the
same reasoning, choosing to keep the payments equal but to
reduce the monthly benefits for women. That doesn't fly,
either. In each case the courts, up to and including the U.S.

Supreme Court, have ruled that the practice discriminates against women. The Arizona ruling handed down in 1983 has sent the insurance industry, the Congress, and all employers, public and private, into tizzies.

All sex-based actuarial tables, whether for pensions, life, automobile, or casualty insurance, or whatever, are now suspect. Policies are frantically being reviewed by employers and their insurers all over the country in an effort to comply with the new concept of the applicable law. The Internal Revenue Service, which was using sex-based actuarial tables to estimate estate taxes, has lost a case in a district court and is revising its tables. Women's organizations are claiming a great victory and are ecstatic. The press is having a ball. The administration, sensing an opportunity to improve its relations with women's groups, welcomes the decisions as Solomonic in their significance. Congress, for the same reason, is rushing legislation to wipe out all considerations of sex for any purpose. In its zeal it is proposing to make the legislation retroactive. Many insurance companies with inadequate reserves are preparing to sell their actuarial souls for relief from retroactivity. Corporations already smarting under the stigma of sex discrimination are publicly hailing the decisions but privately damning them.

What will be the result of all this brouhaha? Probably not much other than an enormous administrative cost to society. The professional women's organizations will get a big boost, not only in prestige but also in dues income. Politicians will proudly point out their concern for women's rights, although most will not understand the issues or be aware of the adverse consequences of their support of them. Insurance companies will stress the horrors of bankruptcy and the consequent loss of jobs and will talk the politicians out of the retroactive provisions while they adjust their premiums to the new state of affairs. Corporations will get rid of their lifetime annuity options as too costly, to the detriment of all their employees.

For women it will probably pretty much even out: perhaps a slight loss, but certainly no big gain. Women currently pay less for life insurance because they live longer. They pay less for automobile insurance because they have fewer accidents. Under the new unisex provisions they will pay less for pensions and annuities in accordance with the court decisions, but more for life and automobile insurance. Depending on your point of view you can work the figures to suit your fancy. I am no expert on the matter, but I have done a lot of reading. My prediction is that professional women with significant pensions will do better, while all other women will do a little worse.

Insurance works by having many persons share the risk of certain dangers. The many individuals are represented by an insurance company acting as a middleman to handle the money and to charge a fee for its services. Insurance can work only when the possible losses to the insured can be measured. Since insurance looks to the future and no one can know which individual is going to suffer losses, techniques have been developed to measure the average loss.

These techniques have been worked out with great precision; experience has shown that they are quite accurate. The techniques rely heavily on some mathematical laws known as the Laws of Probability, and primarily on one of the laws known as the Law of Large Numbers. If we toss a coin a few times, we may get a number of heads, or a number of tails, in a row. This is known as good luck or bad luck, depending on which way you are betting. But if we toss a coin many times, we are almost certain to get a fairly even distribution of heads and tails. The same law applies to fires, earthquakes, automobile accidents, mortality, or longevity. We know fairly well how many fires there will be in a given city, or how often earthquakes will occur in a given region, or how many more automobile accidents there will be in a city as contrasted with its suburbs, or how many people will die next year, or how much longer a sixty-year-old person is likely to live.

Insurance companies employ batteries of mathematicians known as actuaries who calculate all these things and then assign an average cost to each event being insured against. These average costs, plus a reserve in the event that too many tails come up in the beginning, plus the costs of providing these services, are assessed against the insured in the form of a premium. It is vital to know these probabilities with a high degree of accuracy. If the calculations come up with numbers that are too low, the insurance company loses money and eventually goes broke. If the numbers are too high, some other insurance company gets the business, and that eventually leads to unemployed actuaries.

Insurance is a highly competitive business these days. The time is long gone when your friendly neighborhood insurance man showed up in the parlor to collect the weekly premium and to tell you how much it would cost to insure the new baby. A great amount of insurance is purchased by employers whose groups are fundamental to cutting administrative costs and reducing risks. This is especially true in health and accident insurance and in pensions. Pensions are a kind of reverse life insurance in which the policy is paid to a living recipient rather than at the death of the benefactor. The same basic actuarial mortality tables apply. If we know, on the average, how many people are going to die in a certain period of time, then we know how many people are not going to die and can set pension benefits accordingly.

To be fair, efficient, and competitive, actuaries try to set premiums in relation to the risks involved. For earthquakes, people in the wheatfields of Kansas are charged less than those who live along the San Andreas fault in California. Similarly, hurricane insurance costs less in North Dakota than it does in Florida; and automobile accident insurance costs less in the suburbs than it does in the large cities. Humans can be classified in the same way: young people pay less than old people for life insurance; nonsmokers pay less than smokers. As our information revolution progresses, actuaries will be able to collect data with greater precision and adjust more quickly to societal changes. It is important that they be able to assign premiums more equitably according to risks, as young people and nonsmokers will attest. The history of life insurance for women demonstrates how the system adjusts as health care improves and society changes.

In the late 1800s women were charged more for life insurance because maternity deaths were so high, as they still are in many countries with poor sanitation. As sanitation improved, so did women's mortality, until the rates became equal during the 1920s. From the 1920s to the 1950s, the life expectancy of newborn baby girls grew dramatically, from 1.2 to 5.7 years more than baby boys, putting competitive pressure on the insurance companies to give preferential rates to women. The combination of better longevity and the increased entry of women into the job market led a few insurance companies to offer lower-priced policies to women. By the late 1950s preferential treatment for women was standard in the industry. This was not because actuaries liked women better or wanted to discriminate against men (actuaries are about as steely-eyed and unbiased a group as you can find), but simply because they recognized the impersonality of the laws of statistics and biology. The corollary step, of course, was to make women's pensions more expensive, since, if they lived longer, they should pay more than men for the same monthly payout or receive a lower monthly payout for the same amount paid in. You can't have it both ways. This sound actuarial, statistical, and biological practice was approved by state regulatory agencies that had jurisdiction over such matters.

These practices were also followed at the federal level. Social Security, by far the largest job-related pension system in the world, used essentially the same actuarial systems as did the various state and federal retirement systems, many of which were administered by private insurance companies. For twenty years very few of the tens of millions of individuals enrolled in the many public or private pension systems, including Social Security, had any objection to the allocations. It would seem that if the system were considered grossly unfair, some significant number of those people would have brought the issue to debate or would have taken it to the polls in some of the thousands of state and federal elections which took place over that period. I can find no indication of such action.

During that time the Congress enacted the Civil Rights Act of 1964, a monumental piece of legislation spearheaded by Senator Hubert H. Humphrey of Minnesota. Senator Humphrey, soon to become vice president of the United States after the assassination of President John F. Kennedy and the succession of Lyndon B. Johnson, had been an ardent and tireless advocate of civil rights throughout his political life. He proudly and quite properly considered the Civil Rights Act to be the touchstone of his career in the Senate, and was recognized as the legislative nonpareil on the subject, both for energy in execution and in expertise.

The essence of the act is in its Title VII which, in an all-encompassing clause, makes the statement that it is an unlawful employment practice "to discriminate against any individual with respect to his compensation, terms, conditions, or privileges of employment, because of such individual's race, color, religion, sex, or national origin."

The clause was written by Senator Humphrey. During Senate debate, wherein those senators not conversant with proposed legislation traditionally seek clarification and guidance from proponents, particularly the floor manager, Senator Jennings Randolph asked the question.

MR. RANDOLPH: Mr. President. I wish to ask of the senator from Minnesota [Mr. Humphrey], who is the effective manager of the pending bill, a clarifying question on the provisions of Title VII. I have in mind that the Social Security system, in certain respects, treats men and women differently. For example, widows' benefits are paid automatically, but a widower qualifies only if he was disabled or if he was actually supported by his deceased wife. Also, the wife of a retired employee entitled to Social Security receives an additional old age benefit, but the husband of such an employee does not. These differences in treatment, as I recall, are of long standing.

Am I correct, I ask the senator from Minnesota, in assuming that similar differences of treatment in industrial benefit plans, including earlier retirement options for women, may continue in operation under this bill, if it becomes law?

MR. HUMPHREY: Yes. That point was made unmistakably clear earlier today by the adoption of the Bennett amendment, so there can be no doubt about it.

Reassured, Senator Randolph and other concerned senators voted for the bill, which passed both houses with flying colors and was signed into law by a jubilant President Johnson.

Nothing much happened for a dozen or so years until a class-action suit was brought into the district court on behalf of present or former female employees of the Los Angeles Department of Water and Power. It charged that the department's pension plan was in violation of Title VII of the Civil Rights Act of 1964 because it taxed female employees at a higher rate than male employees for the same pension benefits. The department argued that the basis for the differential was longevity, not sex, and that sex, like age, was one of the prime determinants of longevity. The court ruled that there was discrimination under the act and that the state should make retroactive retribution. The case wended its way up to the Supreme Court. In April 1978, fourteen years after the passage of the act, the Supreme Court, in a narrow and mixed decision, ruled that the practice was discriminatory, but that retroactivity was too harsh a remedy, and struck down that portion of the lower court's judgment.

In 1983 the Court, in the Arizona case, determined that a somewhat different payment mechanism was also discriminatory. The state of Arizona offered its pensioners three options: (1) a single lump-sum payment upon retirement, (2) periodic payments of a fixed sum for a fixed period of time, and (3) monthly annuity payments for the remainder of the employee's life. The first two options were the same for men and women because they represented the "present value" of the state's obligation to the employee. Most employees preferred to take the third option because it allowed them to defer income taxes for a longer period. If the employees elected the third option, women received smaller payments than men because, on the average, they lived longer. This the Court ruled discriminatory.

The Court, to its credit, found nothing wrong with sex-based actuarial tables per se; nor did they find anything wrong with insurance companies selling, or people buying, annuities predicated on sex-based actuarial tables. The ruling applied only when the action was job-related, and then only on its interpretation of a single clause in a nineteen-year-old statute. The decision centered on the point that employees be treated as individuals rather than as part of a class.

In its latest ruling the Court stated that Title VII's "focus on the individual is unambiguous." In so doing it used a device that I as a nonlawyer have never noticed before. To bolster its authenticity the Court quoted extensively from its 1978 opinion, which was written by the same group of people, using essentially the same line of reasoning. The 1983 decision states: "This underlying assumption — that sex may properly be used to predict longevity — is flatly inconsistent with the basic teaching of Manhart (1978): that Title VII requires employers to treat their employees as individuals, not as simply components of a racial, religious, sexual or national class."

The whole decision boils down to a single word, *individuals*. The Court, in interpreting the wording of ambiguous statutes, is expected to look back to the intent of the Congress at the time of enactment. In the case of a nineteen-year-old statute, this is sometimes difficult to do; but in this instance, the intent of the Congress was crystal-clear. The debate between Senators Humphrey and Randolph was as unambiguous as you can get, and the fact that Senator Randolph and others relied on Senator Humphrey's reassurance was equally telling. The Court majority, in its opinion, rejected the Humphrey statement out of hand. They further neglected to quote the statement in the previous opinion that "we do not suggest that the statute was intended to revolutionize the insurance and pension industries."

Justice Powell, in his dissent, pointed out this omission, and went on to state:

Congress has chosen to leave the primary responsibility for regulating the insurance industry to the several states. The McCarran-Ferguson Act reflects the long-held view that the "continued regulation . . . by the several states of the business of insurance is in the public interest." Given the consistent policy of entrusting insurance regulation to the states, the majority is not justified in assuming that Congress intended in 1964 to require the industry to change long-standing actuarial methods approved over decades by state insurance commissions.

Nothing in the language of Title VII supports this preemption of state jurisdiction. Nor has the majority identified any evidence in the legislative history that Congress considered the widespread use of sex-based mortality tables to be discriminatory. . . . Rather the legislative history indicates precisely the opposite.

The majority of the Supreme Court, in this narrowly legalistic and highly questionable interpretation of a single word in an old statute, did set the pension and insurance industry on its ear, whether or not it intended to. But what if that same narrow interpretation were extended to all legislation? Literally dozens of statutes on the books do classify individuals into racial, religious, sexual, or national classes for the very purpose of *preventing* discrimination. All the Equal Employment Opportunity laws set up categories of women, blacks, Hispanics, and others for job-related purposes to ensure that these groupings are not discriminated against in the marketplace. Affirmative action programs, mandatory in most large companies and required under most government contracts, set up similar groupings, particularly to measure the progress of women and minorities into management positions. There are the perennial questions of separation of toilet facilities and sleeping accommodations; there are day-care centers, pregnancy benefits, and the exclusion of women from the draft.

Most job-related decisions are a zero-sum game. Only so many jobs are available. If an employer acts in favor of one group as a group, he or she automatically discriminates against another group as a group. The courts have been ducking this question for years, but everyone knows that it is true.

There is nothing wrong with these statutes. They were set up to serve a social purpose and they serve that purpose well. A decision which says that an employer must treat every employee only as an individual is pure nonsense. It means that jobs will go primarily to the quick and the strong. It would have the opposite effect from what was intended and would undo decades of social progress.

•   •   •

Why does the Supreme Court act this way? The most simple explanation goes back to the appointment of Earl Warren as chief justice in 1953. During the 1930s the country was overwhelmed by the Depression, with survival of the democratic capitalistic system the main concern of the decade. The 1940s were dominated by World War II, with the survival of democracy on this planet the main concern of this country. As the decade of the 1950s developed and the safety of our country was established and our economy was booming, the citizens of the United States began to concern themselves with long-outmoded codes of civil justice. The Congress, sensitive to the political problems of civil rights legislation, institutionally dragged its feet. The Eisenhower administration, buoyed by the booming economy, concentrated its attention on the new position of the United States as the world's dominant economic and military power. Warren, having been both a governor and a prosecuting attorney, took a very broad position on the function of the courts, the Supreme Court in particular.

Warren once told Dean Rusk, the former secretary of state, that he believed the primary political function of the courts was to break the impasses inherent in any structure of balanced powers. In his view, he was a sort of referee who stepped in, took control, and made decisions when the Congress and the administration slowed up the game. This was pretty heady stuff, which probably never even occurred to the most wild-eyed authors of the Constitution.

It was also pretty dangerous, because if the courts are going to break impasses, only they can define "impasse." Under this thesis the limits on court power are not set by the Constitution or by discoverable law, but by the tolerance of the other two branches of government.

Heady and dangerous as it may have been, it was appropriate to the times and it worked. Though Warren did not dominate the Court, he exercised a steady and consistent influence as one of a small liberal majority. His most famous decision was the one in which he announced for a unanimous Court that the mere fact of racial segregation in public schools was a violation of the Fourteenth Amendment. During his sixteen-year tenure the Court made the Bill of Rights more explicit than ever before. The terms "Warren Court" and "judicial activism" became anathema to reactionaries and civil rights opponents, and Warren was vilified by newspaper editorials and billboards, particularly in the South.

But times have changed, and the sensitivity of our society to injustice has improved immeasurably. No longer is it necessary to prod the Congress or the executive into action on civil rights issues. What had been a political liability thirty years ago is now a big vote getter. Even the most dedicated civil rights advocate will agree that the statutes on the books are adequate, especially for minorities. The problems now are in implementation. If you are in the minority, you probably perceive progress as being too slow; if you are not, you may perceive the implementation as being too fast or just about right. These conflicting opinions are the essence of a democratic society.

• • •

But back to the subject of this chapter. One major aspect of the rights issue has not yet been resolved satisfactorily: the issue of women's rights. There can be no doubt that our nation has had a long and unfortunate history of sex discrimination. Traditionally, such discrimination was rationalized by an attitude of "romantic paternalism," which had the practical effect of putting women not on a pedestal, but in a cage. As a result of this notion and other crude macho concepts concerned with physical and organizational dominance, our statute books became laden with gross, stereotyped distinctions between the sexes.

Throughout most of the nineteenth century the position of women in our society was in many respects comparable to that of blacks under the pre–Civil War slave codes. Neither slaves nor women could hold office, serve on juries, or bring suit in their own names. Married women were denied the legal capacity to hold or convey property or to serve as legal guardians of their own children. And even though blacks were guaranteed the right to vote in 1870, women were denied that right until the Nineteenth Amendment was adopted half a century later.

It is true that the position of women in America has improved markedly in the last few decades. But the problem is very difficult to handle. It is subtle but pervasive. Organized women's groups relied heavily on the Equal Rights Amendment, which had to be ratified by two-thirds of the state legislatures, but was not. The reasons for failure are complex. Many were simply reluctant to fool with the Constitution; others felt that there were already adequate provisions on the books; some were scared off by visions of unisex toilets and women in combat; others were alienated by the assertiveness of the proponents. But there is no question that a good part of the problem came from the male-dominated old-boy networks in the state legislatures. In any event, the problem remains. It is exacerbated by the rapid movement of women into the job market in the last few decades. My own experience in a large corporation is that sexual discrimination, particularly sexual harassment on the job, is the most difficult problem to handle in the entire industrial relations field — because of its subtlety.

This was the state of affairs the courts had to deal with in the unisex insurance cases. They had been exercising restraint in decision making because the Equal Rights Amendment was in the ratification process, and they did not want to make decisions that could be upset by a change in the Constitution. They were certainly influenced by the Warren concept that the Court should break impasses in the legislative process, and also guided by the Dooley doctrine that "the Supreme Court reads the newspapers." The issue was an emotional one and, on the surface, quite simple.

Most women, organized or not, were outraged. It just didn't seem fair that women should be paid less than men in annuities. The standard arguments about the unreliability of statistics when applied to individual cases were trotted out. There is also an innate suspicion on the part of the press and the general public concerning those who use statistics. "Figures don't lie, but liars figure" is the applicable cliché. It was

a simple, straightforward issue, made to order for sensationalism and media manipulation.

Still, the Supreme Court should have known better. In a
democracy we cannot expect the general public to make an
effort to understand complex issues like the "present value"
of a pension liability, or the enormous impact of changes in
pension systems on the national economy, or the crucial importance of the integrity of actuarial tables to risk assessment,
which form the very fundamental fairness doctrine of risk
distribution. That is what we have institutions for. They should
not be swayed by simplifications and sensationalism. In this
case the Court made a fundamental error: the issue was not
sex, but longevity. Gender, like age, is one of the most accurate measures of longevity. Any argument that can be brought
up about sexual discrimination can be applied to age discrimination. Why should an eighty-year-old person pay more for
an insurance policy than a nineteen-year-old when teetotaling
octogenarians abound and teenagers are succumbing daily to
the effects of drugs and alcohol? The answer, of course, is that
on the average nineteen-year-olds live longer than eighty-
year-olds. The fact that there are individual exceptions does
not destroy the integrity of the system.

What is the effect of this kind of erroneous decision, this
attempt to adjudicate the laws of mathematics? It messes up
our entire system, that's what it does. In the first place, it
sensationalizes and diverts attention from the more basic problems of sexual discrimination. Second, it doesn't help women
at all.

The state of Arizona promptly eliminated the annuity option
from its pension plan, and administrators of many other plans
have followed suit. This means that men and women will now
be offered identical lump sums or payments over a fixed period
of time as they were in the first place. But neither men nor

women will be able to string out the payments over a lifetime. So everybody in Arizona loses.

Every pension plan in the United States is being reviewed in light of the decision. Actuarial consultants are making a mint, but at the cost of tens of thousands of dollars per review for the hundred thousand pension plans in existence. The numbers get to billions of dollars very quickly. We must remember that these are unproductive billions of dollars that must come ultimately out of someone's hide — the pension recipient's, most likely.

When we try to manipulate the laws of nature, we often end up with some peculiar side effects. The phenomenon is facetiously known as the Law of Unintended Consequences. Most corporations, and probably most public agencies, have a desirable pension feature known as Joint and Survivors. Under this provision, the surviving spouse continues to receive a pension on the death of a pensionee. Under the new rules a female employee who elects this option must accept a smaller payment because her surviving male spouse must be assumed to have unisex longevity.

Gets pretty complicated, doesn't it? But what the Court has done more basically is to be shortsighted in taking away from women one of the real advantages they have in this battle for sexual equality — their longevity. One of a woman's disadvantages in job competition is her desire to take time out to have and raise children. No matter how many laws we pass, we will never be rid of the fact that you have to be on the job to get promoted. We all notice that women not only live longer than men, but girls mature faster than boys. We should investigate whether it would make sense to enroll girls in school at an earlier age than boys, or perhaps set an older retirement age for women, to make up for lost time in the middle of their careers. These specific suggestions will probably be hooted down as typical masculine chicanery, but I mean them constructively. Many biological differences exist between men and women. We'll get nowhere pretending that they don't.

Repercussions from judicial activism are quite different in 1985 from what they were in 1953. At that time, even when the Court made the most sweeping decisions, it was difficult to get legislative bodies to respond. These days it is difficult to hold them back. When the Supreme Court acted in 1983, it refused to make its decision retroactive because the parties had acted in good faith and because the costs would be too great. No sooner had the ruling been handed down than bills were introduced into both the Senate and the House requiring that all insurance be made unisex and that the changes be retroactive. This was far beyond anything the Court had considered.

Universal unisex insurance constitutes very poor actuarial practice and skews the risk assessment mechanism into inefficiency. Insurance companies can live with it, however, by passing along the costs to their policyholders. But retroactivity would be catastrophic. Most life insurance companies, even the very largest, are mutual organizations. They have no stockholders; the policyholders own the company. The managers are just that — managers. They own no more of the company than does any policyholder.

If these bills had been enacted as proposed, they would have cost the policyholders $14 billion, since the policies with lower benefits would have had to be "topped up" to equal those with higher benefits. To many millions of small policyholders the paid-up value of their life insurance is the largest single tangible asset they own. Many of the smaller life insurance companies would have been wiped out.

It is hard to think of a bigger potential rip-off of the common man in the name of political opportunism. Yet Senator Bob Packwood of Oregon, who introduced the Senate bill, and Congressman John Dingell of Michigan — the same John Dingell who wrote the Endangered Species Act — who introduced the House bill, brought along support from 130 women's groups and civil rights and labor organizations and immediately picked up 125 cosponsors in the House. Who reads the fine print?

The large insurance companies panicked. Faced with the political problems of fighting both unisex and retroactivity, the board of the American Council of Life Insurance (ACLI) caved in. They swallowed their actuarial pride, decided to rise above principle, and endorsed unisex but not retroactivity. Leading the retreat was ACLI board chairman Robert A. Beck of Prudential. The Pru figured that retroactivity could take a $1.5 billion piece out of the rock — and out of Richard Schweiker, former Reagan cabinet member and current president of ACLI.

The insurance rank and file reacted with outrage. They raised a million dollars for an advertising campaign with this message: under a unisex system women will pay $700 million a year more for auto insurance and $360 million more for life insurance. As this P.R. blitz crescendoed, the ACLI membership voted overwhelmingly to repudiate their board's compromise. The ACLI promptly jumped in with full-page newspaper ads proclaiming "Women live longer than men. Congress shouldn't penalize them because they do." Score one for the little guy (and little girl?). The insurance companies are now split down the middle, and the congressional supporters of unisex are ducking for cover as usual. The whole issue was confused and confounding.

The executive branch and the lower courts were quick to join the parade and add to the confusion. The Social Security

Administration quietly revised its tables to eliminate all sexual differences. This time the men made out better because widowers were raised to equal status with widows. Such equalization naturally added to the costs of the system and increased the administration's funding problems.

Recently a district court ruled that the Internal Revenue Service's actuarial tables for estate tax assessment were sexually discriminatory. The judge obviously misinterpreted the Supreme Court's decision, which was strictly employment-related. The Treasury Department meekly decided not to appeal and instructed the IRS to revise its tables. And so it goes, on and on. No one knows what the costs of all this nonsense will add up to, but it is certain to be many billions of dollars, to be paid ultimately by the citizens of this country, men and women alike.

• • •

Unisex insurance is but one sad example of the effects of judicial activism coupled with legislative irresponsibility and voter apathy. The legal reinterpretation of one word in a nineteen-year-old statute can send waves cascading down into multiple sectors of our society, sapping them of their sufficiency and substance. There are other, more insidious pervasive examples of the courts usurping the legitimate functions of the legislature, the executive, and even the electorate. The original school desegregation ruling was monumental in scope. The courts should have stopped there and allowed the other branches of government, guided by the electorate, to apply the proper remedies.

Two decades after the ruling, desegregation and the quality of primary school education is in a sorry state. Nobody likes the myriad of busing programs except a few ultraliberal legislators who can afford to send their children to private schools.

The integrity of neighborhood schools has been breached; children spend hours riding around on school buses when they should be at home studying. Mothers have no way to take their children home if they get sick during the day. White and black children alike are frightened by unfamiliar and hostile neighborhoods. Cooping up children in crowded buses for hours each week leads to lack of discipline and unruliness. And the flight from the cities by parents concerned with the quality of education has, in many cases, caused imbalances worse than those which existed twenty years ago.

The city of Boston is a classic case in point. For more than a decade the schools have been under the iron-clad control of one man, Judge Arthur W. Garrity. In the name of justice this judge has seen the system decline in quality and numbers until there is serious question whether it can ever recover. Community frustration and parent and student dissatisfaction have touched off racial violence in the schools to the point where Boston is perceived by nightly television news viewers as simply one big bastion of bigotry.

During Judge Garrity's one-man control, mayors, city councilmen, and school committees have been elected — to no avail. The judge rules on. It is obvious that one man with no administrative experience, staff, or responsibility to the electorate, and no training except in the law, cannot possibly cope with the complex and explosive problems of operating the school system of a major city. By now it would seem that the voters should know what they want from a school committee, but they have literally been disenfranchised and can do nothing about the issue until the judge says they can. The judge's rulings have been appealed many times, but who can expect an appeals court to rule against one of its brethren on a matter of judicial authority. It doesn't seem possible in this democracy of ours, but the only legal remedy available to the citizens of Boston is an amendment to the Constitution of the United States!

Then there was the one-man, one-vote decision made back in 1962. The Supreme Court decided that the state of Tennessee had acted unconstitutionally in apportioning its state legislative districts by geography rather than by population. This was the first major intrusion by the courts into the political process. Justice Felix Frankfurter, the great humanitarian liberal, was horrified by the action of the majority and expressed his concern in an eloquent dissent. Frankfurter stated that "there is nothing in the Equal Protection Clause or elsewhere in the federal Constitution which expressly or impliedly supports the view that state legislatures must be so structured as to reflect with approximate equality the voice of every voter." He further warns that "there is not under our Constitution a judicial remedy for every political mischief, for every undesirable exercise of legislative power. The Framers carefully and with deliberate forethought refused so to enthrone the judiciary. In this situation, as in others of like nature, appeal for relief does not belong here. Appeal must be to an informed, civically militant electorate. In a democratic society like ours, relief must come through an aroused popular conscience that sears the conscience of the people's representatives."

Frankfurter's concern was prophetic. The cloud no bigger than a man's hand discerned by Frankfurter has grown into a storm of redistricting cases in which considerations of equality of population, integrity of political units, contiguity of districts, and representation of racial and ethnic minorities compete for precedence.

The courts are not equipped to handle these problems. In Boston yet another federal judge threw out a municipal election after sitting on the case for a year. His response was so late that the election had to be postponed. Several candidates ran out of funds as a result and had to drop out. The judge probably influenced the outcome of those elections more than any single individual. Never having had to run for office, he had no idea of the havoc he had created.

In New Jersey a judge threw out a congressional redistricting plan that varied from the census by only a few percentage points, well within the statistical limits of accuracy of the census at the time it was taken, and certainly within the variations in demographics in the intervening years since the data was collected. The judge had probably never had a course in statistics; he certainly did not understand the concept of limits of accuracy in data collection.

I may not have had the correct education either, because I have never understood the concept of one man, one vote. I recognize that there should be a reasonable degree of proportionality in voting, but I also recognize that differences between urban and rural areas must be considered, as well as differences between industrial and agricultural areas. Reflecting these differences, the Constitution stipulated a bicameral Congress, with one branch set up by geography and one by population. The Framers left the task of ascertaining the degree of proportionality to the state legislatures, wisely recognizing that each state would have different kinds of issues to address through representation.

And now one person, one judge, is deemed to have the omniscience to discard a redistricting plan because it differs by a few percentage points from an imprecise census taken at a single moment in time in a rapidly changing population. And there is no recourse. The higher courts have stuck together every time on this issue. In no case have they reversed.

It is frightening to consider what would happen if some judge declared the United States Senate unconstitutional. One will probably do it. After all, the state of Alaska, with four hundred thousand inhabitants, has two senators, and the state of California, with 24 million inhabitants, also has two senators. Is that one man, one vote? I realize that the Constitution is explicit on this point, but Chief Justice Charles E. Hughes once remarked that the Constitution means what the Supreme Court says it means. And President Woodrow Wilson said that the Supreme Court resembles a constitutional convention in continuous session.

We have become a litigious society. We can hardly move without ending up in the courts. It is not possible to build a power plant or even a sewer without ending up in litigation. Courts are funding school systems and public housing all over the country. They are operating mental health systems and prisons. They are telling us how we must elect our representatives and who shall go to medical school and who shall be a firefighter, tasks for which judges are not equipped (Frankfurter again), "to adjudicate by legal training or experience or native wit." In fact, to many people's surprise, they are not even equipped for much of it by the Constitution itself. One searches in vain to find a statement in the Constitution that grants the power of judicial review to the Supreme Court. It is not in Article III, in which categories of federal court jurisdiction are enumerated; moreover, in Article VI, it is "the judges in every state" who are bound by the supremacy clause, with no mention of a federal court to review and make uniform the state courts' decisions.

In the Convention of 1787 the Framers debated at some length the need for an authority to confer power on some judges and on the executive to share the veto over legislative acts, but the proposal was voted down. It all started in 1803,

when Chief Justice John Marshall wrote the opinion declaring
a minor provision of the Judiciary Act of 1797 unconstitutional,
thereby creating a precedent for judicial review of federal
legislation. From there it just grew until it is deeply imbedded
in our concepts of the law today. If, however, the courts were
to decide to back off a bit, nothing in the Constitution would
prevent them from doing so.

The litigious atmosphere that exists in our society is hurting
us badly in world competition. We have 620,000 lawyers in
the United States, one for every four hundred people. Japan,
our principal world competitor, has only eleven thousand lawyers, one for every ten thousand people. These statistics give
us a small indication of the relative complexity of the two legal
systems. The fact that the Japanese system was established
by Americans less than forty years ago makes the situation all
the more disheartening.

We need to step back and take a look at where this exponential increase in judicial activism is leading us before we
bind ourselves in legal red tape so tightly that we cannot be
extricated. We should heed the warnings of sages who have
gone before us as we review our perceptions of the Supreme
Court.

Thomas Jefferson (1804):
The opinion which gives to the judges the right to decide what
laws are constitutional, and what not, not only for themselves
in their own sphere of action, but for the Legislature & Executive also, in their spheres, would make the judiciary a
despotic branch.

Andrew Jackson (1832):
[The decision of the Supreme Court] ought not to control the
coordinate authorities of this Government. The Congress, the
Executive, and the Court must each for itself be guided by its

own opinion of the Constitution. Each public officer who takes an oath to support the Constitution swears that he will support it as he understands it, and not as it is understood by others. . . . The opinion of the judges has no more authority over Congress than the opinion of Congress has over the judges, and on that point the President is independent of both. The authority of the Supreme Court must not, therefore, be permitted to control the Congress or the Executive when acting in their legislative capacities, but only to have such influence as the force of their reasoning may deserve.

Abraham Lincoln (1861):
If the policy of the Government upon vital questions affecting the whole people is to be irrevocably fixed by decisions of the Supreme Court, the instant they are made in ordinary litigation between parties on personal actions, the people will have ceased to be their own rulers, having to that extent practically resigned their government into the hands of that eminent tribunal.

Chief Justice Richard Neely of the West Virginia State Supreme Court is an ardent proponent of judicial activism. He stated flatly in his book *How Courts Govern America*, "American courts, both state and federal, are the central institution in the United States which makes American democracy work." But even he admits that "most people are aware of only a few court decisions which concern their geographical area, social class, or industry; if everyone were aware of the extent to which the courts turn other people's lives upside down every day, the level of concern would be substantially higher. In the past twenty-five years there has been no appeal to politically accountable, elected officials from court legislation, because the decisions of life-tenured, anonymous judges are, for all practical purposes, beyond the reach of the democratic process."

The Supreme Court has been making sociological judgments, not legal judgments. The legal aspects of cases are treated extensively in the lower courts. If there is a definitive legal point, it is delineated in the districts and honed in the appeals process. Only when the statute is imprecise, or the case law inconclusive, does the highest court even deign to intervene. The record shows that the Supreme Court is uncomfortable in this role. Those who rise to this exalted status are the ultimate, highly skilled practitioners of their profession. Like all professionals their judgments are bounded by their experience and training and ill suited to the exposure to extrapolations beyond those bounds. Little wonder then that forced to make sociological decisions outside their ken, they reach frantically for quasi-legal fig leaves to cover their exposure. But such fig leaves are brittle and fragile. They crumble and fade away when the strong winds of statistics, biology, logic, or sheer human experience blow upon them and test their strength.

I make a simple suggestion: that the next appointee to the Supreme Court not be a lawyer. The law is too precious in this rapidly changing culture to be left to the lawyers anymore, just as war is too important to be left to the generals. When we live in a world in which extinction can be minutes away, we cannot afford to fritter away our energies on minor legalistic concepts. Our international competitors are not concerned with snail darters or unisex insurance. No conceivable way are they willing to delegate the question of who votes for whom or who goes to what school to minor judicial authorities. When we make our own sociological decisions, we cannot be constrained by the historic nitpicks of the legal precedent.

We cannot legislate, we cannot litigate, we cannot adjudicate the laws of nature. Command as we may, King Canute we cannot be. And no matter what the learned justices proclaim from the highest court or from the highest mountain, I will continue to believe that there is a difference between men and women.

Vive la différence.

4

¿Parlez-Vous Español?

¿QUÉ es esto? Es el libro.

¿Es esto el lápiz? Si, es el lápiz.

¿Es esta la caja, señor? No, señor, no es la caja, sino la pluma.

El lápiz es pardo. El libro es azul. El cielo raso es blanco. El sombrero es verde.

El lápiz negro es largo.

El lápiz rojo no es largo; es corto.

¿Es largo el lápiz negro? No, no es largo. Es corto.

La avenida es ancha; la calle es estrecha.

El libro pardo es largo y ancho.

La ventana es grande; la mesa es pequeña.

¿Es grande el libro verde? Si, es grande.

¿Soy yo norteamericano? No, usted no es norteamericano; usted es Español.

Mi sombrero está encima de la mesa.

La puerta está delante de mi.

Yo soy el profesor.

Usted es un alumno.

Usted está sentada delante de la ventana.

Suppose you were a five-year-old suddenly immigrated to Mexico with your family. Suppose that the family was poor, your father out of a job, your mother unable to speak Spanish and illiterate. This is your first day of school, a frightening experience for any child surrounded by strange faces, strange sounds, and strange buildings. You open the first page of the textbook given to you, and the teacher begins to read what is printed above.

What is your first reaction? It would obviously be "I want to go home." But your mother has told you that if you leave the classroom, you will be punished. If you are like most children, you will just sit there, doing nothing. You don't know how to learn the language unless someone teaches it to you. If no one does, you will just wallow in the classroom until you are old enough to get a job, and then quit school.

This is a sad and disheartening experience for a child, but not at all unusual for children who, for centuries, have been immigrants all over the world. Over the years adult immigrants who did not speak the language of their adopted country had two options: one was to retreat into a ghetto and teach their children themselves; the other was to allow the educators in their new homeland to teach their children. In the United States both solutions have been tried. In the early years of our nation, many immigrants established their own neighborhood schools. The Germans, who arrived here during the eighteenth century, used this approach. To a lesser extent the same practice was followed by the Poles and the Swedes. The Jews tried both methods. But because they were crowded into the big cities, and had traditionally been shopkeepers rather than farmers, they soon found it desirable to learn the language of the country in order to conduct business and prosper. But the secret of the melting pot — to learn English — was understood by all immigrants by the end of the nineteenth century. Not only did adults mandate this for their children; they themselves began to attend English classes in increasing numbers, particularly to qualify for their citizenship papers. By the middle of the 1920s, almost everyone spoke English.

A different immigration pattern began to emerge after World War II, especially in New York City and along the Mexican border. In almost all previous immigrations, immigrants broke off most of their ties to their native lands when they left home. Some, like the Irish and the Italians, returned, but chiefly to marry or provide assistance to relatives who wanted to emigrate. The commitment to the new land was complete.

For Mexicans and Puerto Ricans life was different. They tended to maintain close contact with their native land because their immigration coincided with the development of easy transportation during the last two decades. As a result, they have been less willing to assimilate into the traditional American melting pot. Without parental pressure to learn English, the children had little interest in mastering the language of their new home, and the dropout rate of Hispanics from school became alarming.

Educators developed a heightened concern for the linguistically disadvantaged, particularly the Hispanics, during the 1960s. In 1967 hearings were held on a bilingual education bill introduced by Senator Ralph Yarborough of Texas. It was pointed out that the dropout rate of Mexican-Americans in Texas was considerably higher than that of blacks, and twice that of Anglos. Something had to be done.

Here was a classic sociological problem. It had a classic

sociological solution. Teach the kids English. The lessons of
the melting pot were clear.

But to American politicians and the bureaucracy, simple
solutions are anathema. The hearings attracted little public
attention, and the record amply foreboded the complexities
to follow. Experts on language and primary school instruction
were not called on to testify. The hearings were dominated
by ethnic lobbyists, primarily Hispanic. To the amazement of
the few disinterested people who followed the proceedings,
the problem to be solved ended up being the opposite of what
it had started out to be. Instead of searching for ways to
assimilate these linguistically disadvantaged youngsters into
an English-speaking American society, the problem became
one of how to keep the children from being assimilated.

The times were ripe for such a switch. Politicians and social
activists were crying from the rooftops about the ills of American society. It would be cruel, the argument went, to force
these poor children to lose their cultural heritage and to mix
with an alien society. No less a personage than the United
States commissioner of education called for the abandonment
of the melting pot ideal. "Perhaps a better image" could be
used, he said. "It is the image of the mosaic which has a great
variety in it, and which gains its strength from variety." What
a marvelous piece of gobbledygook. Congressman James H.
Scheuer of New York said, "I think we have discarded the
philosophy of the melting pot. We have a new concept of the
value of enhancing, fortifying, and protecting people's differences, the very differences that make our country such a vital
country."

What a cruel concept. To force these children into a cultural
and linguistic ghetto in the name of political expediency was
about as low as a politician or a government bureaucrat could
stoop. The reason the parents of these children came to the

United States in the first place was for economic opportunity. They had not been forced to leave their native land as a result of political or religious persecution. They came to get jobs. Unless the ghetto could become a viable economic unit on its own, these people would have to enter the mainstream of American society in order to prosper. Yet without facility in English, they would be doomed for life to the lowest levels of American society.

The chances of the ghetto becoming a viable economic unit were nil. Every immigrant group had found that out. Germans, Poles, Swedes, Irish, Jews, Italians, French, Chinese, Japanese, and Armenians had all learned that the key to survival and success was assimilation. Each group, however, had a strong desire to preserve its own original culture and proved that the best place to accomplish this task was in the home, where the degree of preservation could be tailored to each family's desires.

No one quite knew what bilingual education was, anyway. To the general public it was some sort of mechanism to assist students in their own language while they were learning English. To the ethnic ideologue, it was a means to preserve ethnicity, that is, separateness in the schools as well as in the home.

This was special-interest legislation clothed in the sanctity accorded all civil rights legislation of the 1960s. And it was packaged well. Images of needy children, poverty, discrimination, and potential psychological damage were all floated before congressional eyes. The public wasn't watching. The expenditures envisioned were relatively small. The proponents were organized, but the opponents were not. The bill would have been politically costly to oppose, but potentially lucrative to support. Few senators or congressmen even bothered to attend the hearings.

The Bilingual Education Act was passed in 1968. It was "designed to meet the special education needs of children of limited English-speaking ability [LESA was the inevitable acronym] in schools having a high concentration of such children." The programs could be bilingual; they could be designed "to impart to students a knowledge of the history and culture associated with their language"; they could consist of "efforts to establish closer cooperation between the school and the home"; and so on. It had the essential ingredient of all special-purpose sociological legislation: it was very vague. This trick allows the administrators of the legislation to interpret it to their own inclinations.

The act did have one glaring omission. It did not explain how the LESA was going to learn English while receiving instruction in another language.

Administration of the act was assigned to the Division of Bilingual Education of the Department of Health, Education and Welfare. The bureaucrats of DBE-HEW may not have known how to teach the English language, but they knew a boondoggle when they saw it. The DBE-HEW was quickly staffed with ethnic militants, following a great American government administrative tradition: staffing programs for a particular group by fervent members of that group. The antitrust division of the Department of Justice is staffed by budding trial lawyers; the Department of Labor by labor union activists; the Department of Commerce by Chamber of Commerce types.

The beginnings were quite appropriately innocuous and unobtrusive. Appropriations for fiscal year 1969 were only $7.8 million, but by 1974 they had worked their way up to $58.3 million and were climbing. Then came a stroke of good fortune for the bureaucracy. The Supreme Court entered the picture.

This time the Supreme Court wasn't the bad guy. In a case known as *Lau* v. *Nichols,* the Court found that Chinese-American, non-English-speaking students were denied equal education opportunity under Title VI of the Civil Rights Act when instructed in English, a language they did not understand. The Court ruled that schools must "rectify the language deficiency," but did not specify how that should be accomplished.

Indeed, the Court recognized that there were several alternatives: "Teaching English to the students of Chinese ancestry who do not speak the language is one choice. Giving instruction to this group in Chinese is another. There may be others." The Supreme Court was on its best behavior. It was even gracious enough to quote Senator Humphrey in a statement he made during floor debate on the Civil Rights Act of 1964, since this particular statement agreed with the position of the Court. "Simple justice requires that public funds to which all taxpayers of all races contribute, not be spent in any fashion which encourages, entrenches, subsidizes, or results in racial discrimination."

To the civil servant an applicable Supreme Court decision is like the keys to Fort Knox. It is like a Nobel Prize of bureaucracy. The Office of Civil Rights was now able to join in the fray. They put out a confusing series of memoranda, which stipulated primarily that the Civil Rights Act applied to any school district that had more than twenty non-English-speaking students, thus roping in practically every school district in the country. But the pièce de résistance of linguistic obfuscation was masterminded by Terrel H. Bell, then commissioner of education, later secretary of education. He appointed a task force that issued a report specifying procedures for eliminating those deficiencies ruled in violation of the Civil Rights Act. They were known as the *Lau* remedies, thus cloaked in the robes of the highest judicial authority. But the *Lau* remedies bore practically no resemblance to the Supreme Court's *Lau* decision. The remedies stated that the students should be taught in their native language — only one of the possible alternatives noted by the Supreme Court. They also directed that the students receive instruction in their native culture, an issue that was not even addressed by the Court.

I have complained in previous chapters that our government authorities do not understand the law of large numbers, but I have to take off my hat to them for understanding how to manipulate small numbers. The Bell task force found out how to make two equal one. They had embraced a Supreme Court decision, ignored it, and transformed bilingual education into monolingual education.

From there on, it was a new ball game. Those two home-run hitters of government spending, Senator Edward Kennedy and Senator Alan Cranston, stepped into the batter's box and drove expenditures out of the ball park. They backed the renewal of the Bilingual Education Act, hoping for a bill that would put the federal government behind full-time native language and cultural instruction as *the* means by which the LESAs would learn. The programs envisioned would have been maintained through the full twelve years of elementary and secondary schooling. As presidential hopefuls, they well recognized the size of the Hispanic vote and that this issue had become the rallying point for the ethnic activists. "When the United States is the fifth largest Spanish-speaking country in the world, and when a majority of people in this hemisphere speak Spanish," Senator Kennedy said, "surely our educational system should not be designed so that it destroys the language and culture of children from Spanish-speaking backgrounds."

The senators didn't get everything they wanted, but they

got most of it. The act was renewed in 1974 and again in 1978. By that time appropriations had jumped from the original $7.8 million to $135 million. The number of projects rose to 565 and the number of language groups served to seventy. It's hard to believe that seventy different languages are spoken in the United States, but if more than twenty people speak one, the Department of Education will find them. The city of Chicago alone must provide instruction not only in Spanish but also in seventeen other languages, including Assyrian, Gujarati, Urdu, and Serbo-Croatian. The job-creation opportunities in these programs are literally limitless; no wonder the professional educators love them. When we read of the complexities of instructor certification to teach in the English language, imagine the bureaucracy needed to certify an instructor in Gujarati or Urdu.

After 1978 the inevitable disillusionment began to set in. By that time enough data had been collected for an evaluation of the efficacy of the programs to begin. A four-year study of 11,500 Hispanic students by the American Institute for Research concluded that most of the students did not need to learn English; that those who did were not in fact acquiring it; and that with few exceptions, the programs were aimed at linguistic and cultural maintenance. The study also found that to the degree the children were already alienated from school, they remained so.

At this point, I must confess my own biases on sociological research. As one who has spent a lifetime associated with research in the physical, chemical, and biological sciences, I don't consider sociological research to be research at all. Most of it is just data collection. All actions in the physical and social sciences are influenced by a large number of variables. The trick in first-class research is to eliminate all variables but one, and to study the effects of that one. This is not easy to do, even in the laboratory, but it is almost impossible to do in large-scale sociological studies, particularly those involving demographics. Also, in any kind of research it is very difficult for the researcher to eliminate personal bias. If a researcher is looking for a particular result, he or she will go to great lengths to find it (as, of course, I have here). Every experienced researcher also knows that additional research grants do not materialize for those who come up with negative results. That is why peer review is so important in the physical sciences. A research conclusion is not accepted if it cannot be duplicated and verified by others. In sociological research this is impossible, so that most of the studies turn out to be simply collections of data. I do hope that my particular collections of data will turn out to be more accurate than some other people's collections of data. On the subject of bilingual education this is particularly true. In reviewing dozens of articles on this subject, I have to conclude that a study can be found to support virtually every possible conclusion.

Without good data on the current programs, we must rely on common sense and general past experience to make our points. Our best data comes from the experience of the millions of immigrants who have come to this country in the last four centuries. That experience is overwhelmingly in favor of assimilation. Maintenance of cultural ghettos or barrios can only lead to inhabitants who are unable to compete in the mainstream of American society. The new world economy will dictate a more knowledge-oriented work force in the United States with lower-skilled industrial jobs performed in countries like India or China, where current wages are less than a dollar a week. With the transportation, information, and communications revolutions, we will no longer import workers, we will export jobs. That means that barrio inhabitants will have available to them only the most menial of service jobs, or public welfare.

The second piece of experience is that cultural maintenance is better done in the home or in the neighborhood, not in the schools. American immigrants have been vehement on this point, perhaps too vehement. Speaking a foreign language has been considered degrading in the American culture, to the point where Americans know too little about foreign competition.

I like to tell the story of my uncle Pat, who worked in the sewer department and had a brogue so thick you could cut it with a knife. When Pat learned that I was studying Latin and Greek in high school, he was scornful. "Them furrin lenguages won't do ya no gud," he said. I tried to convince him that they would help me in later life, but he was adamant. "Let me tell ya something, lad," he continued. "If the English language was gud enough for Jaysus Christ, it's gud enough fer me." Pat may have been a little extreme, but all the immigrants, whatever they felt about languages, managed to keep their cultures alive in their homes, churches, and neighborhoods, and do it without a nickel's worth of government assistance.

As for making this nation bilingual, that notion is ridiculous. We have only to look at the agonies of our neighbor to the north, Québec, to understand the divisiveness of that daffy idea. Besides, what would we do with the people who speak the seventy other languages we support, make them trilingual? Or perhaps septuagesimal-lingual?

From our melting pot experience, we Americans are very leery about other languages and know little about how they are learned. I just happen to be a language hobbyist. I have been able to make myself understood in the languages of a number of foreign countries, specifically French, German, Spanish, Italian, Russian, Japanese, Arabic, and Hebrew. Each language has an appeal all its own and, to some degree, reflects the temperament of the people in the country. The Oriental languages, Japanese and Chinese, are a little inexact. Because they are based on a limited number of Chinese characters, each character has to have several different meanings. It is for this reason that I think Orientals seem somewhat vague and inscrutable. The German and Russian languages are just the opposite, with a bewildering number of word endings, each implying a different shade of meaning. The Germans and Russians reflect this, seeming to be very stiff and precise. Spanish is sibilant and sexy, like a Spanish señorita peeking out of the curtains above her balcony. The Italian language, with practically all its syllables ending in vowels, is very musical, like its people. The Semitic languages are gutteral, suggesting the mysteries of the Middle East. The French language, like its people, is always in a hurry. It never finishes a word before starting the next one.

If there's one thing I've learned, and which all good language schools teach, it's that immersion is by far the best way to learn a foreign language. Get into it and stay with it. You can't learn one language while speaking another. The present system isn't working. We have spent more than half a billion dollars now on language and cultural maintenance programs in the schools and have conducted dozens of studies. After fifteen years we don't know whether they do good or harm. We only know that they are very expensive. The so-called *Lau* remedies are still being used, even though they were not required in the first place. Attempts are finally being made to allow flexibility in the curriculum. Revised regulations are being prepared to allow local districts to choose between language maintenance and English immersion. I have a simpler solution.

The educators are trying to do something that can't be done. If two children in good health and of equal intelligence, with similar family and economic backgrounds, enter school at the same age, but one speaks English and the other does not, the one who does not will be six months to a year behind the one who does. This is not discrimination or anything else; it's a fact. The linguistically disadvantaged child will have to spend time catching up, time that cannot be spent on other subjects. Language maintenance programs only postpone the day of reckoning. Why not recognize that, and plan accordingly? Educators are not certain if very young children can learn subjects like arithmetic, but everyone knows that children start to learn language at birth. Why not start the linguistically disadvantaged child six months earlier and teach nothing but English? This can be done in a kindergarten or a day-care center, and can be purely voluntary. Any reasonably intelligent child can become proficient in spoken English in six months. Then the child can join its peers to learn to read and write. Such a program would be very simple and inexpensive, because the teacher would not have to be proficient in anything but English. This plan might not satisfy some ethnic militants, but it certainly would give the child a better education. It has another subtle benefit. The linguistically disadvantaged student becomes linguistically advantaged because that child is bilingual, and the others are not.

• • •

When we realize how fouled up a single educational problem like language deficiency can get, it is no wonder that our society cries out for a revamping of the entire system. At least three commissions prepared reports on the system's deficiencies in the last year. Since I was a member of one of them (the one chaired by Governor James Hunt of North Carolina), and since I once served as chairman of the Board of Higher Education for the commonwealth of Massachusetts, I feel entitled to make a few observations about education in general.

The concept of equality for all is deeply embedded in our Constitution and our overall system of justice. But our system can only guarantee equality of opportunity, not equality of result. Our society's refusal to admit this is the fundamental problem bedeviling our whole educational system. Some people are taller than others, so we can't guarantee equality for basketball teams. Some people run faster than others, so we can't guarantee equality for track teams. By the same token, some people are smarter than others, so we can't guarantee equality in education systems. As I have said before, we cannot legislate, we cannot litigate, we cannot adjudicate the laws of nature.

We complain about the quality of our schools, pointing out that the quality has been deteriorating for years. This is true, particularly in the high schools. The achievement of today's high school graduate is well below the average of twenty-five years ago, a great deal below that of the graduate of fifty years ago, and tremendously below that of the graduate of seventy-five years ago. But that is comparing apples and oranges. We must realize that the high school dropout rate was about 25 percent a quarter century ago, over 50 percent a half century ago, and that only 10 percent of the student population finished high school at the turn of the century. Granted that most of them dropped out for economic reasons, but the high school graduate in those days had to be highly motivated to finish at all. There were tough courses in Latin and Greek, physics, chemistry, and modern languages. If the student couldn't hack it, he or she was politely invited by the principal to leave. This was considered quite legal and proper, since there was no public stigma attached to dropping out of high school. The schools were run by the scholars; politics had not yet invaded them.

The idea that in a democratic society every child should be able to receive the same high school diploma is more idealistic than practical. It would be too wrenching a concept to propose that students be allowed to drop out of school when they cannot keep up with their peers, because modern society, particularly in the cities, uses the schools to keep young people off the streets. But we should allow them to learn what they can learn at the pace at which they can learn it. A very large fraction of the students in the public schools today cannot master physics or chemistry or the literature of a foreign language or higher mathematics. Why not admit it? It may not be easy to tell a parent that Johnny can't understand algebra, but Johnny knows it, and so does his teacher. The commissioners who have done all the studies don't know it, or won't admit it, or can't persuade the professional staffs who write the final reports that it is so.

Many European countries that cannot afford the inefficiencies of the American school system recognize reality and do not attempt to achieve academic excellence with their whole population. It may not be egalitarian, but it works. They turn out a steady stream of students who are well educated and able to take up the burdens of government and business to the overall benefit of the nation.

In this country we have tried to use the schools to solve the problems of society as a whole; the schools can't do that. We have stuck our heads in the sand and brought the level of education down to the lowest common denominator. We need to create a truly excellent curriculum for those who are

highly gifted, another for average students, and a special curriculum for those who are slow and reluctant learners. If a
student is doing well at a lower level, it should be made easy
for him or her to move up to a faster pace, after some special
coaching for catch-up. Diplomas should indicate clearly which
curriculum the student has completed.

This is heresy. I have never dared propose it to the staffs
of the educational organizations with which I have been connected. Any good staff knows how to run a suggestion like
this off the road and how to banish the heretic out to the
oblivions of bigotry. But what are we doing now? We are
refusing to admit that these differences exist. Whom are we
hurting? The very children we are trying to protect. It is the
bilingual education example on a massive scale. But wouldn't
the lowest curriculum level be disproportionally filled with
children from the minorities, the poor, the disadvantaged, the
bright students from broken homes and from poor family backgrounds? Certainly it would. But the schools did not spawn
these children or make them poor or break up their families.
The schools can only take the material that comes to them
and mold it to the degree that it can be molded. But is this
fair? Fair to whom? Fair to the gifted student who is now held
back to the point of boredom? Fair to the slow learner who
is pushed too hard and finally gives up in despair? Fair to the
teacher who quits from the frustration of trying to squeeze
highly disparate and nonmiscible material into the same mold?

We call for quality in our schools. You can't have quality
and equality at the same time; it is a contradiction in terms.
If we are going to have high-quality output, we are going to
have to cater to high-quality input. If we insist on egalitarianism, we'll end up with pabulum. If we truly want social
justice for the slow learner and the sociologically disadvantaged, we are going to have to tailor whole curricula for them,

and admit it. It's no stigma on the child; the other kids know full well who can do what. It is we who are stigmatized.

Let's stop meddling. Take the issue of school prayer. I can understand the original issue and not get very excited about it. There is merit on both sides. I think it is a good cultural tradition, but I can appreciate the sincere objections of those who feel otherwise. Some states have found a compromise, a moment of silence when the child can think of whatever comes into its mind. The moment of silence is now being thrown out in some courts as unconstitutional, and this really fries me. The federal courts have no constitutional right to invalidate state laws in the first place, as I have said before. Why are they acting this way? Are they afraid that some children might think religious thoughts? They won't unless someone tells them to. They'll think about going to the bathroom, or wishing they could go out to play, or how they are going to get rid of the peas on their plate at lunch. Who is the court to be concerned about what goes on in the mind of a five-year-old?

My only New Year's resolution for 1984 was not to mention the name of George Orwell under any circumstances, but when I consider the frightening implications of a society that forbids silence, I confess that good old George's warnings flit fleetingly, and perhaps unconstitutionally, across my consciousness.

I think that a moment of silence is a good thing. The Greek philosophers had a word for it — *omphaloskepsis*, which means contemplating one's navel. Rodin's famous sculpture *The Thinker* showed a Greek philosopher on a momentary break from omphaloskepsis. I had trouble getting the word into this book. At first the spelling program in my word processor objected to it with solemn beeps and groans, until I found how to gently but firmly override it. Then I discovered that it was not in Houghton Mifflin's dictionary, so my staid old publisher's computer refused to print it. (Here comes Orwell again, damn it.) I'll have you know that this section was hand set on an old Gutenberg press that I found in my basement. It was done on a Sunday morning when the Houghton Mifflin printing computer had crashed with a blown fuse.

Do me a favor. Break the law if you must, but take a moment of silence. Consider how we, the citizens of the United States of America, have screwed up our society. Consider that while our Marines were being blown up two thousand miles from home, and while the White House is being walled in with concrete barriers, and a nuclear Armageddon may be no more than an hour away, that grown men and women, sitting at high benches amid hushed surroundings, are omphaloskeptically contemplating through mentally transparent black robes whether or not Thomas Jefferson in 1787 intended it to be illegal for five-year-olds to stand for one moment in silence at the beginning of every school day. Shouldn't we be ashamed of ourselves?

It's a good thing that I don't have kids in elementary school. I'm afraid that I would finally practice civil disobedience myself. I'd tell them that they should go ahead and keep quiet for a minute, whether the Court liked it or not.

•   •   •

If we want to have quality education, we must have quality instruction. The reports that have been published in the last year have not been kind to the teaching profession, although they have been fair in assessing the reasons for poor performance. Some of the factors inhibiting teaching performance are low pay, adverse external meddling (such as the school prayer issue), inability to enforce discipline, deterioration of the family, and the poor image of the profession. Low pay tops the list and is receiving some attention, although the last reports show little correlation between teacher pay and student performance. External meddling and discipline can be remedied if our government servants put their minds to doing so. The schools cannot do much about the deterioration of the family resulting in a poorly prepared student. But something can be done about the image of the profession.

I believe that the educators are driving out the teachers. The basic problem is that the instructional cognoscenti have succeeded in transforming a delicate art into a dull and deadening profession. For example, teaching mathematics is a profession for which the professional must study mathematics. Teaching literature is a profession for which the professional must study literature. Teaching medicine is a profession for which the professional must study medicine. The act of teaching, however, is an art which, like singing or sculpting or composing, can only be peripherally professionalized. You have to have it in you.

Most people who think about such things as teaching wonder why humans spend so large a proportion of their lifetime in adolescence compared, for example, to birds, which conquer the miracles of flight within days of emerging from the egg. I think that it is because the human child has so much more to learn than a baby bird. A bird stops learning in a week; if it hasn't learned all the necessary survival skills by that time, something gobbles it up. Through the superiority of its brain, the human animal has conquered all enemies except itself, so its offspring are protected from predators during the years it takes to learn all the skills, primarily language, that they need to be productive in a collective society. The wonderful aspect of learning is that for the fortunate and the skilled, learning can go on all through life.

Learning is instinctive. Study as we may, we still know very little about how a young child learns. If learning is instinctive, much of teaching must also be instinctive. That's very fortunate, since through the eons of evolution, there were very few teachers' colleges around. Parents are instinctive teachers, as are playmates. Some parents are better teachers than others; and some playmates are "good influences," while other playmates are "bad influences," a circumstance to which parents are also instinctively attuned.

We have all known and long remember the good teachers in our lives. Some of them may have had courses in classroom and student motivation, or in psychology of interpersonal relationships, but not many. It just flowed out of them. This is not to say that instinctive skills cannot be honed. Jack Nicklaus takes golf lessons and Luciano Pavarotti has a singing coach, but these professionals spend most of their time on the links or on the stage, not on learning the mechanics of their trade.

The professional educators force teachers to spend so much time on the mechanics that teachers are not adequately prepared in the subjects they intend to teach. You can't teach something you don't know. We all know of certified mathematics teachers who don't know enough to teach long division, and of English teachers who can't parse a sentence. Yet Albert Einstein could not be certified to teach high school science or Shakespeare poetry.

The professional educators got themselves into trouble back in the heydays of progressive education. School was not supposed to be hard work, so the doctrine went; school was meant to be fun. Progressive education emphasized such concepts as active learning (experiences and projects) rather than passive learning (reading); cooperative planning of classroom activities by teachers and pupils; the goal of "effective living" rather than acquisition of knowledge; and the use of books, facts, or traditional learning only when necessary as part of students' activities and experience. The schools of education were sucked into the concepts of progressive education and became strongly identified with the follies and fads that followed. The ideas were soon submerged by the realities of World War II, but before they ran their course, horrible examples of excesses occurred, as in Ann Arbor, Michigan, a major university center. A progressive administration eliminated all textbooks there and let it be known that "teachers were free to do what they wanted in the classroom, but they were not free to use a textbook."

Progressive education is long gone as a significant factor, but the concepts keep bubbling up from the professionals, searching for the elusive, arcane elixir which, in the mechanics of teaching, will make teaching and learning as pleasant and painless as administering or taking a pill. But there is no magic potion. It is just a tough job. Why is it so difficult for so many American educators to acknowledge that writing a sentence, speaking clearly, playing the piano, or learning inferential statistics is simply difficult work?

All that the professionals have given us is a set of artificial barriers to the attraction of qualified teachers into the educational process. Why is it desirable and sometimes necessary to have a master's degree in education to teach in the elementary schools? We have some fine teachers in our medical schools, in our law schools, in our engineering schools, and in postdoctoral education. None of these schools requires a degree in education. In most of them a degree in education would be looked at askance. What they do require is good, solid credentials in the subject to be taught and the motivation to teach it.

This last point raises the question of why we need schools of education at all. For the last decade schools of education have attracted fewer, less capable students. The students complain that the course work is boring, perhaps worthless. Some educators propose scrapping teachers' colleges altogether and training America's teachers with a year or two of classroom apprenticeship after college instead. "Do away with them. Do away with teacher colleges," says Joseph Murphy, chancellor of the City University of New York. "I have never been convinced that an education major is better prepared for a teaching career."

Shoemakers, look to your lasts.

•   •   •

American education is going to get better. And it is going to get better fast. Part of the reason for the improvement will be national attention being given now to these problems I have listed. But the most fundamental reason why schools will get better soon is sheer economic necessity. The schools have deteriorated because the payoff for knowledge has deteriorated. Perhaps this statement seems contradictory in our complex technological society, but it is true. The standard of living enjoyed in the developed countries of the world is based on the exponential rise in productivity over the last century, a rise caused almost entirely by improvements in machinery.

Even the dramatic productivity gains in agriculture, allowing us to feed a hundred Americans with two farm workers, compared to the thirty farm workers it took a century ago, is attributable to improvements in farm machinery. This was not a case of spontaneous generation or deus ex machina, either. Someone had to invent the machines; someone had to provide the tooling; someone had to learn how to build them; someone had to develop the management skills to coordinate the entire effort; and someone had to provide the capital.

In the early industrial revolution capital was scarce. Factories and machines were not understood, so the pioneers who provided the seed capital deserved a handsome return for their foresight and willingness to take risks. Unfortunately, the providers of capital had the upper hand, and their returns became much too handsome. In their greed they demanded too big a piece of the pie, with no one strong enough to cry foul. The conditions under which factory workers labored were abysmal yet tolerable, because the only alternative for the immigrants who manned the lathes and looms was starvation.

The skilled technicians who invented the machines and forged the tools and managed the effort became hired hands, but they lived comparatively well and were respected in their community. Before the days of strong unions the only path to upward mobility was knowledge. The immigrants wanted their children to learn to read and write and, above all, to speak the language. They wanted them to learn history and arithmetic and business so that they could understand this strange, new land and become foremen in the factories or merchants to supply the needs of industry. They slaved and sacrificed to keep their kids in school. The Jews understood it best from centuries of the Diaspora. Those destitute immigrants demanded and achieved superior school systems in the large cities, and woe to the child who complained or failed to finish his homework. They weren't the only ones; the movies of the 1920s relished the portrayal of the young "schoolmarm" arriving in Iowa or Kansas from New England. The first thing she was told by the elders of the community was, "If you run into any troublemaker, or have any boy that doesn't want to learn, you let us know and we'll take care of him." No discipline problems there. Knowledge paid off, and they knew it.

Ultimately, the robber barons at the top became too greedy and the whole system went topsy-turvy. Labor insisted on its just deserts, and the strong labor union was born. As in so many cases, the system overcorrected. The image of the down-trodden garment worker laboring under sweatshop conditions ten hours a day, six days a week, with no overtime pay, Social Security, life or health insurance, sickness pay, unemployment compensation, or workmen's compensation for injuries is, thank God, long gone. In its place is the $50,000-per-year steel worker on an eight-hour day with coffee and lunch breaks, a forty-hour week with ten paid holidays, and all the fringes that earlier workers lacked. I have no objection to any individual worker, or football player, or rock star, or even business executive making as much money as he or she can get, but the recent packages for steel, rubber, chemicals, and electrical machinery cover so many millions of workers that our whole reward system has been skewed out of shape, and we have lost our international competitiveness.

These are called semiskilled jobs, but they are not. Any assembly-line job can be learned in a couple of weeks. It requires no more skill than that of the loom operator of a century ago. By far the largest portion of our nation's productivity improvement has now gone to unskilled labor. Knowledge and training don't pay off the way they used to. Parents used to be happy if their children could get jobs as salespersons in retail stores. These were white-collar jobs; they had more prestige and paid more money. They still have the white collar and the prestige, but they are paid about one-third as well as the blue-collar job.

Doctors used to make five times the pay of blue-collar workers. Now, after twenty years of schooling and several more years of internship and training, they are lucky if they gross more than twice as much as workers who can learn their jobs in less than three weeks. If the doctor counts in his training time and the lost income, he may not net out much at all. In former times teachers made about three times as much as blue-collar workers. Now, even after adjusting for the teachers' shorter working days and longer vacations, the blue-collar unionized workers are making more money.

If you are of an egalitarian mind, you consider these developments desirable and, indeed, nothing more than simple justice. Justice or not, the bottom line is a steady denigration of the value of knowledge and skill, and with it a whittling away at the incentives for maintaining the performance capacity of the schools. What does a parent who has sacrificed to put a son through college only to have the boy next door outearn him on an assembly line at the automobile factory think? The blue-collar unionized worker, in turn, is nowhere near as motivated to keep up a quality school system as was his counterpart a century ago. Logically, such a worker will pay his union dues but vote against an increase in his town's school budget.

This state of affairs is changing rapidly. The $50,000-a-year American steel worker cannot compete with the $3000-a-year Korean competitor in this new one-world economy. Unskilled jobs are being exported from the United States at a breathtaking pace, which poses a severe problem for the unemployed blue-collar worker and for our domestic economy and our society as a whole. In the short run, we have a big problem, but in the long run we will all be better off.

We must switch to a knowledge-based economy. The machines that make the final assemblies will be operated by unskilled labor, but our skilled work force will design and program the machines that make the machines. There will be fewer factory jobs as automation takes over to ensure higher productivity, but these will be made up elsewhere. We are already in the transition, and it is painful. But painful as it is, we have no choice. As this switch is made, there will come a stronger outcry for better teachers, for discipline in the classroom, for curricula with more substance. This time it will not come only from the politicians, the educators, and the businessmen.

This time it will come from the parents and the students.

5

Not in My Backyard

NUCLEAR POWER in the United States of America is dead, finished, kaput. After some fraction of the number of plants in construction is completed, the probability of any new nuclear-powered electricity generating station being started into construction in this century is practically zero. The probability of any commercial nuclear plant coming on-line within the working lifetime of any reader of this book is also practically zero. It is a great tragedy of our time that after unlocking the vast energy resources of the nucleus, our society has chosen to proliferate the evil aspects of that energy and to proscribe the good.

To follow the unfolding of this tragic history, I will consider three aspects of nuclear energy: first, the biological effects of nuclear radiation, then power plant safety, and finally, the disposal of high-level wastes. Before your eyes start to glaze over, I can assure you that the first two can be understood without any scientific background, and that the third will require only the simplest, slightest smidgeon of nuclear physics.

Since I've never had a course in nuclear physics myself (they didn't teach it when I went to school), you can be sure that I will be gentle with you.

According to the "big bang" theory, the world began as a single massive blast of nuclear radiation. The development of the galaxies was started by this initial radiation, leading ultimately to the development of our own solar system, and to the emergence of life on this planet, fueled to this day by the nuclear reactions in the sun. As you might expect, there is still a lot of residual radiation kicking around after these cataclysmic events. As long as life has existed on this earth, it has been bathed in nuclear — more technically, ionizing — radiation. The amount of radiation has been gradually decreasing as the universe winds down, but it is still all around us and in us. We get it from cosmic rays from outer space; it emanates from radioactive materials in the soil below us and from the floors and walls and roofs of the buildings we live in. It is in the air we breathe and the food we eat. The potassium in our vegetables is radioactive, with a half-life of 130 million years, although what difference that makes I don't know. Every one of us is radioactive; each healthy person produces about 28,000 deeply penetrating gamma rays a minute and about 190,000 beta particles. Certainly we can live with this radiation. A more interesting question would be whether we could live without it. Radiation has most likely caused some of the mutations by which we have evolved to our present form. Who knows what we would have been like without it, or what life would be like in the future if it suddenly ceased? Who knows what viruses or bacteria are suppressed by our own internal bombardment of gamma rays and beta particles?

We can live in the presence of this radiation as we live in the presence of oxygen and sunlight. But even oxygen and sunlight are harmful in very large doses. The question is, How much ionizing radiation can we tolerate? To answer that question we must turn to some numbers.

The unit by which radiation is measured is named after Wilhelm Roentgen, the man who discovered x-rays about a hundred years ago. Before that, no one had even suspected the existence of ionizing radiation. Since radiation has different effects on different nuclei, a unit was devised to be the equivalent of a Roentgen in its effects on living tissue. It is known as the Roentgen, equivalent, man, or rem. That unit is too large for describing the low-level effects of radiation, so we use a unit that is one thousandth of a rem, or millirem. (Scientists use Latin prefixes for fractions of a unit, like *milli* for one-thousandth and *micro* for one-millionth, but they use Greek prefixes for multiples of a unit, like *kilo* for one thousand times and *mega* for one million times. I don't know why. Some medieval academic compromise, I suppose.)

The average background radiation level in the United States is about 100 millirems per year. This background varies significantly from place to place, higher in the mountains, which receive more cosmic radiation, also higher where there are more radioactive rocks, but lower at sea level and in marshy areas. Cities like Denver, Colorado, receive twice the average level, and low, watery areas like southern Florida receive about one-tenth the average. The variations in other countries are much wider. At Kerala in India, villagers get 2800 millirems per year. In parts of Brazil, some people get 25,000 per year. In the Iranian city of Ramsar, the dose is about 44,000 per year, and on the French Riviera, the dose reaches 88,000 millirems per year. Some form of life has existed in all of these areas for billions of years, so it is pretty clear that nature has adapted to very high levels of background radiation. This is all very frustrating to scientists, because there seems to be no discernible difference between people or animals or plants or bugs in any of these locations. In Denver, for example, cancer incidence should be much higher than average; in fact, it is significantly lower, indicating that background level probably has little effect on cancer incidence. Nature has obviously adapted over millennia, and we are probably never going to know what the effect, if any, of small variations in low-level radiation will be. Most likely, I believe, there isn't any. I believe that there is a "threshold," developed over eons of time, below which natural defenses mitigate the effects. I don't know what that threshold is, but it must be many hundreds of millirems.

As levels of radiation increase, the effects become more predictable. We know a great deal about the effects of radiation at high levels. This information is available from animal studies, from a carefully followed group of eighty thousand Japanese atomic bomb survivors, from excess doses of x-rays given to British arthritis patients, from treatments given to German tuberculosis sufferers, from American women who moistened radium-tipped paint brushes with their tongues in a New Jersey luminous watch dial factory, and a host of other sources. We also know that the rate at which a given dose is received is important. The Brazilians who live in an environment of 25,000 millirems per year with no ill effects would not be able to easily absorb such a dose in a second if it were given in an x-ray. Above 100,000 millirems, all of the data checks out very well, and scientists have a great deal of confidence in their conclusions. The problem is how to project this data to lower levels of radiation. Scientists have agreed on a very conservative method known as the linear hypothesis. This is a very esoteric title for what we were taught in the fifth grade as proportions. Simply enough, it says that the effect is proportional to the dose, right down to zero, with no threshold. With the exception of two thoroughly discredited studies, all measurements show that the linear hypothesis is very conservative and predicts effects far more severe than anyone has observed. I have the highest regard for the scientists who set these standards, and, at moderate or high radiation levels, I applaud their conservatism. I also have the highest respect and concern for the effects of nuclear radiation. As those of you who have read *Nuclear Hostages* are aware, I might not be alive today if I didn't have. But I don't buy the linearity concept at low levels.

It is very risky to invoke concepts of common sense or good judgment in scientific matters where data is available. But where data is not available, as in low-level radiation, it is bad science not to. In virtually all biological reactions, there is a threshold below which the body's own defenses can cope with an intrusion that might be harmful at high levels. This is true of alcohol, aspirin, cholesterol, sunshine, heat, cold — you name it. Since both phenomena involve dissipation of energy in the body, the analogy of falling off a cliff applies. If a thousand people fall off a thousand-foot cliff, they will almost certainly all die. If a thousand people fall off a twelve-inch-diameter log, the linear hypothesis says that one of them will die. We know that is not so. They might sprain an ankle perhaps, but not die. There is a big difference between falling off a cliff and falling off a log. The human body has not evolved to handle thousand-foot falls, but it is perfectly capable of handling a one-foot fall. So it must be with low-level radiation. If it can accommodate radiation background levels ranging from tens of millirems to tens of thousands of millirems, variations of a few millirems get lost in the noise level.

The linear hypothesis is excellent for workers dealing with radiation in a laboratory or a hospital or a nuclear power plant. It's conservative and safe, and that's good. But it confuses the general public and the press and provides ammunition for the nuclear opponent intent only on mischief. The public is now so frightened that some people are refusing necessary x-rays and others are refusing to work at video display terminals. It is time for reputable scientists to stand up and say what is true. *There is no evidence of deleterious biological effects from additional low levels of ionizing radiation.*

Nuclear power plants are safe. If there is a hurricane predicted, or a tornado, or an earthquake, head for your nearest nuclear power plant. The containment can easily withstand a house or a tree or an automobile being thrown against it by a tornado; it can easily withstand the high winds of a hurricane or the flooding from a tropical storm; it can easily withstand a direct hit from a crashing airplane or the force of a chemical charge detonated against it; it is by far the safest place to be in an earthquake. It is as close to being impregnable against outside forces as you can get.

The reasons that nuclear power plants are so protected are straightforward. The people who design and work in nuclear power plants, like the people who design and fly in airplanes, are very concerned for their own safety. There is a saying among commercial airline pilots that there are old pilots and there are bold pilots, but there are no old, bold pilots. The same is true for those who work in the nuclear environment, be it power plants, hospitals, or research laboratories. The nuclear environment is a harsh one; the key to survival is safety. The individual who is callous, careless, or cavalier is soon recognized by the system and is quietly but firmly ejected. I know. I have spent a lifetime in that environment.

Fortunately, the very concentration of energy that makes the environment potentially hazardous is the factor that allows designers the freedom to take elaborate safety precautions. Nuclear reactors are quite small for the amount of energy they contain. They are not like the Empire State Building or Hoover Dam or Golden Gate Bridge, which are too huge to be protected against natural disasters. A nuclear reactor is only 12 feet in diameter and 65 feet tall. The inner containment in which the reactor is encased is a hermetically sealed, welded steel casement many inches thick, designed and tested to withstand very high internal pressures. The outer casing is constructed of three-foot-thick concrete walls heavily reinforced by massive steel rods welded into a honeycomb around which the concrete is poured. It would be structurally impossible to build a dam or a bridge or a building with this much protection.

At one time, the general public believed that a nuclear reactor could explode like a bomb. That myth has long since been put to rest. It cannot explode; it can only get hot and, under certain circumstances, melt. It is the possibility of melting to which reactor designers and operators devote so much attention. They want to be as certain as possible that the reactor fuel rods do not get to a high enough temperature to melt and, if they do, that no radioactivity escapes from the containment building.

To date, the record of the reactor designers and operators has been exemplary. There have been no fatalities in the history of operation of commercial nuclear-powered electric generating plants. This has been an unbelievably perfect record; a multi-multibillion-dollar commercial industry developed without a single fatality. It has no parallel. Certainly not in coal- or oil-fired power plants, steel, copper, rubber, automobiles, airplanes, shipping, chemicals, bridge building, or any of our basic capital-intensive industries.

And there have been no significant emissions of radioactivity into the environment. Consider that! With dozens of nuclear power plants in operation, some for twenty years or more, emissions have been minuscule for all of them put together. Compare that with coal- or oil-fired plants, with steel mills and rubber factories, with automobiles and oil refineries, all of which, with the best available technologies and under the severest environmental surveillance, are still spewing out carcinogens by the thousands of tons.

Yet the industry is moribund.

The third aspect of nuclear power generation to be considered is the disposal of high-level nuclear wastes. The answer to this problem is so simple that I am embarrassed to present it to you. Because the energy to be released is concentrated in the nuclei of fissionable elements, it is highly concentrated, as is the residue after the energy is extracted. In fact, the residue produced in a reactor per person per year is about the size of an aspirin tablet. If reprocessed, all of the high-level waste to be produced in this century in this country would fit into a seventy-five-foot cube. To put it another way, it would be only enough to cover a football field six feet deep. This is an absurdly small volume of material. To say that we have no place to put it in this vast country of ours is an insult to our collective intelligence. It now appears that commercial reprocessing will not be economical, so the industry is making plans to store the fuel rods themselves for an indefinite period of time. Spent fuel is currently stored in pools of water adjacent to the reactors. These storage pools will be filled some time in the next decade; time is getting short for the selection of a more permanent storage site. Even if the fuel is not reprocessed to remove extraneous materials, it represents a very small volume and, from that standpoint, could be handled at many locations throughout the country. The problem, of course, is with the residual radioactivity.

Now we come to the smidgeon of nuclear physics I mentioned earlier. A commercial nuclear reactor core consists primarily of uranium, the heaviest element existing naturally on earth. (Heavier elements used to exist, but they have long since decayed away.) The neutron is a large particle, freed in great quantity from the nuclei of fissioning atoms during the reaction. A neutron has no charge, so it is free to pass through or be captured by other nuclei as it comes in contact with them. If it is captured by a target nucleus, two very different kinds of things can happen. It can split the nucleus into a number of smaller parts, or it can remain captured and form the nucleus of a heavier atom. If it splits or fissions the nucleus, the reaction is a violent one, releasing a great deal of energy and additional free neutrons to sustain the reaction. The fission fragments are highly radioactive, losing half their radioactivity in about thirty-five years. This is known as their half-life. If the neutron remains captured, the nucleus is heavier and forms an element such as plutonium, which is known as a transuranic, or beyond uranium, element. Plutonium is radioactive, but comparatively quite stable, with a half-life of more than twenty-four thousand years.

Spent fuel consists of a mixture of fission fragments and transuranics. Unless a person eats or inhales spent fuel, only the fission fragments are troublesome, because they have the shortest half-life. All the original nuclei have about the same amount of energy. The fission fragments dissipate half that energy in about thirty-five years, the plutonium in twenty-four thousand years. Obviously, the fission fragments are about a thousand times more radioactive than the plutonium. Furthermore, the emissions from plutonium are not penetrating and can be stopped by a sheet of tissue paper. After the fission fragments have decayed, the remainder is no more dangerous than the background radiation in many parts of the earth. The statement that we must guard nuclear waste storage sites for hundreds of thousands of years is false. It is not long half-life that makes a radioactive element dangerous, it is the intensity of the radiation. Consider again the potassium we eat to sustain life. It is radioactive with a half-life of over a hundred million years, but because of that long half-life, its intensity is so low that our bodies accommodate it quite comfortably.

To conclude that spent fuel does not have to be guarded for many hundreds of thousands of years does not mean that the problem is trivial. On the contrary, the problem is a serious one, but it is manageable. If we confine our primary attention to the fission fragments, we still have to worry about them until the intensity decays by a factor of about one thousand. This takes about three hundred years, with each year getting a little easier. But three hundred years is not three hundred thousand years; there is a big difference. We all know of engineering works that have lasted more than three hundred years — houses, dams, factories, and bridges, for example. It is well within the state of the art to design storage sites that will retain their integrity for that length of time and much longer. Since the volume to be accommodated is so small, a number of sites around the country would serve very well.

The most obvious solution to the spent-waste storage problem is to put the fuel rods into the ground, either in a hole or into the side of a mountain. The only danger is that they get put into a water table and contaminate it. The best prospective storage sites, then, are in arid areas, a number of which are currently under study. To me, the best storage site is in Nevada, at the Nevada Proving Grounds, about a hundred miles from Las Vegas. This is where all of the underground nuclear weapons tests have been conducted. The company with which I have been associated for the last thirty-seven years has prime contracts in the area, so I have both some knowledge of and prejudice toward that location.

The Nevada Proving Grounds has been in operation as a nuclear testing area for thirty-five years, already one half-life of fission fragments. The water table is a closed basin with no access to other off-site water tables. In the thirty-five years that the water table has been under the strictest of scrutiny, it has not migrated more than one-half inch, and no measurable radioactivity has been detected beyond the borders of the Proving Grounds. From the standpoint of leakage, the site can be considered secure for centuries. More significant, there have been at least three hundred announced nuclear weapons tests carried out at the Proving Grounds with the residual radioactivity from the detonations contained underground. Naturally, the area is closely guarded, controlled, and monitored, and it will have to be guarded and monitored for hundreds of years because of the radioactivity already in the ground. It is an ideal location for a commercial spent-fuel site; one section has already been set aside for the purpose. Because of the small volume of the spent waste compared to the vast area required to isolate weapons tests, the site could easily accommodate ten times the spent fuel to be generated by the power plants now in operation or under construction. The handling, guarding, and monitoring costs will simply be incremental to the main function of handling weapons and their residue. In fact, the current spent-fuel assessment on nuclear power plant owners will be adequate to cover all costs of handling, transporting, and monitoring spent-fuel storage at the Nevada Proving Grounds. Political problems will hold up the actual designation of the site for some time, but the "not in my backyard" syndrome applies to any hazardous waste storage, nuclear or nonnuclear. The important point is that once we understand the difference between highly-radioactive short-lived fission fragments and weakly-radioactive long-lived transuranic elements, the basic scientific aspects of the problem disappear; they become engineering tasks, the solutions to which are well within the state of the art.

If my argument is correct, if the biological effects of low-level radiation are overstated, if nuclear power plants are as safe as I say they are, if spent-fuel rods can be stored safely and economically, how come the industry is in such a mess? The answer is a long and complex one of scientists, reactor vendors, utility managers, government regulators, and nuclear opponents, all believing that they are acting in the public interest and their own interests, but all reading the flow of events erroneously, and all sequentially and systematically shooting themselves in the foot to the detriment of our society as a whole.

The science was born in violence, in the horror of a great war, in a period when millions of soldiers died in battle, when millions of civilians died in air raids, when millions of the persecuted died in gas chambers and prison camps, in a period when, as Winston Churchill saw it, "To avert a vast, indefinite butchery, to bring the war to an end, to give peace to the world, to lay healing hands on its tortured peoples by a manifestation of overwhelming power — at the cost of a few explosions — seemed after all our toils and perils a miracle of deliverance."

• • •

Enrico Fermi's first reactor went critical in December 1942, under the stands at Stagg Stadium in Chicago. No attention could be given, no resources diverted, no plans made for peacetime uses under the pressures and constraints of the great war. How different it could have been if the logical, careful plans for the development of a peacetime industry could have begun at the time of that first controlled chain reaction. But that was not to be. The scientists were fully preoccupied, and quite properly so, for the next several years with the wartime application. When the first Atomic Energy

Act was passed in 1946, great hopes were raised for peacetime applications, but these had to be put aside with the pressures of the cold war and the crash program for the development of the thermonuclear weapon. In 1954 the first light-water reactor for propulsion application was put into service in the submarine *Nautilus*. By that time, the pressure for commercial applications of the new science had been building up relentlessly. Also in 1954, under President Dwight D. Eisenhower, the Atomic Energy Act had been amended to provide for private ownership of nuclear reactors, lifting wartime restrictions. The scientists were eager to get on with peacetime applications, in no little measure to expiate their perceived wartime sins. The reactor vendors were ready for business, the utilities were drooling with the prospects of electricity "too cheap to meter," and the politicians and the public were clamoring for the promised paradise of the peacetime atom.

It was a heady time for the whole country, and for the whole world. American industry and American science reigned supreme. The scientists had conquered the atom with a speed and a skill that were the marvel of that or any age. Not only had they developed a fission weapon and a thermonuclear weapon, but they had developed a propulsion reactor for submarines that would revolutionize naval warfare as the weapons had revolutionized strategic warfare. The ability of the submarine to remain submerged and undetected would make it the successor to the battleship and the aircraft carrier as the backbone of the fleet. What could be simpler than to adapt this marvelous propulsion device to the electricity generation needs of the civilian economy?

This is exactly what was done. Ground was broken by President Eisenhower in Shippingport, Pennsylvania, on September 10, 1954, for the world's first commercial nuclear power-generating station. In the remarkably short period of three

years and four months, the plant was delivering 60 megawatts
of power to the customers of the Duquesne Light Company
of Pittsburgh, another major triumph for the nuclear scientists
and engineers. Although the Shippingport plant was financed
by government funds, it was only two years later that the
world's first large-scale, privately financed nuclear power plant
began feeding 200 megawatts of electric power into the grid
of the Commonwealth Edison Company. Orders began to flow
into the vendors by the dozen. Nuclear power was on its way.

But there were clouds on the horizon, some of them atomic.
The development of commercial applications of technology
usually takes longer than military applications do. The reasons
are that military applications start with a well-defined market
need, that competing technologies are eliminated early in the
game by fiat, and that costs are secondary to performance.
Technology has free reign in the military market and, with
few exceptions, defines the product that the military customer
is ordered to use, whether it fits the exact requirements or
not. The problem of technology transfer from military markets
to civilian is one which haunts us to this day. It is a major
reason for the loss of many of our present technological markets to Japan, where research and development is carried out
for commercial purposes only, while ours is dominated by
military applications. The problems of technology transfer were
not understood in the early postwar years. Most wartime technological developments were adapted gingerly, in small incremental steps, limiting the risks and testing the civilian
markets over many years. This was the case in the use of jet
engines for civilian transport, in the adaptation of radar to
color television, of magnetron oscillators to microwave ovens,
of buzz bombs to space shuttles, and of the massive military
number crunchers to today's personal computers.

Not so with nuclear power. It went from submarine pro-

pulsion to commercial electricity generation in the space of
three years. The two minor adaptations of the basic light-
water technology were quite literally set in concrete by 1949.
There is nothing wrong with that technology; it may be the
best there is. I don't know. But I think in hindsight that we
may have been better off to have moved more slowly, to have
tested the waters of public acceptance more gingerly, to have
evaluated the safety-economy tradeoffs of heavy-water or gas-
cooled technologies more carefully before making the commitment.

The initial blame can clearly be laid in the laps of the scientists and engineers. They had developed the first fission
weapon in three years in the midst of wartime shortages. They
had developed the first thermonuclear weapons in five years,
starting without even a workable theoretical basis. They had
developed and built a working submarine propulsion reactor
in four years. After those triumphs, electric power generation
seemed like a cinch. They were cocky, competent, secretive,
and sometimes arrogant. Very few had had any commercial
experience, and certainly none had marketing experience.

It was the Ming mentality at its apex. It would never have
occurred to a soul to ask the public what kind of power reactor
it wanted, any more than it would have occurred to them to
ask the public what kind of a bomb or what kind of a submarine
it wanted. Backed up by a president extremely eager to cap
a lifetime military career with a peacetime application of the
dreaded atom, and with a compliant Joint Committee on Atomic
Energy endowed with the deepest of pockets, they needed
only to say the word to get the strongest administration support and unlimited funds from the Congress. Not only were
they oblivious to the uneasiness of the general public about
all things nuclear, they were oblivious to the activities of their
scientific brethren who were firing off fission and fusion weap-

ons like firecrakers on the Fourth of July, causing a major campaign issue about fallout as early as the 1956 election. Nobody stopped to evaluate the 1958 moratorium on atmospheric weapons testing, prompted by worldwide concern about fallout, or the 1963 limited Test Ban Treaty, which was the number one priority of the new president, John F. Kennedy. The technologists knew that nuclear power plants were safe, and they were arrogant and disdainful of those who said them nay. What they didn't understand is that for the public and the politicians, perception has priority, not facts. It doesn't make any difference how safe nuclear power plants truly are, or how many slick ads or substantive statistics are produced, the general public will always be uneasy. The nuclear age was born in violence; to the vast majority of our citizenry, its aftereffects are silent, subtle, and insidious. The technologists did not understand that at the beginning, and they do not understand that to this day. No amount of either sweet talk or solid statistics will sweep away that image.

The reactor vendors should have known better. They were supposed to be hardheaded businessmen, not visionary scientists. It is axiomatic in business to start out a new product slowly, to make the inevitable errors in small sample lots, to build and test, build and test, until the product is honed and whittled to where it can be introduced to a sample market for feedback and redesign. That iterative process is the essence of a market-driven economy. Woe to the producer who brings forth a product full-blown and untested in the marketplace, be it an Edsel automobile, a Nehru jacket, or a synthetic potato chip. This is what happened with nuclear power. The first commercial reactor delivered 60 megawatts of power, the second, 200 megawatts. It takes a number of years to shake down an undertaking of this size, but the vendors couldn't wait. Before the concrete was cured on the 60-megawatt plant they were finishing the designs of 500-megawatt plants and scaling up to 1000 megawatts and higher. In capital-intensive undertakings costing hundreds of millions of dollars, it is a risky business indeed to scale up by factors of ten or more without extensive experience with pilot plants.

In retrospect, the mistakes are understandable. As with the technologists, the managers and decision makers lacked commercial risk-taking experience. Practically no power plants of any kind were built during the thirties. Almost everything that was built during the forties and early fifties was financed by government guarantees with no risk to the constructor. None of these managers had faced a high-risk investment decision in their working lifetimes. Besides, scale-ups by factors of ten were routine in their wartime experience. These were the same managers who had built the massive Oak Ridge separation plants without knowing what kind of a separation membrane they would use, the same decision makers who began the design of the Hanford plutonium reactors, the largest United States wartime construction project, with only a millionth of a gram of plutonium to work with. There was no energy shortage, no inflation, no skeptical government regulation, and nary a nuclear protester when they made their decisions.

But they paid the price, and their companies paid the price of their market inexperience. In their haste to line up customers, they offered fixed-price, turnkey contracts to their customers, the utilities, who could not afford to be risk takers. When inflation finally came and costs went out of sight, the vendors were still stuck with many of these fixed-price contracts, particularly for uranium fuel. For one company the financial exposure threatened the viability of the whole enterprise, even though nuclear power was but a fraction of its business. To this day, none of the prime equipment vendors have recovered their investments or earned a dime of profit for their efforts.

The electric utility managers were the fall guys. Electric utilities, although mostly stockholder-owned, profit-seeking corporations, occupy an unusual slot in the American economic spectrum. By their nature, they are truly monopolies and must be regulated. Because they are highly capital intensive, and because the consumption of electricity is constantly on the increase, even in these days of conservation, it is in the public interest that they be allowed continuous access to capital markets. This is quite a different consideration from other regulated industries, such as airlines, which are limited by the number of flights they can schedule, or banks, which are regulated by the dollar amount of the loans they can make on their capital structure. Electric utilities are regulated primarily by return on capital. There must be a minimum they can earn for access to capital markets, but there must also then be a maximum to prevent profiteering. Rates are generally set close to the minimums by public utilities commissions. Because the rates of return are limited, electric utilities do not attract risk capital, so it is considered in the public interest to protect those who do invest from undue risk.

At first the electric utility managers were intrigued by the new technology and the prospects of a more competitive position against fossil fuels. They were quite familiar with the pace of developments in the Middle East, where vast quantities of oil were being discovered so close to the surface that recovery costs were less than ten cents a barrel. Initially, the Middle Eastern discoveries were a threat to more expensive domestic supplies, so that tariffs were set up to control imports. As the U.S. economy boomed, however, the demand for energy became insatiable, the domestic supplies were gobbled up, and the United States became a net importer of energy. The utility officials worried about this impending dependence on fuel supplies from countries with unstable governments many thousands of miles away, as well they might. They were also concerned about the growing environmental movement and welcomed a technology that reduced toxic emissions practically to zero. They were intrigued by the prospects of growth and dependability of supply, but not particularly by the prospects of increased earnings because of the regulatory limits on return on capital. Maligned they are, and mistakes they have made, but I find electric utility executives more customer and public service oriented, or at least less profit oriented, than the general cut of American industry. It is probably the limit on capital return that sets the risk-reward ratio, and thus establishes the culture for the industry.

For whatever set of reasons, the electric utility managers went for the nuclear option hook, line, and sinker. Experienced in coal- and oil-fired steam-generating plants that had not changed in basic technology for decades, they were totally unprepared for the management problems of huge nuclear power plants. The first plants did very well. They were small, and they received a great deal of attention from the experienced government technologists and the reactor vendors, who also had a good cadre of experienced personnel. As the industry began to expand at breakneck speed, the ranks of the experienced grew thinner and thinner, and the utilities were left more and more to cope for themselves. At first only the larger and broader-based power companies went nuclear, but as the program caught on, smaller and poorly capitalized companies jumped on the bandwagon, exacerbating the problems of trained operating personnel and experienced management. Disaster was on the horizon.

There was always a basic opposition and concern for the

expansion of anything nuclear. The nuclear weapons developers were heroes for about a week, from Hiroshima to the Japanese surrender. Soon after, a reaction began to set in. Many scientists deplored their participation in the weapons program, and even J. Robert Oppenheimer declared in his famous speech that "the scientists have known sin." Some responsible citizens were dubious about extending the technology into the public domain, citing the dangers of proliferation and general safety. Most of the country and the world was enthusiastic about the potential of this vast new energy source, however, and those who weren't recognized its inevitability, so the programs went forward vigorously.

But the power program was vulnerable, vulnerable to a degree not ever imagined by its proponents. It was tied to the weapons program, born in violence. Nuclear radiation was eerie, invisible, untouchable. Most of the information about it was secret, tied to weapons. No one felt comfortable even thinking about it. Nuclear power plants were strange futuristic objects, with their massive cooling towers in place of familiar smokestacks. They didn't stink, they didn't make noise, they didn't pour out smoke, they were too clean looking to be doing any good. Nothing went in and nothing came out. The American public was used to factories that were dirty and grimy, that poured out smoke and gave off noxious odors, that had truckloads of material going in and truckloads of material going out, with hundreds of people going in and going out all day. The nukes just didn't fit with the American psyche. The situation was made to order for the professional protesters.

Protesters have an easy life compared to performers. It is always easier to complain than to construct. A protester has the fascinating advantage of being free of selecting alternatives. During the fifties and sixties the United States was on an energy-consumption binge, and certain industries such as oil companies, coal companies, and electric utilities had the task of providing that energy. The reason for the energy binge was a public policy of long duration that called for the rapid industrialization of the American economy and a rapid colonization of the American hinterlands. The capital-intensive factory and the gas-guzzling automobile were the means to these ends. The policy was expressed in a series of investment-encouraging and tax-sheltering bills that had been passed by a number of successive Congresses and approved by presidents from the days of Woodrow Wilson. It was clearly the will of the people, and it worked. The United States had built up the mightiest war machine in history and beaten back the forces of totalitarianism. Further, it had used its industrial base, fueled by cheap energy and a magnanimous public policy, to rebuild the war-ruined nations of the world, friend and foe alike. Cheap energy had built up the American standard of living to the highest ever seen on the face of the earth. But the era of cheap energy was coming to an end, and somebody was going to have to do something about it. There was a series of alternative policy choices, all having some good points and all having some bad.

Petroleum was the key. All the shallow wells in the traditional oil-producing states were beginning to run dry; the newer discoveries were in deep wells or more difficult geological sites, making the finds more expensive. Absurdly cheap oil was being produced in Iran and Saudi Arabia, but these sources were halfway around the world and in a politically volatile area. The United States was fast becoming a net importer of energy. Some farsighted legislators suggested increased energy taxes or import controls to discourage energy use or reduce political exposure, but the electorate would have no part of it. There was plenty of coal, but it was dirty and environmentally unpleasant, so that local regulators were pushing the utilities to convert from coal to oil, exacerbating the petroleum problem. Hydroelectric costs were high, wood even higher, and solar energy costs out of sight. As the environmental movement picked up speed, it became apparent that fossil-fuel plants were pouring thousands of tons of lung irritants and carcinogens into the atmosphere as energy use increased. The specters of acid rain and carbon-dioxide-caused climatic changes were on the horizon. Nuclear was a natural.

The protesters didn't see it that way. With no responsibility to consider alternatives, they were free to emphasize the perceived negatives of nuclear. For years they claimed that a nuclear power plant could blow up like a bomb. As a generation of citizens grew up with at least some high school physics, that argument faded away. Then came the proliferation threat. Since a nuclear power plant produced plutonium, it was argued, terrorists would break into a reactor and steal the plutonium to make bombs. As the public began to understand the subject a little better, the idea that a group of terrorists could break into one of these massive plants, putting out the lights in the whole surrounding area, disassemble a fifty-ton header, pull out highly radioactive fuel elements, and stick them in the back of a station wagon to be reprocessed in their basement chemistry laboratory became so ludicrous that it was soon discarded. No self-respecting terrorist would consider breaking into a nuclear power plant when he could go back home and make all the plutonium he wanted in a small research reactor.

As the more lurid fantasies faded, the protesters settled on the more esoteric aspects of the nuclear equation to block the progress of the industry. Their big break came from the scientists who made the disposal of high-level spent-fuel rods into a much bigger problem than was necessary. Fuel rods don't take up much space. They can be handled and stored just as they are, but the scientists wanted to reprocess them to concentrate the radioactivity. The more you concentrate them, the more you get a hotter and hotter potato, very difficult to handle. They next failed to educate the public about the difference between short-lived, highly radioactive fission fragments and long-lived weakly radioactive transuranic elements. Then they proposed to store the residue in some salt mines that leaked water. How dumb can you get? What the country needed in those days was fewer Ph.D.'s in nuclear physics and a few more high school courses in political science.

The protesters had a field day. They managed to build a nonproblem into a national issue that isn't understood to this day. Many states have laws prohibiting the construction of additional nuclear plants until the waste problem is solved. Federal legislation calling for the selection of a site some time in the late eighties has been passed, but the issue has now become a political, not a technical, problem, and I doubt that the selection will be made in this decade.

The next issue was the likelihood of core meltdown and the resultant escape of radioactivity to the atmosphere. In the early seventies the protesters claimed that the emergency core-cooling systems wouldn't work. This was the issue on which the protesters developed their most powerful weapon, delay. One group held up administrative hearings for a solid year. This group, purporting to speak for concerned scientists, had only one individual, a college professor, who could have been remotely considered to be a scientist. The real scientists were not concerned at all. Eventually, after years of delay, tests confirmed that the emergency cooling systems worked perfectly, and were very conservatively designed.

Then came the regulators. The original Atomic Energy Act called for the development of peacetime uses of atomic energy and charged the Atomic Energy Commission (AEC) with that task. Later it was decided that the same government agency shouldn't be both promoting and policing, so the Nuclear Regulatory Commission (NRC) was split off to be the policeman. The AEC, after shedding its skin a couple of times, became the Department of Energy. The Nuclear Regulatory Commission was soon caught between a rock and a hard place. On one side was a big-buck industry, moving fast — probably too fast — to promote nuclear power. On the other side were the protesters, who didn't want to move at all. They had developed their art into a profession, a profession that had become self-sustaining, and they were well skilled in the politics delay. The regulators, smarting under allegations that they were partial to industry, bent over backward to demonstrate their impartiality, and slowed down the licensing process. Industry grumbled at the delay, but was fairly complacent until the Three Mile Island accident changed all the rules.

That accident caught everyone by surprise. It was not an event involving nuclear safety at all, but a horrible example of how poorly prepared we are in this country to handle the management of potential crises. There was never more than a remote possibility that radioactivity would be emitted to the atmosphere in harmful quantities. The utility management was inept, with inadequately trained operators, poor supervision, and a complete ignorance of how to handle public relations. The operators and management made every mistake in the book, yet the integrity of the safety system was maintained. Subsequent investigation has shown that at least fifty additional safety actions were available to be taken when the system was brought under control. Commissions and committees were appointed ad nauseam, and the accident has been studied to the nth degree over the years. Not one study has concluded that there was any significant danger to the populace at any time. But the utility panicked, the regulators

panicked, the press panicked, and the state government panicked. This is the lesson of Three Mile Island. We did not
and do not yet have a coherent system for analysis of potential
crises, for assessment of the danger to the populace, or for
communication of that assessment to the press and the public
in a simple, understandable manner. The absence of even a
rudimentary system of crisis management is a national dis-
grace in these days of wanton, reckless, organized terrorism,
where dams and buildings can be blown up, water supplies
poisoned, noxious chemical gases released, or nuclear weapons detonated. Such actions are much more probable than
release of radioactivity from a nuclear power plant.

The OPEC oil embargo of 1973 seemed at first to be a boon
to nuclear power. Oil prices skyrocketed, and nuclear electricity became the biggest bargain in town. That was true if
the plant was finished or near completion. If construction had
not started or was in the early stages in 1973, it was another
story. The reason is that nuclear power plants are capital
intensive. Any energy source that is capital intensive uses a
great deal of energy in the fabrication of its component parts.
This is also the reason that alternate forms of energy never
got off the ground. Solar power, the darling of the seventies,
never made it because solar energy is highly capital intensive
in its collectors, converters, and ancillary equipment. As the
price of oil went up, the cost of nuclear, solar, and synthetic
fuel plants went up with it. The alternate energy sources were
highly subsidized by the government, but when oil prices

went down, component prices were held up by high interest rates, and the alternate energy sources remained uneconomical even with subsidies.

The final blow was inflation and high interest rates. Many people think that conservation and the current excess of generating power was a primary cause of the nuclear decline, but that is not correct. Nuclear plants are heavily front-end loaded. If they can be built, they are much cheaper to operate than fossil-fuel plants. The problem is that the utilities can't get them built, or if they build them, they can't get operating licenses. Three quarters of the excess costs of plants under construction are money costs. The inflation built into components in years gone by, the high cost of money, and the regulatory delays in backfitting are the culprits in the demise of nuclear power. It now takes twelve to fifteen years to get a nuclear plant built, licensed, and on-line. Public utilities commissions will no longer allow payment for construction work in progress, so a potential lender would be at the mercy of a regulatory agency fifteen years in the future to decide how it could recover its investment and what rate of return it should receive. With no way to predict the political climate in which a regulator would act a decade and a half from now, no lender with a scratch on his brain would lend a nickel to a nuclear power plant. Nuclear power plants are simply not financeable. It wouldn't make any difference if there were another oil embargo, if the public decided that nuclear plants were as safe as their mothers' arms, or if the radioactivity in the spent-fuel rods suddenly decayed to zero. The bureaucracy is too entrenched, and the professional protesters now have kids to put through college. Even attempts to legislate a shortening of the licensing time would be held up in the courts for many years, and there would be no money available until the issues were decided. Nuclear power has had it for this century.

What can we learn from this sad story? We first find that scientists can be too conservative as well as too enthusiastic. Their enthusiasm in nontechnical matters led them to underestimate the social and political obstacles to commercial acceptance of nuclear power, while their technical conservatism in setting low-level radiological standards and spent-fuel rod disposal specifications led them to interpose unnecessary barriers to success. The reactor vendors have found that they could not develop a commercial market with a wartime crash program mentality. The electric utilities have found that a devotion to producing economical electric energy is not enough in this cruel world; they must take into consideration the existence of an uninformed public and press, unsympathetic regulators, professional protesters, and the existence of a host of externalities, such as oil embargoes, inflation, interest rates, and the general reluctance of rate payers to pay for something that they are not going to get.

A special word about protesters and the press. Many in the industry blame the news media for most of their troubles. I don't believe that. Nuclear is news. It has been since August 5, 1945, the day of Hiroshima. And it should be. The development of nuclear weapons is the most significant single event that has occurred in the history of mankind. It has revolutionized warfare and world politics. It has put into the hands of an unprepared world populace the power to annihilate civilization instantly. It has frightened thoughtful people all over the world, not only for their own survival but for the survival of their children and their children's children. Nuclear power is inextricably linked to nuclear weapons in the minds of the public. The ordinary citizen cannot visualize a nuclear weapons test in the side of a mountain in a remote desert, or a MIRVed missile deep in a silo in an undisclosed location, but it can visualize a nuclear power plant when it shows up on the television screen. Whatever happens or does not happen to a nuclear power plant is, and always will be, news. The technology is complex, but the public wants simple answers. The press understands that it will get simple answers from the protesters because the protesters have no responsibility to be precise. This is not an excuse for the press, merely an explanation. The leaders of the media, particularly the instant media — newspapers and television — have a responsibility to society, which they are not fulfilling. It is a responsibility to assign competent, trained personnel to as complex a subject as nuclear reporting. I have never yet encountered a knowledgeable nuclear news reporter. In the trade press, yes, and in magazine reporting, but in day-to-day coverage, newspaper or television, no. It is no wonder that they fall for the quick, glib answer, and not the studied, sober response of the producer.

I place the responsibility for the demise of nuclear power in the United States primarily onto the professional nuclear protesters. They have accomplished their victories by distortions, deceits, and delays. In the long and sorry history of administrative hearings, I have found not one instance where they have added anything to the reliability or safety of nuclear power plants. On the contrary, by their delaying tactics they have held up research and testing that might have prevented fiascoes like Three Mile Island. There have been mistakes galore made by scientists, reactor vendors, utility managers, regulators, and the press, but the international record comparing the United States to the rest of the world bears out the contention that the professional protesters are the prime obstructionists.

In Canada, Great Britain, Japan, and Europe, particularly France, nuclear power has been a great success. Japan, the most sensitive country in the world in matters nuclear, currently operates twenty-five nuclear units and expects to double its nuclear capacity by 1990. In France, over half the electricity is nuclear generated. In the United States, the number is 13 percent. In Canada, it takes only six years to put a nuclear plant on line, less than half the time it takes in the United States. In fact, the Canadians have offered to sell us nuclear-generated electricity at a price well below our cost from oil- or coal-fired plants.

Each of those countries was far behind the United States in the original development of nuclear power. Except for Canada, each is densely populated, with nuclear units close to centers of population. Each uses basically the same technology, in most cases equipment built here and engineering services provided by American companies. Each has a highly vocal and independent press, while government bureaucrats are the same all over the world. What none of them has is strong and well-financed professional protest groups. Are they wrong and we right? Is low-level radiation dangerous only in this country? Is the danger of core meltdown confined to our fifty states? Is it only in the United States that seventy-five cubic feet of space can't be found to store reprocessed fuel rods or a few hundred acres to store them as they are? These questions have added to the costs and caused the delays in plant construction in this country to the point where the nuclear option is no longer financially viable.

Ultimately, the professional protesters will be called to task for these delays. But it will be too late. Energy constitutes 12 percent of our gross national product — about the same as agriculture. To the extent that we are internationally uncompetitive in energy costs, the difference will have to come out of our hides somewhere else — from health care, or welfare, or education, or national defense, or the arts, or simply leisure time. Internationally, it is a zero-sum game, and we can't make the rules any longer. One of the prime reasons for the high standard of living in the United States has been the availability of inexpensive energy. That advantage is slipping away from us, and we are losing our competitive edge. The single question we must ask ourselves as a citizenry is this: In listening to these professional protesters, are we acting in the public interest, or are we merely shooting ourselves in the foot?

6

What's Good for General Motors

THE MYSTERY of the Mona Lisa is no more. The celebrated smile of La Gioconda, the lady from Florence, is simply the satisfied smirk of the recipient of a secret. Leonardo da Vinci was the first to come up with the idea of a self-propelled land vehicle, which he was obviously describing to her as he painted. As he talked and painted, she thought and plotted. Finally, she broke out into a sly grin, realizing the importance of this revolutionary concept and the effect it would have on La Borsa Valori, the Florentine stock market. Unfortunately for her, Leonardo had a few higher priorities, such as canals and fortifications and cannons and battering rams, on his research and development time schedule, so his invention was never reduced to practice, and history is left with only that fleeting moment of contemplation. But she lives on with us as the first recipient of an automotive sales pitch and as the first potential satisfied customer.

Two hundred fifty years passed before J. H. Genevois, a

Swiss clergyman, suggested mounting small windmills on a cartlike vehicle, their power to be used to wind springs that would move the road wheels. During the middle of the eighteenth century, the idea of compressed air engines became popular. It was stimulated by the invention of the air pump by Otto von Guericke, who was the first to make metal pistons, cylinders, and connecting rods, the basic components of the reciprocating engine. William Medhurst patented the air engine in 1799 and suggested a grid of compressor stations to service vehicles propelled by it.

As happens in all developing technologies, a wide and wild variety of engines and propellants was proposed and tested. Christian Huygens, a Dutch inventor, produced an engine that worked by air pressure developed by explosion of a powder charge. Denis Papin of France built a model engine on the vacuum principle, using condensation of steam to produce the vacuum. Philippe Lebon patented a coal gas engine and was the first to mention electrical ignition. Isaac de Rivas made and patented a gas-powered vehicle in Paris in 1807; the engine used hydrogen gas as fuel. The valves and ignition were operated by hand, and the timing problem understandably seems to have been very difficult.

Gradually, during the latter years of the seventeenth century, the steam engine began to take prominence. The first working model was made by Ferdinand Verbiest, a Belgian Jesuit missionary, in 1668. Amazingly, it was produced while the inventor was attending at the court of the Emperor K'anghsi of the Chinese Ming dynasty. It is generally agreed that the first true automobile was constructed by Nicholas Joseph Cugnot of Lorraine in 1769. A large, heavy, steam-powered tricycle, it ran for twenty minutes, carrying four people, at two miles per hour. However, it had to stop every five minutes to build up steam; on its second trial run it went off the road and was wrecked.

By the turn of the century steam engines were in operation all over Europe and in the United States. In 1805 Oliver Evans demonstrated the first American motor vehicle in Philadelphia. It was a forty-thousand-pound combination steam wagon and flatboat that operated on both land and water; Evans used it to help dredge Philadelphia's harbor. In 1829 Sir Goldsworthy Gurney, a British inventor, built a steam carriage that broke all distance records of the time. He drove it two hundred miles from London to Bath and back at an average speed of fifteen miles an hour. By 1830 English steam carriages carried up to fourteen passengers each. But many people objected to the snorting monsters, which frightened horses and children and ruined the roads. Railroad and stagecoach line operators also opposed steam carriages because they feared the competition. As a result of their opposition, England passed the Red Flag Law in 1865, which required a man to walk ahead of any steam carriage traveling on the highway. In daytime he had to carry a red flag, and at night a lantern. This law, which was not repealed until 1896, did not exactly encourage automotive entrepreneurship. Nevertheless, steam-powered carriages persisted for a good many years, being produced well into the present century. The famous Stanley Steamers, first introduced by the Stanley brothers in 1897, were still being manufactured in 1925.

But the public wanted something better; people felt nervous about sitting on top of a boiler of live steam. Furthermore, the burners and the boilers often developed trouble. For a while it looked as though electric cars might be the answer. The first ones were built before 1850; by the year 1900 they were the most widely used automobiles. People liked them because they had silent motors, did not give off poisonous fumes, and were not in danger of blowing up. But electric cars lost favor because they could travel only about a hundred miles before their batteries had to be recharged. It is a fascinating fact that even today, after more than a hundred years of research, no way has been found to convert chemical energy to electricity much more efficiently than was possible at the turn of the century, with the result that electric cars are still too heavy and underpowered for general highway use. If a more powerful battery is ever developed, it would be a boon to the beleaguered electric utilities, which could charge batteries at night at very low incremental cost, and even less cost to the environment, since electric cars are virtually non-polluting. I have worked on that problem at our company, but there is no solution in sight.

The compromise, of course, was the gasoline engine. Its origins go back to Herr Doktor Nicholas Augustus Otto, who built the first operating engine using the four-stroke cycle that bears his name. Otto's first engines used illuminating gas, which was quite readily available. He later switched to a volatile distillate of petroleum. This liquid was a nuisance to refiners because more of it was produced than they could use. A small amount of it, called stove naphtha, was burned in a type of cookstove built especially for the purpose. After Doktor Otto put it on the map, the name was changed to gasoline because of its ease of vaporization.

Otto built a number of stationary and semiportable engines to compete with the well-established steam engines, founding the Otto Gasmotorworke in Cologne, with Gottlieb Daimler as his technical director. Daimler was a top-notch mechanic, having started out as a gunsmith before attending engineering school and becoming a technical administrator. He was convinced that Otto's cumbersome engines could be reduced in

size and simplified for application to a road vehicle, so he quit
and formed his own company in 1882. It took him seven years
to build a four-wheeled, four-seat, single-cylinder road vehicle; the engine was in the rear, and it was steered by a tiller.
Daimler's modified carriage approach was an instant success.

In the meantime Carl Benz, a visionary inventor operating
out of Karlsruhe, was dedicated to the proposition that the
automobile would supersede the horse and revolutionize the
world's transportation. He persisted in his efforts to build a
gas-fueled automobile in the face of many obstacles, including
lack of money to the point of poverty and the bitter objections
of his associates, many of whom considered him unbalanced
on the subject.

Benz ran his first car, a three-wheeler powered by a two-
cycle, one-cylinder engine, early in 1885, a happy and triumphant day. He circled a small track beside his factory, his
workmen running beside the car, his wife running, too, clap-
ping her hands; the little machine made four circuits of the
track, stalling only twice before a broken chain stopped it. A
little later, Benz attempted a public showing of an improved
model. He became so excited that he forgot to steer, and
smashed it against a brick wall surrounding his own house.

In 1891 a French firm secured the rights to both the Daimler and Benz engines, forming the Daimler-Benz company.
A couple of years later one of the French owners commis-
sioned a specially built Daimler racing car and named it after
his daughter, Mercedes. The car was so successful that Daimler's name was eclipsed, and the company's number one product is known today as the Mercedes-Benz. Surprisingly, Daimler
and Benz never met.

In the United States, meanwhile, scores of mechanically
minded men in garages and machine shops all over the country, completely oblivious of the goings-on in Europe, were

attempting to perfect a stationary gasoline engine and then reduce it in size so that it could fit into a carriage. As the new century began, all the early greats of the new industry were active. Charles and Frank Duryea gave up their bicycle repair business to form the Duryea Motor Wagon Company, selling two-seaters for $1000 and four-seaters for $2000. America's first new car buyer was George H. Morill, Jr., of Norwood, Massachusetts. As was the trade custom of the day, he paid cash. Ransom E. Olds built the first curved-dashboard vehicle. His name survived for decades in the Reo, and to this day in the Oldsmobile. Other pioneers included Alexander Winton and James Packard. The first trade association, the American Motor League, started with six manufacturers and a trade journal, *The Horseless Age*. With it, an industry was born.

There are three basic components to every successful industrial enterprise — product, money, and the management of the delicate balance between the first two. The development of the automobile industry in the United States is a gargantuan but intricately quintessential example of the three-dimensional ebbs and flows of these major factors. Fiercely independent, yet closely coupled as they move through time, now one dominant, now all indistinguishable, like some Olympian Trinity, they are inseparable but never at peace with one another.

In the beginning product had it, hands down. The pioneers were mechanics, bicycle makers, railroad men, shop foremen. They lived from week to week, moonlighting, working nights and weekends, scrounging parts and materials from wherever they could find them. Finance was an arcane activity practiced by bankers, and the word *management* was not in their vocabulary.

Another word not in their vocabulary was *entrepreneur*.

But that was what they were — entrepreneurs extraordi-
naires. Generally self-taught, they worked on extremely complicated engineering and production problems with
excruciatingly short time schedules against enormous odds.
In 1904 there were five thousand cars built by sixty companies.
In the next ten years, 550 companies were formed, most of
which went belly up. In 1908, the year the Model T was
introduced, sixty-five thousand cars were produced; nine years
later, the number was 2 million. In 1923 there were 180 car
makers; by 1927 there were only forty-four. Today, domestically, there are three and one-half.

For each of the 550 companies formed, there must have
been at least four or five that did not get to the point of formal
incorporation, and many others that ended up with a half-
finished model. The odds against success were very high,
probably as high as ten thousand to one. But that doesn't faze
the entrepreneur. By his very nature, he is unrealistic, else
he would never enter the contest. The true entrepreneur is
always confident that he can overcome all the odds and obstacles — I've never met one yet who didn't think he was one
in a million. (This chapter is written entirely in the masculine
gender. It is not completely macho on my part — it is just
that I have never run across a female entrepreneur in industry.
I am sure that they are out there, and I hope to meet one
someday. She should be a delightful and powerful combination of characteristics.)

Individual creativity, of which entrepreneurship is a subset,
is a rare and delicate quality, often found in the crudest and
least likely of settings; witness the oft-recounted oddities of
artists and thinkers over the ages. Creativity thrives on communication and competition, the raison d'être of the great
universities. From time to time the interaction of a few individuals initiates an almost critical reaction akin to the great

natural nuclear reactor which, through an improbable concentration of fissionable uranium, burned for thousands of
years, unattended and unnoticed, in the gelatinized granite
of Gabon. It happened with the philosophers of Athens; it
happened with the painters and sculptors of Renaissance Italy;
it happened with the writers of Elizabethan England; it happened in recent years with the great scientists of Budapest in
Hungary, with the critical mass of nuclear developers at Los
Alamos in New Mexico, and with the computer creators along
Route 128 and in Silicon Valley. So, too, the American automobile industry crystallized around the unlikely little region
of Detroit in Michigan.

They all showed up at one time or another. Alexander Winton, Ransom Olds, the hot-tempered, hard-drinking Dodge
brothers, James Couzens, later prominent in the United States
Senate, Henry Leland, founder of both the Cadillac and Lincoln Motor Car companies, Jonathan B. Maxwell, Charles
Sorenson, William Knudsen, Walter P. Chrysler, and the only
experienced financier among the pioneers, William C. Durant, the founder of General Motors. But the kernel about
which the crystal formed was a farm boy from nearby Dearborn, Henry Ford.

In the nineteenth century the state of Michigan was doubly
blessed with vast tracts of timber and exceptionally fertile soil.
The stands of timber, among the finest in the world, made
Detroit a leading center for the manufacture of ships, carriages, railroad cars, and furniture, drawing a large supply of
skilled mechanics and other craftsmen to the area. The lure
of the soil, described by a kinsman as eighteen inches deep,
drew William Ford, a Protestant tenant farmer, from famine-
plagued county Cork in southern Ireland in 1847. Had the
lumber-based industry and the fertile farmland not been so
closely coupled, young Henry would not have been able to

hone his skills in mechanics while attending to his farm, a scant eight miles away. Henry hated the farm; at age thirteen he first saw a steam-driven vehicle while driving to Detroit with his father on a farm wagon, and knew that this would be the world for him. His family were strong willed and persuasive, however, and his farm girl wife, Clara, knew no other world, so he oscillated between farm and factory jobs until he was almost thirty years old, the indecisiveness unusual for the entrepreneur he was soon to become. Tragically, a part of him never left the farm.

When he finally made the choice, neither he nor Clara ever looked back. He had a scheme for a horseless carriage, which he outlined for Clara on the back of a sheet of organ music; she came to believe in it as strongly as he did. He landed a job with the Edison Illuminating Company in Detroit and soon rose to the position of chief engineer, which meant that he was chief trouble-shooter, on call twenty-four hours a day. The job was ideal in that it gave the couple sufficient income to support themselves and their newborn son, but still left Henry plenty of time to work on his new engine.

A born scrounger, Henry made use of every bit of scrap material he could find. He used the handwheel of an old lathe as a flywheel. He made a cylinder out of a piece of discarded pipe. As his sister, Mary, remembered it, he

> reamed out the piece of pipe to a one-inch bore, tooled up a homemade piston fitted with rings, and attached this by a rod to the crankshaft. A two-to-one gear arrangement operated a cam, opening the exhaust valve and timing the spark. A piece of fiber with a wire through its center served as a spark plug; it made contact with a wire at the end of the piston, and when the piston moved away, this contact was broken and a spark leaped the gap, exploding the gasoline. He used house current to supply the electricity. He clamped the mounting board to

the kitchen sink, and handed Clara an oilcan filled with gasoline. She held the oilcan in one hand, and with the other adjusted a screw to let the gasoline trickle slowly into the cylinder. Henry spun the flywheel, the air and gas were sucked into the cylinder. The kitchen light flickered. He made a slight adjustment, tried again, and the engine roared into action, the sink shaking with vibration, flames shooting from the exhaust. He ran the engine for a minute, then put it aside to begin the construction of a two-cylinder engine. The engine worked, and that was all that he needed to know.

Ford could not finance his horseless carriage alone, but finance wasn't the problem; Henry was. He easily raised money for his first venture, the Detroit Automobile Company, from local citizens, but when he kept experimenting rather than building cars, his backers grew weary and dissolved the enterprise. With Ford out, the company was reorganized, and Henry Leland took it over under the new name, the Cadillac Motor Company.

Undaunted, Ford started all over again, with a company under his own name. He picked up partners with ease, luring the Dodge brothers, John and Horace, away from Oldsmobile to build his chassis. With the Dodge brothers in the fold, the Ford Motor Company became a going concern. Within thirty-seven days of its incorporation on June 16, 1903, the first Ford car, a two-cylinder dubbed the Model A, was sold for $850. By October 1 the fledgling company had delivered two hundred cars, and the orders began to flow in. The company produced eight different models before the famous Model T in 1908, some costly, some inexpensive. The inexpensive ones sold better, but the large, costly ones were more profitable. A battle broke out in the board, one which would repeat itself many times in automotive boards in years to come. The board wanted to build big cars because they were more profitable.

The automobile was a luxury item, a status symbol for those who could afford a horseless carriage. The ordinary citizen didn't need one, couldn't afford one, and, besides, all of the competition was building large automobiles. This did not fit in with Henry's concepts; he dug in his heels. He wanted to build low-cost small cars that the average man could buy. He argued that building more and selling for less would deliver more profits in the long run. The board did not agree.

The instant success of the Model T is known to all as the premiere accomplishment par excellence of American industry, but all was not peaches and cream in the Ford Motor Company. Henry was a determined and obstinate man. With the success of the Model T, he had enough money to buy out the big-car enthusiasts on the board, establishing majority control in his own hands. The inevitable conflict of personalities built up with the Dodge brothers, who used their profits to break off and start their own company. He bought out his bookkeeper-partner, James Couzens, who used his proceeds to run for the United States Senate, whence he harassed his old associate for many years.

No sooner was the company formed than it was hit with a patent infringement suit. To the surprise of the industry, George Selden, a patent attorney, had obtained a basic patent on the automobile. The royalties were modest, and most of the companies decided to pay tribute rather than fight it. Not Henry. He was incensed. For six years he battled in the courts. He finally prevailed, but almost lost his company in the process. At one point he became so discouraged that he almost sold out. William C. Durant, the financier, was taking a different approach to manufacturing and selling automobiles. He was buying up companies started by financially inexperienced entrepreneurs and raising the capital for production in the eastern financial markets. He had already picked up a number of

small companies, including Buick, Olds, Cadillac, and Oak-
land-Pontiac. The addition of Ford would round out the product lines in his new General Motors Corporation. After Ford
had lost a preliminary skirmish in the court, he was lying on
the floor in his New York hotel room, immobile with lumbago,
when he received an offer from Durant through Couzens.
Durant offered to buy the Ford Motor Company for $8 mil-
lion. "Tell him he can have it if the money's all cash," countered the suspicious Ford. Durant was able to raise only $6
million in cash, offering notes for the balance. But Ford wouldn't
budge, so the deal fell through.

Soon after the aborted General Motors deal, things started
looking up for Ford. Profits more than adequate to cover the
costs of litigation were rolling in; finally, in 1911, the New
York State Court of Appeals ruled that the automobile was in
the public domain and that the Selden patent was invalid.
Ford was literally off to the races. He won speed races, he
won endurance races, he won a transcontinental race. Ford's
name became synonymous with quality and endurance.

But Ford's dream was broader in scope. His idea was to
turn the automobile from a luxury and a plaything into a
necessity. To do that he had not only to put out a quality
product, but he had to do it at an affordable price. This meant
attention to productivity as well as to product.

Productivity is a buzz word these days, with all sorts of
esoteric definitions. Basically, it is the optimization of the
relative contributions of machines and labor to the final product. Ford's approach was first to standardize the product, then
optimize the use of machines, then optimize the use of labor.
The tin lizzie, the Model T, was just that — one model, no
substitutions, no variations. It was available "in any color, as
long as it's black." This simplified inventory control, it sim-

plified production machinery, and it simplified assembly techniques.

In 1908 all automobiles were assembled the same way. The car frame remained in place while workmen scurried around for parts. When Ford conceived his revolutionary Highland Park factory, with the main building a sixth of a mile long, it was obvious that running around this enormous plant would be exhausting. Why not bring the work to the man? After much experimentation, the moving assembly line evolved in 1913. Ford did not invent mass production, but he did invent the moving assembly line. And it paid off in reduced costs, which quickly translated into reduced prices. The Model T cost $950 in 1909 and $490 in 1913.

Yet Ford was still worried. For the first time in its ten-year life, the company could not hold on to workers. Rapid turnover disrupted production. Ford decided that although he had rewarded his stockholders with $12 million in dividends, his executives with hundreds of thousands in bonuses, and his customers with two price reductions, the worker, the crucial link in the production chain, was being left out. Prevailing practice was to pay as little as possible; wages in the area were at a bare subsistence level of $2.50 a day. Ford figured that he could double the wage rate and still be ahead with greater worker productivity. His directors almost collapsed, but he insisted on $5.00 a day. The worldwide reaction was electric.

The Employers Association of Detroit accused Ford of undermining the structure of the capitalist system; the National Association of Manufacturers was typically incensed; the *Wall Street Journal* called it blatant immorality — a misapplication of "Biblical principles" in a field "where they do not belong." But the world public and the press thought it was magnificent. Within only a few years, Ford had become a legend.

Ford is best remembered for his Model T, for his moving assembly lines, and for his $5.00 a day wage. But Ford's basic concept of turning the automobile from a plaything into a necessity in this vast and mobile developing nation was the true contribution. His success turned out to be but a modest prelude to a more widespread revolution. The development of moving assembly line mass-production techniques, the frequent reduction of prices to stimulate volume, and the payment, for the first time in history, of a living wage to stimulate productivity were innovations that changed the very structure of society.

And I don't believe that Ford knew what he was doing. He had no broad vision of society. He just wanted to produce and sell automobiles. He was narrow-minded, bigoted, unschooled, untutored, suspicious of education, wealth, and knowledge. He was rabidly anti-Semitic, unrealistically pacifistic; he brooked no opposition, not even from his son, and not from his grandson until he was on his deathbed. His was the "invisible hand" of Adam Smith, personified. He was the "mad socialist" of Detroit, yet he made more money than anyone in the country. He was stubborn and self-centered, yet he provided the engine and the wheels upon which America rode to an unprecedented prosperity.

Product reigned supreme for nineteen years. The Model T went into production in 1908 and wasn't withdrawn until 1927. But two other elements of a successful industrial enterprise — money and management — were yet to be heard from. Ford didn't need either. With product supremacy, he was making all the money in the world, and, with a single product and absolute control, management consisted of doing what Henry wanted done.

Billy Durant tried the money route first. William Crapo Durant was the antithesis of Henry Ford. Grandson of Henry

Howland Crapo, governor of Michigan from 1865 to 1869, enrolled as an honorary colonel in the state militia at the age of seven, Billy was born with a silver spoon, which soon tarnished with the deprivations caused by an alcoholic father. Raised in genteel poverty, Durant started out working in a lumberyard. He soon graduated to selling patent medicines, followed by postgraduate training as a drummer for a cigar company. He rounded out his schooling by developing a successful insurance agency before taking on the management of an insolvent local waterworks. Within eight months he had the company back on its feet and was branching out into real estate and housing construction, all the while looking for new worlds to conquer. One day an acquaintance offered him a ride in a novel two-wheeled cart with a uniquely stable suspension system. He contacted the manufacturer to secure a sales territory, only to find that he could buy the whole business, patents and all, for $1500. He borrowed the money from J. Dallas Dort, a friend, and started the Durant-Dort Carriage Company.

Billy sold six hundred of the carts before he had manufactured a one, and within a few years became the nation's largest carriage manufacturer. By 1904 Durant was a millionaire many times over, and the leading citizen of Flint, Michigan, at the age of forty-three. Naturally, he was aware of the burgeoning automobile industry.

The opportunity came in his home city of Flint. David Dunbar Buick had had a brilliant idea for a more powerful automobile engine. He would put the intake and exhaust valves in the removable head of the engine rather than in the foot, where they had been located heretofore. This would make the engine more compact and more efficient. Buick knew a lot about mechanics but very little about money. A perfectionist, he went broke four times before he produced his first valve-in-head engine. His fifth effort, the Buick Motor Car Company, was on its way down the drain when Durant was called in to the rescue. Billy knew very little about automobiles, and cared even less about what went on inside them. He was a supersalesman; it mattered little to him whether he was selling automobiles or patent medicines or cigars. Not having Ford's obstinacy, he first purchased a license under the Selden patent, figuring that it would cost him only $15 per car. With an artful agility in both sales and finance, he made Buick the best-selling automobile in the country within four years. Working with the financial resources of the House of Morgan, Durant was in a position to buy up other manufacturers on the road to a single, integrated, dominant automobile manufacturer.

He first worked on a merger of Buick and Maxwell into a holding company called United Motors Company. Later, Oldsmobile was brought into the fold through an entity called International Motors. The deal fell through for a while, so Durant had to find a new name. Somebody made up a list; Durant scanned it casually. The name didn't matter to him, and he finally picked one: General Motors Corporation.

By the end of 1909 Durant had acquired eleven automobile makers, two commercial-vehicle makers, and eight automotive-parts manufacturers; the jewels were Buick, Cadillac, Oldsmobile, and Albert Champion's A-C Spark Plug Company, all acquired for General Motors stock.

But Billy had moved too fast. By 1910 his rapid expansion had run him out of cash. It was a product-dominated market, and Billy didn't understand automobiles. Ford, disdainful of the six-cylinder engines on the new high-performance cars, stating that he had no use for an engine "that has more spark plugs than a cow has teats," was taking away the bulk of the market with his low-priced Model T, and when Buick's sales dropped off, the bankers moved in. A consortium of investment bankers put up the money to rescue the company. They set up a voting trust to run it, and Durant was squeezed out. He had lost control of General Motors.

But Durant was persistent. He wanted to start over again, but he needed an automobile to start with. He found it in the person of Louis Chevrolet, the premier race car driver of the day. Like David Buick, Chevrolet was an excellent mechanic who cared little for finance. Durant set up the Chevrolet Motor Car Company with himself in control, using Louis's six-cylinder design as the prime product. Through a dazzling series of stock market maneuvers, he merged Chevrolet into General Motors, ousted the voting trust, and took control again. This time his partners were Pierre S. Du Pont and his treasurer, John Jacob Raskob. His management team consisted of Charles Nash as president of the company and Walter P. Chrysler, who had risen from a farm boy to the presidency of the flagship Buick division.

By the beginning of the second decade of the century, the automobile business had become quite complex. Product was still dominant, but styling, distribution networks, installment financing, capital budgeting, inventory control, and all the other elements of a maturing industry began to come into the equation. It was too much for the wild and woolly stock market manipulator. Durant held on until the recession of 1920, then lost control for the second and last time. The business had outgrown him.

Du Pont and the House of Morgan put up the money to tide the company over the recession, and Pierre Du Pont, representing the largest shareholders, became the chief executive officer. The Du Pont corporation, whence he came, was a powerful, mature chemical and munitions giant, which had prospered handsomely in the war and had the organizational stability of a third-generation management team. General Motors was a complex shambles. It had a varied and complicated product line put together by the whims and wiles of Billy Durant; it was in a dynamic, rapidly changing industry, where companies sprouted up and expired almost weekly; and it was on its fourth set of managers — Durant twice, the bankers' voting trust, and now Pierre Du Pont.

Du Pont, a chemist with a degree from the Massachusetts Institute of Technology, liked to have technically trained men about him. He found the ideal associate, Alfred P. Sloan, Jr., already in the company.

Sloan had also graduated from MIT. A precocious, bookish, aloof person, he had earned a degree in electrical engineering in just three years, graduating as the youngest member of his class. He started as a draftsman in the Hyatt Roller Bearing Company, which was on the verge of bankruptcy when he arrived. Sloan's father and a friend invested $5000 in the company and turned it over to Alfred Jr. to run. Enamored of the new scientific management techniques pioneered by Frederick Winslow Taylor, Sloan ran a tight shop in a rough-and-tumble industry, managing to build it from a twenty-five-employee, ramshackle collection of antiquated machinery into a precision-based factory with thirty-eight hundred well-paid piece-rate production workers. He sold bearings to all the major automobile manufacturers, but the bulk of the sales was to General Motors and Ford. Fearful of being squeezed, Sloan had sold out to Durant in 1916 for $13.5 million in General Motors stock. It didn't take him long to realize that his investment was still in jeopardy. With seventy-five factories in forty cities, and more than fifty executives reporting directly to a harassed Durant, General Motors was just too large to operate as a one-man fiefdom. The tidy mind of Alfred P. Sloan was troubled; with all his fortune tied up in General Motors, Sloan set out to write a complete plan of reorganization for the company. Durant wouldn't give it the time of day. Sloan decided to resign and took a month's vacation in Europe to mull over his future. By the time he returned, the ball game was over. Durant was out, and Du Pont was in.

One of the most pressing problems confronting Pierre Du Pont when he moved into the chief executive's office was management reorganization. He was vaguely aware of Sloan's earlier proposals; when he studied them in detail, he liked what he saw. To Sloan's delight, he approved them with only minor modifications. The age of management was born.

For twenty years the automotive industry had been dominated by mechanics and money manipulators. Ford and the product people were still dominant, but the industry had become too complex for the manipulators like Durant. Led by Sloan, a new breed of professional managers, demanded by the changing nature of the business, was about to emerge. Ford had set out to make the automobile a necessity; he had succeeded brilliantly and would be dominant in the market for years to come. But buyers in sizable growing markets in the prosperous roaring twenties wanted something in addition to just transportation. They wanted styling or power or comfort or prestige. They wanted self-starters and lower running boards for women and colors other than black.

The men in charge at General Motors set out to satisfy those markets. They could not match Ford's low prices in the utilitarian vehicle, but they could produce higher-quality transportation with a number of models at progressively higher prices, confident that the markets were growing toward them. They settled on six basic models — Chevrolet, priced just above Ford; Oakland, later to become Pontiac; the Buick four-cylinder; the Buick six; the Oldsmobile eight, then priced above Buick; and the top-of-the-line Cadillac. Since each of these models came in a variety of styles, with a variety of

options and colors, the management challenges at General
Motors were very different from those at Ford. Divisions
inevitably overlapped and became competitive; distribution
systems and selling techniques differed at the several divisions; there was competition for advertising and promotional
funds; all divisions used some common parts, so there were
direct cost and overhead allocation problems. In short, General Motors was becoming the first modern diversified business.

Sloan set up a line and staff organization similar to that
perfected by the military but without the military's rigidity.
Each division was an operating company on its own, with staff
committees providing coordination and asset allocation. Policy
direction came from the board through an executive committee. Many of the executives from the old Durant days
chafed under the centralized coordination and control; those
who could not adapt were gradually weeded out. Within a
very few years Sloan had a management team and system that
was a model for generations of business school students and
has survived at General Motors for more than fifty years.

The new management system was remarkably flexible. A
new product idea or a styling change could be tried out in
one division without risking a total corporate commitment.
Less expensive cars could be pushed during difficult times,
and the larger, more expensive ones when prosperity returned. Most important was the concept of upgrading. The
rising young executive could start with a Chevrolet, gradually
work his way up the line as his fortunes improved, and, when
he reached the pinnacle, there he would be, for his neighbors
and all the world to applaud, in the ne plus ultra, the Cadillac,
preferably chauffeur-driven, of course. As the twenties worked
their way into the thirties, there came into being that periodic
reminder, that need for status reassessment, that point of

decision, in good times and in bad, the annual model change. Product began to give way, not only to management, but to such other parameters as prestige and personality.

You'd never have known it at Ford. The twenties started with the Model T overwhelmingly dominant in the market and Mr. Ford as the dominant personality in the United States. The automobile had revolutionized rural America. The farmer could get into town to buy and sell and socialize; for the farm woman, it was heaven. For the first time, medical care was available, since doctors were the first professionals to take advantage of the increased mobility, but equally important was the ability to meet with her neighbors, to assemble at the granges for the exchange of pies and cakes and to square dance, to get to church on Sunday, to organize the children into 4-H clubs, and to spend the full year preparing for the climactic event of the year, the annual county fair. The automobile had started the revolution, the tin lizzie was its mechanical symbol, and Henry Ford was its George Washington. In the cities, the legend of the $5.00-a-day wage, like the Model T itself, lived on beyond its time. Except for the Jews, who recognized him as the most dangerous anti-Semite in American history, Ford was the hero of the country. He was a strong supporter of President Wilson in the 1916 campaign, placing a series of signed full-page ads in five hundred newspapers throughout the industrialized states, and had a significant influence on Wilson's narrow victory. When the president persuaded him to run for the Senate in 1918, he disdained to put in a single campaign appearance, but lost by only 6000 votes. He went on well-publicized camping trips with Harvey Firestone and Thomas A. Edison, his successful inventor friends, occasionally condescending to bring along the awed and grateful new president of the United States, Warren G. Harding. A very strong Ford for President movement built up during the early twenties, and had not Harding died suddenly, catapulting Calvin Coolidge into the presidency, this most thoroughly unqualified man could very well have been elevated to the most important office in the country.

He paid little attention to the business, but wouldn't let anyone else run it. He turned over the title of president to his only son, Edsel, but that kind and gentle man never had a chance. Henry kept no office hours, held no regular meetings, had no cost-control system, did no formal planning, set no long-range goals. While Sloan of General Motors was setting up the management system of the century, Henry ran the country's largest industrial enterprise like a corner grocery store. He had one product, one color, one style, one price — take it or leave it, that was it. Would you believe that the momentum set up by the Model T sustained the company for thirty-six years, from 1908 until 1944? Many capable people tried to change it, the most notable being William S. Knudsen.

Knudsen, a massive, hard-driving Dane, learned his first two words of English, "Hurry up," from a customs inspector when he landed in Hoboken from Copenhagen in 1899. They became his motto as he worked his way up with a variety of production jobs in manufacturing companies on the East Coast. He came to Ford with an acquisition in 1911 and soon became the top production man in the company. An earthy man whose colorful broken English and smoking and drinking habits set him aside from the usual Ford executive, he argued long and hard for variety in the product line. Recognized as a production genius, he persuaded everyone but his boss. Henry, who wanted no geniuses around him, would brook no product changes. Citing his profane language and personal habits, Henry had Knudsen fired over a minor disagreement. To Henry's chagrin, Knudsen went on to become one of the giants of the industry at General Motors. Knudsen took over the ailing

Chevrolet division, straightened it out in three years, and within seven brought so much strength into it that Chevy sailed right past Ford to become the best-selling car in the United States. Knudsen went on to corporate immortality by following Sloan as president, then finished his career as overall czar of war production for President Roosevelt during World War II.

In 1927 Henry bowed to the inevitable. He discontinued the Model T after nineteen years and started production of a new car. The Model A was a good car, as was the V-8 of the thirties, but the Ford Motor Car Company was living on sheer momentum. Henry withdrew more and more from operations. Although Edsel was nominally in charge, the old man thought him too soft; he relied more and more on Harry Bennett, a thug whom Henry had hired originally as a bodyguard for his grandchildren. For some reason, perhaps the contrast with his son, Henry placed all his confidence in the former pugilist who, with his security force of ex-convicts and other brutish goons, gradually took over complete control of the company. The company staggered through the thirties, losing market share steadily to General Motors and the emerging Chrysler Corporation; it was propped up only temporarily by the start of production of military materials prior to the war. Henry had a couple of strokes, withdrawing more and more in favor of Bennett. When the beloved but betrodden Edsel passed away in 1943, the father's grief was assuaged only by his firm belief in reincarnation. Bennett took over unofficially but completely, and the company began to sink into insolvency in the midst of unprecedented wartime prosperity. It was only the personal intervention of the secretary of the navy, concerned about war production in a company now run by "crackpots, ex-convicts, and Nazi subversives," that convinced President Roosevelt to release the grandson, young Henry II, from active naval duty to attempt a rescue. It was not the classic shirtsleeves to shirtsleeves in three generations, but almost shirtsleeves to insolvency in two.

Sloan at General Motors had organized to let the market come to him, and come to him it did, smoothly and inexorably. With Knudsen as the production genius, and with the concepts of upgrading and the annual model change, GM had a car for every customer. Sloan's managers recognized the importance of distribution and finance, setting up a cohesive sales force with a sophisticated feedback system to keep management well informed on market shifts and the General Motors Acceptance Corporation, to become the largest installment finance agency in the country. It soon recognized the importance of women as the ultimate decision makers in this primary family prestige purchase. The husband kicked the tires, but the wife picked the color and the style and the convenience items, and, more often than not, the ultimate make and model. In the match between monarchy and management, management won going away.

With Ford's insistence on an obsolescent product and GM's concern for the big picture, the disparity was so great that there was even room for something in between. Walter P. Chrysler was not an immigrant or a farm boy like many of the automotive pioneers. His father was an engineer on a crack Union Pacific passenger train, and young Walter grew up with the smell of steam in his nostrils. He took to automobiles while in high school, and early dreamed of having an automobile company with his name on the door. He had worked his way up to plant manager of an automotive division of the American Locomotive Works when he caught the attention of James Storrow, the banking head of the 1916 voting trust at General Motors. He joined GM as an assistant to Charles Nash at the Buick division, taking over the division presidency when Nash moved up to head the company. A brilliant engineer with a flamboyant personality, a hot temper, and an equally hot vocabulary, Chrysler didn't like Billy Durant's financial hokey-pokey when Billy regained control. When Durant made some financial acquisitions that included poor-quality products, Chrysler, whose technical pride was outraged, told off the boss and quit.

But he had learned some financial acumen under the bankers and financiers. That experience, coupled with his innate engineering ability, rounded him into a formidable business executive. He was immediately offered $1 million to save Willys-Overland, a company that had suffered during the economic slowdown after World War I. Save it he did by instituting financial controls. He was then asked to take on Maxwell, a popular car that was not selling well because its axles often broke. Chrysler simply redesigned the axles himself, and Maxwell's reputation was saved. Surrounding himself with super-quality engineers, he brought several of the companies and a car of his own design together into a new venture under his own name. When he was able to pick up the Dodge Brothers Company in 1928, the Chrysler Corporation became number three in the automotive industry, gaining its reputation by sheer engineering quality of product. As Ford faltered, Chrysler moved into the number two spot for a time, with its solid product line of Plymouth, Dodge, DeSoto, and top-of-the-line Chrysler. For a time, just before the war broke out, it looked as though the upstart Chrysler Corporation would make a serious run for first place against the well-disciplined management system of the General Motors Corporation. Walter Chrysler had shown in a very few years that when the chips are down, and the product quality is available, the customer will opt for product.

All of the big three automotive companies made superlative

contributions to the war effort, but each took a different path to satisfying the pent-up demand of the impatient American public.

The situation at Ford was critical. Young Henry had been released from active duty to stem the deterioration of that once proud and powerful enterprise, but it took him almost two years to take control from his senile grandfather and the crude Bennett; even then, it was accomplished only through the intervention of his mother and grandmother, who threatened to sell their stock unless control changed hands. Realizing that he knew next to nothing about making automobiles, he cast in all directions for assistance.

In November 1945 a group of ten air corps officers finishing active duty as management experts at the Pentagon sent Henry a telegram: "We have a matter of management importance to discuss with you." To their amazement, they received a dinner invitation from the president himself, and were hired on the spot. None of them knew anything about the automobile business, so for the first few months they simply circulated around the company, asking questions. Pretty soon everyone called them the Quiz Kids, an appellation later modified to the Whiz Kids, and though few of them liked it, the name stuck. Whiz Kids or not, they were professional management experts, a new breed, and they were winners. Tex Thornton, their leader, soon left to form Litton Industries, but Arjay Miller went on to become the president of Ford, and Robert S. McNamara, a third member of the group, not only became president of Ford, but secretary of defense and head of the World Bank.

The Whiz Kids were not enough; Ford needed experience. He settled on Ernest R. Breech, president of the Bendix division of General Motors. Breech lost no time in bringing aboard a half dozen seasoned GM executives who quickly stopped the flow of blood and restored the company to profitability. The General Motors management system reigned triumphant. Although Henry II would rule for decades at the top of the heap, the managers at the lower level soon became indistinguishable from their archrivals.

The metamorphosis at Chrysler was less dramatic. The big boss, after his spectacular ascent to prominence, grew ill during the thirties and turned control over to his chief production man, K. T. Keller. During the war production reigned supreme, strengthening his position, but Keller lacked the vision, patience, creativity, and tenacity of Chrysler and was no match for the General Motors behemoth or the revitalized, look-alike Ford. At war's end, while the others were planning new cars, Keller was content to sit on his duff with slight modifications to the prewar vehicles.

Keller had a hat fetish. Seldom seen without his fedora, he vowed that every car Chrysler built would have a roof high enough so that a man wearing a hat could sit up straight in his seat. With a stubbornness and earthiness reminiscent of Old Henry Ford, he resisted the trend toward lower cars. "We build cars to sit in, not piss over," was his pithy philosophy.

Keller was succeeded by a series of nondescript executives. As Ford regained ground with its new GM-inspired management system, Chrysler became neither fish nor fowl. It lacked the brilliance and cohesion of Walter Chrysler's one-man control, never acquiring the in-depth resources of a distributed management system. It handled its labor relations badly, gradually losing its reputation for engineering quality and production. As its share of market decreased, it lost economies of scale to its larger rivals. It simply did not have enough production units on which to spread its overhead costs. Production- and engineering-trained CEOs gave way to financial executives who knew something about costs but little about cars. In order to have enough product to absorb indirect costs, Chrysler fell into the most fundamental fallacy of inept management: it built cars for inventory without having customers for them. Using the old saw, "You can't sell from an empty wagon," the company built up the concept of a "sales bank." Every model year, they continued to pour out product well beyond the ability of the distribution system to sell at a profit. By the numbers, a profit was booked when the product left the factory, but there were not enough customers. Inventory built up in railroad yards, in abandoned drive-in movie theaters, in fair grounds, in parking lots all over the country. You couldn't find a parking space in Detroit at the end of a production year; they were all filled with Chrysler inventory. After the cars had sagged up to their axles in the mud, ice, and snow of a midwestern winter, they were frequently in a sorry state. Reports came in of sales-bank cars stagnant for so long that weeds were growing in the carpeting. Teams regularly roamed the lots, changing tires, recharging batteries, replacing broken windshields. Renting parking space, financing inventory, and refurbishing vehicles all added up to increased costs. As the costs rose, the profits vanished, the company's reputation sagged, the better dealers went elsewhere, morale plummeted, and the inevitable bankruptcy moved closer and closer, until the once proud enterprise submitted to the final ignominy, government takeover and new management under the flamboyant Lee Iacocca.

During the forties and fifties, General Motors' broad product line, its attention to styling, and the annual model change, combined with its seasoned management team, gave it a firm grasp on the market. The troubles of its main competitors, Ford on its way back from insolvency and Chrysler on its way toward it, gave the giant firm the economies of scale that allowed it to govern the market so completely that its competitors lived by its sufferance. "Break up General Motors" was the cry of the trustbusters. Although antitrust enforcement has had its own excesses, it is pretty clear that in those days it worked. It was primarily the threat of antitrust action that kept the company from turning the United States automobile industry into a monopoly. During the sixties the company increased its dominance throughout the world. By the early seventies General Motors had reached the pinnacle. It was the biggest, most profitable, best managed, most admired corporation in the history of the free enterprise system. Within a decade, it would be losing money and appealing to the United States government for protection against foreign competition.

As usual, the troubles started way back. Big bureaucracies, public or private, have a great deal of momentum. Like supertankers, they have little maneuverability and are difficult to steer. Without anticipation, they can be headed for the rocks before the hand at the tiller is aware of the looming danger.

When Afred P. Sloan set up the General Motors operating and management system, he set it up for the conditions of the time. Pierre Du Pont was a chemist and Sloan an engineer. They knew their products and assumed that excellence of design and quality of production would forever be dominant in their company. Sloan recognized that with the coming diversity of product and markets a structured, semidecentralized line and staff management system would be necessary. The economic system was relatively simple in those days. It consisted of three elements — design, produce, and sell. It did not have to consider labor. There was plenty of labor available, dirt cheap. It did not have to consider the environment. Smoke from a smokestack meant jobs, not pollution.

It did not have to consider safety. Everyone knew that automobiles were dangerous. Caveat emptor. It did not have to consider government. Those were the days of Harding, and Coolidge, and Herbert Hoover. It didn't have to consider foreign competition. Shipping costs were prohibitive, and besides, they drove on the wrong side of the road over there.

The first time the system started to come off the track was when it lost sight of its fundamental objective, simplicity and quality of product. Harlow "Red" Curtice was the harbinger. He was the first professional manager, the first of those who were not "product men" to rise to the top at GM. He loved size, he loved speed, he loved gimmickry. His hoods were the biggest, his radiators the most dominant, his chrome the most glittering; his Buicks were classed as "the only hundred-mile-per-hour stock cars in production," in a day when roads could not handle forty-mile-per-hour speeds. The concept sold well, so the others were forced to follow.

As the size of the industry grew, the companies had to face an increasingly difficult dilemma. The annual model change was crucial to sales, but as the capital investment mounted, it was impossible to make material annual modifications to machinery and product. Increasingly, the industry turned to styling and variety of options as its selling points. At one time General Motors had twelve hundred stylists on its payroll, but only 950 research scientists. Year after year the engines and the transmissions and the models ballooned into such complexity that one could not tell product from puff. According to a Yale physicist's whimsical calculation, a 1965 Chevrolet, offered in forty-six models, thirty-two different engines, twenty transmissions, thirty colors (plus nine two-tones), and four hundred options, was available in more combinations than there were atoms in the universe. Just before its collapse, Chrysler was making one hundred fifty-six different engines, seventy-two different side-body lamps, sixty-nine different rear axles, and seventeen different shapes of door handles. In a supposedly high-volume business, some parts were being produced in lots of less than a thousand. Just handling inventory was a task of staggering complexity. It was no wonder that the product men lost out.

General Motors institutionalized the change in 1958. The financial people had come to the fore more and more as the complexity and size of the business grew and as layers of middle managers became necessary to handle that complexity in those precomputer days. As a manager grows more and more remote from the action on the factory floor or the drafting room or the sales showroom, he comes to deal more and more with abstractions. These abstractions can best be dealt with in numbers, giving the financially trained executive an advantage. Frederick Donner was such a man. A thin-lipped accountant with an analytical bent, Donner had acquired detailed knowledge of the company from the executive suites at headquarters, not from the factories of Detroit or Flint or Lansing. In contrast to the swashbuckling, voluble automobile men of the past, Donner was uncomfortable around people and boasted, "I don't even own a slide rule." From the day of his election as chairman in 1958 to today, the chief executive officer of the country's largest industrial enterprise has come up the financial, not the operating, ladder.

Some of the best operating men drifted away. "Bunky" Knudsen, son of the legendary Bill, went to the presidency of Ford, not recognizing that he was going from one disaster to a worse one. John Z. DeLorean, the brilliant, iconoclastic engineer, never recovered emotionally from his frustrations at GM and went steadily downhill after his departure.

Product men didn't fare much better elsewhere. Chrysler was insolvent before it found a manager in the mold of the founder. Ford was no different. Henry II never even liked automobiles and was uncomfortable with strong executives around him. He booted out Ernie Breech, the Bendix executive who had saved the company. Bunky Knudsen didn't last long; Henry II fired him as Old Henry had fired his father. The story of the firing of Lee Iacocca is known to all. The only president with whom he seemed to be comfortable was Robert McNamara, whose background was the Harvard Business School who knew nothing about automobiles. When Henry II finally called it quits, he was careful to call out the incumbent, a colorless character whose primary qualification was loyalty to the boss.

Over the past twenty years automobile executives have all begun to look alike. With the exception of Iacocca, an anomaly the product of crisis, they have become nameless, faceless creatures, not prominent on the national scene, content to serve their five years in the top spot and fade away into obscurity. They live together in Bloomfield Hills, play golf at the same country clubs, attend the same business schools, embrace the same management systems. In their cloistered impersonality they have become remote from America, unchanging with the times, puzzled that the answers are not in the book. It is this remoteness, this utter dependence on management systems, this refusal to recognize the importance of externalities that has turned the industry, in two short decades, from the pride of the free enterprise system into an uncompetitive and unproductive morass, from a proud, independent bastion of business into a virtual ward of the United States government.

The labor record of the automobile industry has been abysmal. It didn't start out that way. Old Henry had always considered himself a laboring man. His $5.00-a-day wage shook up the industrial system, and, when he introduced the five-day workweek, the chairman of the National Association of Manufacturers was horrified enough to assert that "Ford may try to amend the Ten Commandments, but any acceptance of the five-day week means a surrender to easy and loose living." As Henry grew older, however, Harry Bennett and his goon squads took over, spying and reporting on workers to the point where an atmosphere of fear pervaded the factory floor. At one time, it was estimated that one worker in every four was an informer.

At GM Sloan with his system recognized no outside elements, certainly not government and certainly not labor unions. He was violently opposed to Franklin Roosevelt with all his reforms and would not give labor leaders the time of day. The company had an inflexible requirement for a minimum return on investment. When that minimum was threatened during the depression, wages were cut to meet it. There were no exceptions, and there was no appeal. When the inevitable labor unrest followed, GM set up an espionage system to rival Harry Bennett's. Any employee suspected of union activity was summarily fired. These inflexible policies set General Motors up as the ideal target for the first and most important strike in the history of American industrial unionism.

The United Auto Workers (UAW), emboldened by New Deal labor legislation and newly associated with the aggressive Congress of Industrial Organizations and John L. Lewis, its dynamic leader, were ready to go in 1936. General Motors was prepared for the strike with its espionage squads, a cooperative police force, thousands of dollars' worth of stored guns and tear gas, and elaborate plans for lockouts. But the workers fooled them. They simply sat down on their jobs inside the plants. On December 28, 1936, the first sit-down strike, the most important strike in American labor history, started in the Cleveland, Ohio, plant of the Fisher Body Corporation, a subsidiary of General Motors. In spite of long and bitter battles, the most bloody of which was against Harry Bennett's bat-wielding brutes at the Ford River Rouge plant, the union eventually prevailed.

It took ten years of strenuous effort, even though aided by the administration, public opinion, and the full power of the courts, for the union to smash through the determined opposition of Sloan and Bennett to organize the automobile industry. Steeled in the controversy, the UAW became the most powerful, the most antagonistic, the most obdurate union in the country. The tense pattern of labor-management relations for the next forty years was established in that decade. Both sides, like warring nations, battled to their mutual destruction. Work rules were highly regulated and rigorously structured, with formal grievance procedures negotiated in an atmosphere of mutual suspicion and distrust. The cost-of-living adjustment (COLA), through which wages were automatically adjusted for inflation, fattened the workers' paychecks but set the national pattern for the runaway inflation of the seventies. Senior management officials, with average duration in office of less than six years, were determined to have labor peace and the devil take the next administration. There was a "not on my watch" attitude on the part of a succession of CEOs, of which Walter Reuther, as UAW president, took advantage to drive the toughest of bargains. The stage was set for the militantism of the sixties, when the counterculture invaded the younger UAW workers. Absenteeism, tardiness, slipshod workmanship, drugs, racial struggles, and sheer indifference were the order of the day. By the time of the first OPEC embargo, management, systems or no systems, had surrendered control of the production floor.

Management didn't do any better with safety or air pollution. Here they took on not merely their own workers, but the United States government, the press, and ultimately, the American public. As management personnel became more remote and abstract, they became more arrogant and unyielding. Focusing single-mindedly on the short-term well-being of the corporation and its stockholders, the senior executives ignored the responsibility of all societal institutions to support consensual social good, particularly when those organizations were the largest and most powerful in the country. When Peter Drucker, dean of American business writers, criticized General Motors management for lack of responsiveness to society and community in his widely acclaimed treatise *Concept of the Corporation,* he found himself persona non grata in the company. "Fundamentally antibusiness," sniffed one senior official.

General Motors' single most important invention of the sixties was Ralph Nader. If Nader had written the script himself, he couldn't have done a better job. It all started with the Corvair. Chairman Frederick Donner had been on a cost-cutting binge to prop up short-term earnings. He ran smack-dab into Ed Cole, the brilliant engineer who headed the Chevrolet division. Cole had a new hot product in the Corvair, a sporty car with a rear-mounted aluminum engine. Although GM had invested $150 million in the development, Donner watched every part like a hawk. His cost-cutting program extended to the smallest parts, including a $15 stabilizing bar that he stripped from the chassis on the grounds that it was too expensive. Cole's objections were overridden, even though the first prototype rolled over on the test track in the hands of an experienced driver. The battle raged on the fourteenth floor of executive headquarters, Cole finally giving in for budgetary reasons. It was a costly decision. Six years of production Corvairs were in the field before the omission was corrected.

In the meantime the problem had come to the attention of

Nader, an obscure Harvard Law School graduate with a messianic zeal to use the law to cure social inequities brought about by the greediness of major corporations. Interested in auto safety, he brought the problem to the attention of an ambitious freshman senator from Connecticut, Abraham Ribicoff.

The question of how safe the Corvair was for the ordinary driver has never been adequately answered, but General Motors already had a reputation for dragging its feet on safety features, and when Nader published his book about the Corvair, *Unsafe at Any Speed,* he became a national celebrity, while GM managers became the bad guys. Called to what he thought was a routine hearing before Ribicoff's safety subcommittee, Donner brought along the new GM president, James Roche, another accountant. Not only did they have to face Ribicoff, but they had to contend with another freshman senator, Robert F. Kennedy of New York. A skilled advocate, openly contemptuous of the lofty executives, Kennedy ripped them apart. Donner and Roche sat before the microphones, hands shaking and voices quavering before the onslaught. They didn't remember how much GM had spent on safety research, only recalling a one-million-dollar grant the company had made to MIT the week before.

"What was the profit of General Motors last year?" Kennedy demanded.

"I'll have to ask one of my associates," the flustered Donner replied. The icy accountant, who could rattle off statistics by the hour, was unable to answer the most basic of questions about the company.

"One thousand seven hundred million dollars," Roche interjected weakly.

"You made one point seven billion dollars and waited until

last week to spend one million on a safety study?" Kennedy countered incredulously.

From there on it was all downhill. Kennedy wouldn't let the two executives recover and, according to the *Washington Post,* treated them "much as if he were examining a couple of youthful applicants for a driver's license who hadn't done their homework."

You would think that after that dismal performance, the company would have been more careful. On the contrary, it next blundered into a preposterous episode, which can most charitably be described as dumb. The corporation's chief counsel, angered at Nader and the senators, ordered a private investigation of the young attorney, hoping to "make a case for him being a homosexual and an anti-Semite," and to so discredit him that "anything he might say or do afterward . . . would carry no weight with the great American public." As part of the investigation, agents were assigned to follow Nader wherever he went. Two of the agents, burly, with crew cuts, felt-hatted and cigarred, followed him into the Senate Office Building on his way to testify before Ribicoff's subcommittee. It's hard to believe, but they lost him in the building and asked a uniformed guard, who happened to be a Ribicoff patronage employee, where Nader had gone. The guard, recognizing the private eyes for what they were, gleefully called Ribicoff's office, and the jig was up. The result was that not only did GM president Roche have to deliver a humiliating public apology before the scornful subcommittee, but the ensuing public scandal smoothed the way for the passage of a much stronger auto safety bill than the subcommittee had even dreamed of.

The industry's record on air pollution control was less dramatic, but equally poorly handled. Continual obstruction and foot-dragging so exhausted the patience of the regulators, the press, and the public that the resulting legislation was much more restrictive and unworkable than that which would have passed had the industry been more cooperative.

Detroit's performance on labor relations, public relations, safety, and air pollution was atrocious, but its miscalculations on product mix, the marketplace, and foreign competition in the new world economy were worse. It all went back to the question of whether the primary market for automobiles was reliable, low-cost transportation, or luxury, gadgets, and prestige. Old Henry Ford had dominated the market in the early days with his concept that what the country needed and wanted was the former, and he was right for almost twenty years. Alfred P. Sloan was right when he designed his system for a spectrum of price ranges, gadgets galore, and the obligatory annual model change. His concepts lasted even longer, but by the seventies they were a half century old and carved inches thick into every piece of granite on every sumptuous skyscraper in the city. Any financier who questioned the biblical injunction that you could not make money on small cars didn't progress past bookkeeper, second class. Detroit's disdainful disclaimer of the low-cost transportation argument was "We do have low-cost transportation systems in this country. We call them used cars."

But the Arabs and inflation had changed everything topsy-turvy and we were back to the days of Old Henry. With the price of gasoline and rising capital costs, people couldn't afford luxury; they opted for reliability and low cost. Unfortunately, Detroit was not equipped, mentally or mechanically, to give it to them.

The small car had always been a loser in Detroit. Bill Knudsen had proposed it in the thirties to no avail. "Engine Charlie" Wilson tried again in the forties, but was shot down by the money men. The small car had always dominated the markets in Europe, where fuel was expensive and roads were narrow, but they made no impact in the United States until the immediately popular Volkswagen Beetle showed up in 1960. Ford grudgingly reacted with the Pinto, and GM with the Vega, but their hearts were not in it. Chrysler, by then being run by a phalanx of CPAs, decided that there was no potential profit in these minuscule vehicles and shelved the whole idea. By the end of the sixties the Japanese, particularly Toyota and Datsun, had become a factor. Detroit viewed the imported interlopers and the subcompacts as somehow anti-American, not the bellwethers of major market shifts. The companies seemed purposely to make their economy cars cheap imitations of their standard-sized models. Quality comparisons with the imports were odious and did much to refute the old "Made in Japan" poor-quality myth. By the time the first OPEC price rise hit, Detroit was outgunned and outmaneuvered. Chrysler, with no domestic small car, immediately went into a nosedive and lost money for two years; Ford and GM were stung, but recovered when the oil embargo was lifted. True to their convictions, the Americans misinterpreted a small bubble of pent-up demand for big cars as a major market reversal, and were caught flat-footed when the second OPEC price rise hit. Chrysler went into insolvency, Ford had three loss years in a row, coming perilously close to the edge, and the monarch of them all, the lofty General Motors, went into the tank and lost money in 1980.

What had happened? Clearly, the Americans were myopic in their market analyses. The first oil embargo was not predictable, but everyone knew that the price of gasoline was slated to go up substantially. It was also obvious that inflation, safety controls, and antipollution requirements were pricing the standard car out of the reach of the low wage earner.

Detroit certainly knew that. It was the reason it fought so long and hard against safety and environmental legislation. If it had put the same amount of effort into adaptive auto design, it would have been much better off in the long run. By the time the industry recognized the market shift, it was too late for any short-term corrections.

American industry is supposed to be adaptive, however. Other sections of the economy adapted to changing conditions. Why not the auto industry? In fairness, it must be pointed out that everything hit them at once — almost literally, the roof fell in. Many of the negatives were not of their doing. No reasonable person could have predicted the first oil price rise, the lull, the second price rise, and then the oil glut. The government was at fault in many ways. It kept price controls on gasoline, ostensibly to protect the consumer, but, as later free market experience painfully showed, provided only a temporary umbrella for OPEC. It maintained a nineteenth-century, domestic market concept of antitrust, blindly preventing industry cooperation to solve common problems such as pollution control. For too long it maintained tax policies that restricted needed capital investment. It continues to run a massive deficit that keeps the dollar uncompetitive, giving imports a competitive advantage of as much as 25 percent.

But the industry itself is at fault for the fundamental problems. Marketing myopia is a big one. A certain arrogance, an insularity, a Bloomfield Hills Brahmin mentality is another. The biggest of all is productivity, which is a combination of management-labor relations and management-management relations. The antagonism built up over the years between management and the unions will take a long time to subside and will make it very difficult for the industry to adapt to the wage differentials and work methods of the new world economy. Both sides will put up good façades in negotiations. But let's face it — they don't trust each other. And they won't until someone finds a way to bridge the massive cultural gap caused by the separation of the decision makers by eight to ten layers of middle management from the population on the factory floor.

We must look to an awakening on the part of the major unions, and I will deal with that in the next chapter; in this one, I'll stick to the foibles of management. Too much isolation from foreign competition in Fortress America has made postwar management soft. In the very basics, research and development and innovative engineering, cost cutting and short-term orientation at the top have caused a technical inferiority to the Germans at the top of the market and to the Japanese at the low end. In fuel injection, disc brakes, and independent suspension systems, the heralded American technology has taken a back seat to the Germans. In the design of lightweight, small displacement engines, the Japanese have forged far ahead. It should be possible for the United States to catch up with the Germans in the designs for the high end, but at the low end, Detroit has given up and the companies admit it. Their solution is to import Japanese technology and production techniques through the guise of joint ventures.

Good management covers a series of disciplines. Paramount among them is smooth, cost-effective material flow. Procurement practices in the American automotive industry have often been primitive. It's difficult to obtain data on procurement practices, but we do know that steel, the most basic and fundamental component in the automobile, was procured by allocation among the large steel companies and not by competitive bid until recently, when the American steel companies also became noncompetitive. We hear much of the Japanese "just in time" methods of inventory control, where suppliers are close by and only a few days' inventory are kept on hand. Americans are rushing to imitate it. That's not the basic problem. Inventories are buffers. They are kept on hand to interface between mismatches in the flow of production, to make up for mistakes in planning and production scheduling, and for work stoppages. It is these deficiencies which must be corrected before inventories can be minimized.

If there is a single, most identifiable flaw in this complex national tragedy, it is probably the dominance of financial men over product men in the management hierarchy. For twenty-five years, as a matter of policy, the chief executive officer at General Motors has come up through the financial ranks. It's probably my own biased technological background showing through, but I think it is time for a little more of Old Henry Ford in his younger days or of Walter P. Chrysler, and a little less of the concepts of Alfred P. Sloan or Red Curtice or Frederick Donner.

Others feel the same way. W. Edward Deming, the man who wrote the book on Japanese quality control, is an American. He is outspoken about the failure of Detroit's quality control, and about who is at fault. "Populating management with financially oriented people has ruined the country," he stated. "Management jobs rob the hourly worker of his right to be proud of his work. Quality is of no great concern to management, since no manager has ever lost a job because he didn't act on quality."

The frightening thing is that management doesn't seem to be learning. Automobile manufacture is no longer in the free market system in the United States. It is a regulated industry. Chrysler is a ward of the government. Lee Iacocca, the only product man in charge of a major automobile company, has done a superb job in turning the company around. But if it were not for the government intervention, Chrysler would certainly have gone bankrupt, and if it were not for the present import restraints, Chrysler would not have made it, Iacocca or no Iacocca. Ford and General Motors have come out of their loss years, but only because of import controls. Management doesn't seem to understand this. General Motors has gone off and bought itself a data processing service company. Diversification is not a bad thing in itself, but it doesn't help sell automobiles. We practice it quite successfully in the company I am associated with, but we started it thirty years ago, and it is an integral part of our corporate culture. For General Motors it's too late. The data processing company may be a good investment if it's kept separate, but the chances of those two corporate cultures coalescing are nil. Hoping for diversification to modify the General Motors management mentality is like leaving the landing lights on for Amelia Earhart. It just ain't going to happen.

The United States and Japanese governments negotiated "voluntary" import quotas on automobiles back in 1981, primarily to save jobs at a time when all of the U.S. companies were losing money and laying off workers by the thousands. It was an appropriate national policy at the time. The flow of blood has been stopped; all of the companies are profitable and some workers have been rehired. But the import controls represent restraint of trade in the purest sense. The Japanese can still undersell the Americans by $1200 to $1500 per car, and they will cream the market when controls are lifted. Under this price umbrella both the Japanese and the American automobile industries are prospering, but at the expense of the American consumer. Since the Japanese can sell all the cars they are allowed to export, they have been raising prices and loading the cars with expensive options. The Americans have raised their prices to match, but the Japanese are still better off. A recent Brookings Institution study points out that the

Americans have raised their profits by $1.4 billion, while the Japanese have made $2 billion on the quotas. That's why you don't hear the Japanese complaining. The quotas cost American consumers $4.3 billion in 1983, or about $100,000 a year for each of the forty-six thousand autoworker jobs that the quotas saved. Spending $100,000 to save a $50,000 job that was too highly paid in the first place doesn't make sense.

In the face of this terribly noncompetitive situation, the American automobile manufacturers had the audacity to pay themselves millions of dollars in performance bonuses. Now, ordinarily, I'd be the last person to complain about executive performance bonuses. I've received some pretty hefty ones myself, but they have been against a record of open, competitive performance, not protectionism. I am also aware that some of the totals included accumulated stock option awards and, in fairness, should not be lumped into a single year. But boards of directors have wide powers of delayed compensation, and they should have had the public sensitivity to recognize the devastating effect of these actions on union negotiations and quota renewals. Talk about cutting off your own nose! These actions have cost the industry hundreds of millions of dollars in wage increases and have certainly been a factor in the future loss of the very quotas that provided the extra incentive compensation. When will they ever learn?

The obtuseness of these recent actions has convinced me that American automobile company managements have not faced up to the new world order; until they do, they will continue to get themselves in trouble, and to need government bailouts. They will need more automation, to be sure. They will need more union wage concessions, although I don't see how they are going to get them. They will need more computers and better inventory control. They will need a new generation of small cars, and better engineering in their large

ones. But these are not the fundamental problems. For Detroit companies to prosper again, they will need new corporate
leaders of sophistication and strength.

An engineer at an automobile test track put it more bluntly.
"There is absolutely nothing wrong with the American industry that a few engineers with some balls and some real
feelings about automobiles couldn't fix with a clean sheet of
paper and a management with enough guts to back them up."

I believe that.

7

One Strike, You're Out!

THE TROUBLE started way back. Most of the men who operated air traffic control posts were former military pilots accustomed to hard-won glamour status among their GI colleagues and emotionally secure in a profession described as mixing hours and hours of stifling boredom with moments of sheer terror. In the quiet hum of the cockpit or the control room, the pilot or the controller must be ever alert to the perils of complacency and the prospects of sudden danger from an instrument error or a miscalculation. It takes a special person, indeed. The concept carried over into their civilian government jobs as monitors and directors of the nation's increasingly crowded air traffic lanes. The Professional Air Traffic Controllers Organization (PATCO) didn't even call itself a union, so confident were its members of their unique status. Its first executive director, F. Lee Bailey, the flamboyant criminal attorney and veteran pilot, was adept at presenting PATCO's case before the public, the press, and especially the Congress. In 1969 Bailey described controllers as "old men at thirty-five" and noted that controlling traffic was a job that "only the top ten percent of the male population is even capable of doing." (The macho attitude is still strong; 95 percent of the controllers are men.)

Controlling air traffic certainly is a difficult way to make a living. The long hours and pressure took a grim toll: men who could not stand the gaff suffered heart attacks, hypertension, and ulcers. Conflict with their lower paid, lower pecking order, more bureaucratic Federal Aviation Administration (FAA) supervisors was inevitable, increasing the tension. But, like pilots, those controllers emotionally compatible with the job loved it. For each of the eleven thousand PATCO members, ten applicants were ready to take the job. The compensation extracted from an impressed Congress was outstanding. At an average age of thirty-five, the controllers, most without college degrees, working for the only employer who had use for their services, drew down $40,000 a year. With overtime and shift differentials many made as much as $60,000. They had one of the best retirement systems outside the military; half pay at age fifty with just twenty years' service, or at any age with twenty-five years' service. Disability pay was like a license to steal. A controller who could demonstrate a psychological disability such as burnout was eligible for 75 percent of salary, tax free and indexed to inflation. The net pay for disability was higher than for working. Small wonder that it was a young man's game, and that controllers were going out at a rate of five hundred per year.

They still weren't satisfied. Guided by increasingly militant leaders, the controllers persistently compared themselves with senior airline pilots in the private sector, whose highest pay could exceed $100,000 per year, rates unmatched anywhere in the government service except for the president himself. In 1980 Robert E. Poli, executive vice president of the organization, ousted his boss on the charge that he was not militant enough in his negotiations with the government. The new leader, forty-four years old, six-foot-two, 235 pounds, with prematurely gray hair and a full beard, was a forceful presence at the negotiating table and on television. He decided to go for broke, demanding a flat $10,000-per-year raise, a thirty-two-hour week, and retirement after twenty years at 75 percent of pay. The ousted leader was flabbergasted. "You mean that you are going to the Congress and ask them for more than they're making?" he asked incredulously. "That's right. We'll force them to give it to us" was the determined reply.

Negotiations had gone on between the Federal Aviation Administration and the union for seven months; at one time a settlement costing $40 million, twice that received by other government workers, had been reached but was rejected by 95 percent of PATCO's members. According to government negotiators, Mr. Poli's new demands amounted to $681 million, seventeen times what had been agreed to. Poli threatened to strike, emphasizing the stressful nature of the controllers' profession. Lynn Helms, administrator of the FAA, was disdainful. "These jobs are nowhere near as stressful as those of window washers on a New York skyscraper," he snorted. "If you want to see stress, join a policeman in the Bronx from eight o'clock at night until three o'clock in the morning, or watch a deckhand on a gasoline barge on a foggy night in New Orleans."

Poli and the PATCO members were adamant. They knew that a transportation strike is the most devastating of all work stoppages, reaching into every geographical section of the country, adversely affecting every sector of the economy, and, because of the international nature of air transportation in the new world economy, immediately affecting the economics and the politics of all nations of the world. PATCO had vigorously supported Ronald Reagan in the 1980 campaign and felt that not only did he owe them one, but that he would soon knuckle under to the combined threats of economic and air safety disruption. At 7:00 A.M. eastern daylight time on August 3, 1981, Poli called a strike. It was a turning point in the history of industrywide labor unions in the United States of America.

Poli was wrong — unbelievably, tragically wrong. The strike was illegal to start with, but illegal strikes had been called before, the perpetrators getting away with little more than a token slap on the wrist. The PATCO members were the highest paid government workers in the country, but industrial unions in the private sector had achieved higher wage increases. It was a strike against the public safety, but such actions had been going on since the Boston police strike brought Calvin Coolidge to prominence in the 1920s. Several thousand controllers were not members of PATCO, and there were enough nonstriking controllers and supervisors to man the control posts for an indefinite period of time, but Poli thought that they would wear out eventually. Although the strike would hurt the economies of other nations, Poli thought he could count on the international camaraderie of controllers who were in constant daily contact. These errors in assessment could not possibly be attributed to lack of information alone; the blinders of arrogance played a big part.

Most of all, Poli misjudged his opponent, the new president of the United States. Poli was imposing when he appeared on the tube, but he was no match for the old pro rising in righteous indignation in opposition to the illegal strike. And not only was it illegal, but it was perceived to be, and was, an open challenge to a president who was at a peak of his popularity, having just survived an assassination attempt and having just defeated Tip O'Neill and the whole Democratic

Congress in the budget process. Poli didn't stand a chance.

The president lost no time. Within hours he issued a public statement praising the supervisors and controllers who had stayed on the job to keep the nation's air system operating safely. He pointed out that he himself had led strikes in the private sector, but that "we cannot compare labor-management relations in the private sector with government. Government has to provide without interruption the protective services which are government's reason for being."

He went on with the following unambiguous statement:

It was in recognition of this that the Congress passed a law forbidding strikes by government employees against the public safety. Let me read the solemn oath taken by each of these employees: "I am not participating in any strike against the government of the United States or any agency thereof, and I will not so participate while I am an employee of the government of the United States."

It is for this reason I must tell those who failed to report for duty this morning they are in violation of the law and if they do not report for work within forty-eight hours they have forfeited their jobs and will be terminated.

The PATCO members were shocked. The public was delighted. The wheels of government moved quickly. The president stuck to his word, terminating the striking controllers and filling the positions with supervisors and nonstrikers. The courts moved in, imposing multimillion-dollar fines against the striking organization. The Federal Labor Relations Authority stripped PATCO of its status as legal representative of the controllers. Drew Lewis, the secretary of commerce, accelerated training programs. When the call went out for job applicants to replace the strikers, 225,000 people applied for the 7000 job openings. Foreign controllers made sympathetic noises for a few days, but they were not about to strike to support their more highly paid American associates. Other unions, particularly the Air Line Pilots Association, had their own sets of problems coming up and were reluctant to show any support. The leaders of the AFL-CIO recognized the unpopularity of the walkout and sensed the threat to organized labor in general; they refused to give any help. PATCO had nothing but its own militancy to fall back on.

It seems incredible that the association's members did not realize the threat to their security and back down, but they followed Poli, even when it became obvious that their cause was hopeless. The press labeled him "the Reverend Jim Jones of the American labor movement," referring to the mass suicides that had recently taken place in Guyana and speculated on how he had talked the members into "drinking the Kool-Aid." But no amount of metaphor mixing can overstate their stupidity in following their leader over the cliff to their own destruction. Poli hung on for four months before he resigned, never realizing that the strike had been over in four hours. The FAA filled the positions with new trainees, and air travelers stood the inconvenience with good grace. It was soon obvious that there had been overstaffing; the industry had record safety years in 1982 and 1983 with far fewer controllers operating the towers. Only recently have there been complaints, but these can be traced primarily to large increases in air travel.

The tragedy is that thousands of careers had been ruined, thousands of families impoverished, and millions of dollars wasted on a strike that should never have occurred. Walter Hendrick, a former controller, summed it up well.

Speaking for myself, I had not before, nor have I since, experienced a sense of achievement, of real worth, that even comes close to the self-satisfaction and pride I felt during the years that I was employed as an air traffic controller. Now I punch a clock for less than one third of what I was earning. Granted, I am thankful to have a job, but compared to what I was earning at an occupation I truly enjoyed, I can only conclude that I was a fool to participate in that ill-fated venture.

Who jerked us around more, the FAA, Bob Poli and his choirboys? Or did we all just kick the stool out from under ourselves?

That is the question all members of American organized labor must ask: "Are we all just kicking the stool out from under ourselves?" Other unions seem to be drinking the Kool-Aid, perhaps not as dramatically as PATCO, but just as fatally.

●　　●　　●

Consider the steelworkers. If ever an industry was in deep, deep trouble in this country, it is steel. I am a firm believer in the democratic capitalistic system, but the actions of all the protagonists in this drama — government, management, and labor alike — are enough to make me reach for the rosary beads to bolster the faith. In the late 1950s, American integrated steel producers were the industrial giants of the world. Plants were modern, iron ore was close at hand, scrap was cheap and plentiful, markets were far from saturation, and although hourly wages were six times as high as those in Japan — $3.75 against $0.58 — productivity was so high that American steel had a considerable price advantage over the Japanese. Pushed on by governments, which considered steel-making capacity a leading indicator of national prowess, all of the industrially developing nations expanded capacity dramatically in the early 1960s, a time when markets were already beginning to be saturated.

The Americans made all the mistakes in the book. As the market leaders, they first made the classic market leader's mistake of investing in capital-deepening rather than capital-widening capacity; that is, they devoted their funds primarily to additional productive units embodying familiar technology rather than to adopting new technologies. The developing nations, with no other way to compete, chose the new technology route, leaving the Americans, to this day, not only with excess capacity, but with excess outmoded capacity.

The large American steel companies are vertically integrated; they own their sources of iron ore, particularly those close by in the upper Great Lakes. But over the years the quality of the available local ores has deteriorated, while larger, richer deposits have been opened up in Brazil and Australia, deposits more accessible to the new supertanker transportation systems developed by the Greek shipping magnates. For all sorts of internal accounting reasons — for example, depreciation and overhead absorption — the Americans were reluctant to abandon their own low-grade sources of supply and gradually lost their competitive advantage in this crucial cost element to the Asians and the South Americans.

American integrated steel companies are oligopolistic, a phonetically appropriate tongue twister meaning that the industry is controlled by a few large companies, the largest being U.S. Steel. Prices were generally "administered." That palliative term meant that U.S. Steel would announce a price increase, followed, after a decent interval like a week, by an identical price increase by all the other producers. If that ain't price fixing, I don't know what is. But it didn't seem to bother the U.S. government during the halcyon days. As costs increased, prices would increase to maintain profit margins. Little wonder in that cozy situation that there was very little pressure on management to reduce costs.

The steelworkers' union had a ball. They were in the catbird seat for sure. Government considered steel to be a crucial national security resource and steel prices a key element in inflation control. Steel agreements always involved three parties: the companies, the unions, and the federal administration. Unfortunately, politicians do not have much staying power at the negotiating table — domestic political problems have short time horizons. Government pressure was generally applied for rapid settlements, and increases in employee benefits were viewed more favorably than increases in steel prices. As an example, the 1956 wage negotiations dragged on until a strike was called. Alarmed, Eisenhower's secretaries of labor and the treasury intervened, convincing the industry to increase benefits by 25 percent over the three-year life of the contract. This action set up an inflationary spiral in which the union pressured the government for price increases as the cost of improved contracts.

When Kennedy came in, he tried to break the spiral. Arthur Goldberg, Kennedy's labor secretary, had been the union's lawyer, and he knew where all the bodies were buried. In 1962 he convinced the union to limit wage increases to productivity growth, allowing the companies to maintain their prices. Accepting the assurances of the administration that all parties would play their assigned roles, the union agreed to a moderate contract well before the previous one had expired.

Less than a week later, U.S. Steel announced a price increase and the other companies dutifully followed. President Kennedy was incensed. The administration mounted a massive media campaign denouncing the company's action. Attorney General Bobby Kennedy, a hardball player if there ever was one, threatened antitrust action and income tax audits. The president summoned Roger Blough, then chairman of U.S. Steel Corporation, to the White House and read him the riot act. Afterward the president allegedly commented, "My father always told me that all businessmen were sons of bitches, but I never believed it until now." At a subsequent press conference, Kennedy stated, "Now the only thing wrong with the statement was that . . . it indicated that [my father] was critical of the business community. . . . That's obviously in error, because he was a businessman himself. He meant the steel men."

U.S. Steel and several other companies announced that they would maintain their prices; others proclaimed price rollbacks. Three days after the original announcement, Blough belatedly blinked, and U.S. Steel followed suit. The industrial dominance of big steel was finished.

The victory was sweet for the union and the Kennedy administration, but it solved no problems. Using its new muscle, the union continually pressed for more concessions, and usually won them. The government continued to intervene, reaching the utmost in crudity during the Johnson administration, when Johnson invited union and company representatives to negotiations at the White House and allegedly refused to allow them to use the bathroom until an agreement was reached. Wages continued to increase, mostly in the form of fringe benefits, from the $3.58 per hour of 1958 to the $25 per hour of today. All this in an industry of declining markets, obsolete technology, uncompetitive raw materials, excess capacity, intense foreign competition, and minimills nibbling at the edges.

The minimills are good examples of the competitive advantages of innovation. Much smaller companies, they use the latest technology — electric arc furnaces, continuous casting — employ nonunion labor, "cherry pick" the most lucrative specialized markets, and generally run rings around the slower moving, more conservative integrated producers.

Big steel is in so much trouble that it is difficult to see how it can ever extricate itself. No one expects the market to recover, since energy prices ensure that less steel will be used in its biggest market, transportation. Synthetic materials are inexorably picking away at weight-sensitive applications, and the domestic industry is woefully uncompetitive. Management finally realizes its problems and is doing its best to solve them, but there seem to be no good solutions. They have tried diversification. That may do some good for the stockholders — a notoriously ungrateful bunch — but very little for the steel business, and it has generated enough bad publicity to be counterproductive. They have been able to get some relief from foreign competition by government action, but that is not going to help in the long run.

The American public demands the less expensive product and the American politician understands that. Furthermore, steel companies have little support in the rest of American industry. The American automobile manufacturers and the knowledgeable autoworkers oppose price supports for their most expensive basic commodity, steel; those price supports will only make them less competitive in their own domestic and international markets. The politicians understand that, too.

A further problem is that steel is a basic commodity, not a consumer item like shoes or television sets or automobiles, in which product value can be difficult to compare. Steel is bought by sophisticated industrial procurement professionals. Cold rolled steel, made to specifications, is the same the world over. The buyer and the seller both know that, and so do the politicians. Even when we dress up protectionism in fancy sounding terms like industrial policy, no one is fooled.

In the face of this bleak reality, the union plods blithely

on, refusing to make the concessions so necessary to bare survival. Bitterness between the union and management is as bad as it has ever been, and both are at loggerheads with the government. To point out how bad the situation is, I'm going to resort to a small table. I'm not much for including tables in books, because I think most people skip over them, but if you will please look carefully at this one, you will find the entire steel labor problem succinctly summarized. I promise you that this will be the only table in the whole book.

LABOR COST OF STEEL		
Hourly wage	Country	Labor cost per ton
$25.00	United States	$300.00
$10.00	Japan	$ 70.00
$ 3.00	Korea	$ 20.00

Steel can be shipped anywhere in the world for an additional $40.00 a ton.

These numbers are frightening in their simplicity. Management understands them, because management is on the firing line, trying to move steel, but the union refuses to accept them, claiming that they are a management trick. There is no possible trick. All they have to do is call up any independent steel broker anywhere in the world, and the numbers can be verified. Just as in the case of the air controllers, the steelworkers will receive little sympathy from the general public. The public will feel sorry for individuals, as they feel sorry for anyone who is out of work. But this is a collective attitude.

Twenty-five dollars per hour is $1000 per week without

overtime — $50,000 per year for fifty working weeks and two weeks' vacation. Who is going to feel sorry for a union member making that kind of money and looking for more? Remember that this is basically unskilled labor. What kind of sympathy are they going to get from the average wage earner making a fraction of that amount, or from the professional who has spent four years in college and maybe more in graduate school and will never see $50,000 per year? It's absurd. This country cannot afford to support these jobs through import restrictions. It would amount to nothing less than high-income welfare. The steelworkers' union is committing collective suicide, not as rapidly as the air controllers did, but just as inexorably.

What went wrong?

• • •

When modern industrial society began to develop in England and Western Europe, it never occurred to an employer to pay any higher wages than he had to, a not uncommon attitude even today. For the most part, the early industrialist felt quite benevolent in rescuing the worker from his only alternative, a life of brutish, back-breaking labor on the land. The fact that so many came from the farms to seek employment in the cities confirms that the workers thought so, too.

Initially attracted by the higher wages and better working conditions, the workers soon lost their independence and came under the complete control of the employers. As bad as life was on the farm, there was generally some fuel and some food and a family home to live in. In the city, when times were bad and there was no work, the head of the family was helpless. He had to steal or starve or accept whatever wage he could get. This lack of bargaining power led to the horrible social inequities depicted in William Hogarth's engravings in the eighteenth century and to the socialist concepts of Karl Marx in the next.

These same working conditions led to the waves of migration to the New World, to a new life where the memories of the Old were strong and bitter. The prejudice against the factory and the plenitude of land kept the new republic a predominantly agricultural country until well into the nineteenth century. Although Alexander Hamilton exerted his extraordinary abilities to the utmost to develop a system of native manufactures, he could not prevail against the contrary philosophy of the Jeffersonians. The latter, repelled by the deplorable social excrescences of early English industrialism, strongly opposed the establishment of factories on this side of the Atlantic. Thomas Jefferson himself condemned them as "panderers of vice and the instruments by which the liberties of a country are generally overturned."

Several other factors retarded the erection of mills and factories in the new republic. Most important was the spirit of equality firmly implanted in our citizenry. Few cared to subject themselves to the servile discipline of the factory. They preferred to farm their land or ply their trades at their own workbenches. The resulting labor shortage greatly hampered the enterprise of the emerging manufacturers, but it did keep wages at a relatively high level.

When the Revolution cut off our supply of manufactured goods from England, native capitalists were spurred into increased activity. Samuel Slater, a highly skilled English technician, came to this country in 1779. Able to produce spinning machinery from memory, he established the first textile mill in Pawtucket, Rhode Island. Francis C. Lowell, another pioneer industrialist, introduced power looms in his mill in Waltham and engaged young women from the countryside as operators. Others opened shops and mills to take advantage of the rising American population and of the canals and turnpikes, which were opening up markets in the interior.

There was no labor movement in this country prior to the establishment of the industrial system of production for the simple reason that during the handicraft stage workmen had no need of it. They were as often employer as employee. Many plied their trades in their own little shops, alone, with an apprentice, or with a few journeymen at the most. Each mechanic worked according to the customs long established by his guild. Primarily interested in maintaining prices and standards of work, he was in a true sense an incipient capitalist.

With the acceleration of the process of industrial production after 1800 — effecting the introduction of power machinery, the accumulation of capital, the increase in population, the improvements in transportation, and the extension of markets — craftsmen began to separate into employers and workmen. The former, able and ambitious, eager for high profits, and pressed by the merchants and capitalists, found it tempting to exploit their employees. As more and more workmen began to depend on the owners of machinery and factories for their livelihood, they were less and less able to cope individually with the increasingly oppressive conditions of labor. Unlike the suppliers of materials or capital or the merchants of distribution, they had no bargaining power. In their groping efforts to strengthen their position with respect to work and wages, they in time resorted to one or another form of cooperation.

The initial efforts toward unionization were feeble and sporadic. Patterned after the trade guilds of the handicraft era, they were mainly benevolent in nature, seeing to such matters as insurance, sickness and funeral benefits, and rules for ap-

prenticeship. Probably the chief handicap confronting unions
was the threat of criminal conspiracy. The common law, archaic as ever, held that any combination of workmen for their
personal benefit was for the purpose of injury to their employer and therefore illegal. In 1806 a group of Philadelphia
shoemakers who had struck for higher wages was indicted on
two counts: a combination to raise wages and a combination
to injure others. The prosecutor reflected the sentiments of
property owners and businessmen — the only ones who could
vote in those days — when he addressed the jury in these
words: "A combination of workmen to raise their wages may
be considered in a twofold point of view: one is to benefit
themselves . . . the other is to injure those who do not join
the society. The rule of law condemns both."

The jury's verdict: "We find the defendants guilty of a combination to raise wages." How's that for enlightened apples?

Conditions in the New England cotton mills were particularly oppressive, largely because most of the workers were
women and children. The first trade association, formed there
in 1831, condemned the practice of exploiting women and
children for thirteen hours a day, six days a week, at beggarly
wages. The association folded after three years, and the oppressive conditions prevailed for many decades. These are not
mere statistics to me. I have living relatives who left school
after the second grade to go to work to help the family survive.
They started at the age of eight, working from morning till
night, never seeing the sun, with no sick leave, no vacations,
no pensions, no air conditioning in the summer, and very
little heat in the winter. It is no wonder that those hardy
enough to evolve from such conditions have lived to be octo-
and nonagenarians.

For most of the nineteenth century the American workman
was as hobbled by his friends as he was bedeviled by his

enemies. Oppressive as the factory was, there was always the opportunity of the land for those who could stand it no longer. Dismal though the conditions were, it was still a free country, and for those who had the stamina and the diligence, there was the opportunity to rise, as my own family did, to relative prosperity. Not so in the old country. There was no land available, no western frontier where the adventurous could forge a new life, no opportunity to break the chains of a rigid class system. In Europe, the workman's cry was not just for wages and working conditions, but for complete social upheaval. The social reformers saw no possibility of modifying the existing stratified system; their only solution was the chaos of anarchism or the dictatorship of the proletariat of Karl Marx.

Many of the social reformers came to this country preaching revolution. But the United States had already had one revolution and was not about to have another. Many of the reformers proposed complete abolition of the wage system, substituting producers' cooperatives. Others went further, proposing complete socialist government, a concept that turned off the citizens of this newly independent, agricultural republic. The mildest of their demands was an eight-hour-maximum working day. In midcentury the reformers' movements coalesced into the Noble and Holy Order of the Knights of Labor. Their demands were politically and economically impossible to achieve. Politically, they repelled more people than they attracted, while economically, their demands were well beyond the capacity of the system to produce. It is certainly true that labor unions have been the prime factor in gaining reduced working hours for their members, but only after the whole of the economic system had improved productivity to the point where such social goals were achievable. It was as ridiculous to propose a forty-hour week in nineteenth-century America as it would be ridiculous today to propose a forty-hour week for a peasant in Bangladesh, compulsory education in Colombia, or social security in the Sudan. The result of all these proposals was to antagonize the entire community while doing nothing, alas, to help the plight of the worker. Proposals for social reform beyond the capacity of the economic and political system to accommodate are often hailed as visionary, but in practice they turn out to be sadly counterproductive.

•   •   •

It was the happy lot of Samuel Gompers to turn the union movement toward pragmatism. Gompers was a cigarmaker and the son of a cigarmaker. The elder Gompers, a Dutch Jew, migrated from Amsterdam to London in the 1840s. Unable to support his family in England, he moved to New York, where, at the age of ten, Samuel had to quit school and was apprenticed to the cigarmaking trade. Bright, lively, and ambitious, his cigar ever present, Gompers went to night school and also found time for the social activities of his neighborhood. Too young and too full of zest to resent the inequity of his lot or the hard life about him, he was still well aware of the sordidness of poverty and the cruelty of child labor. When he was fourteen, he joined the cigarmakers' union. The industry was then undergoing radical readjustment. The introduction of molds and other machinery had increased productivity and reduced employment; Gompers fought successfully to have some of the productivity gains passed on to the workers, a visionary concept for the time. By the time he was twenty-five, he had formed a new union with himself as president. One strike was broken, but gradually Gompers and the Cigarmakers International Union gained experience and credibility, becoming a model craft union.

Once the union was stabilized, Gompers moved on to the

national labor movement, then dominated by the radicals and social reformers of the Knights of Labor. He was no philosopher. He was not moved by theories or abstract ideals. Even in his precocious adolescence, when his mind rebelled against the poverty and misery about him, he had never lost sight of practical realities. He had an orderly and pragmatic mind, and the tactics of the aggressive socialists repelled him.

A number of trade union leaders agreed with him. They regarded the leadership of the movements as confused reformers and rejected their advocacy of political action. What they wanted most of all were higher wages and shorter hours for the members of their unions. Nobler but less tangible goals left them cold. Gompers saw eye to eye with these officials. Indeed he had worked hard to organize his own cigarmakers' union along those lines. But he realized more keenly that to make trade unions more effective it was necessary not merely to strengthen them individually but to unite them into a powerful national federation.

The clash of the two philosophies came to a head in 1886, when the Knights, confident of their strength with seven hundred thousand members, put on a campaign of personal vilification, accusing Gompers of "habitual inebriety" and expelling the Cigarmakers International Union from the Order of Knights. This arrogant injunction gave the advantage to Gompers and his friends. They called for a national conference, which was ignored by the Knights, and calmly proceeded to form a new organization, the American Federation of Labor, with Gompers as president at an annual salary of $1000.

The new federation adopted a conservative trade union policy, limiting its aim to the immediate benefits of higher wages and shorter hours. Eager to build up the individual unions and to gain the advantage of economic solidarity, they limited membership to skilled craftsmen. Certain that they could gain more by collective bargaining than through political agitation, they adopted a policy of political neutrality and agreed to seek favorable legislation through the party in power.

Gompers dominated the labor movement as no man has ever done, continuing as president of the American Federation of Labor from its feeble beginnings to his death in 1924, a span of thirty-eight years. He recognized the enormous increases in the productivity of American industry and was determined that labor receive its fair share through collective bargaining, or through the strike, which he perceived as labor's major weapon in the collective bargaining process. He had no objections to large corporations as such, accepting their managements as his natural adversaries in the economic process.

He condemned antitrust legislation as unnecessary and ineffectual. As rugged an individualist as the industrialists of his day, Gompers regarded trade unions and trusts as necessary instruments of modern industrial conditions. He was on friendly terms with a number of leading capitalists. He fought his archenemy to the right, the National Association of Manufacturers, with the same zeal and openness he devoted to his battles with his archenemies to the left, the socialists and Communists. He was opposed to government regulation of any kind. Maintaining that matters of wages and hours — the foundation and capstone of the AFL — were matters to be settled in the private sector, Gompers unalterably opposed the regulation of either. He reluctantly acquiesced to some regulation for women and minors, but he saw no advantage in a minimum wage.

The fear that government regulation meant curtailment of the use of the strike caused him to reject compulsory arbitration as a violation of the Thirteenth Amendment. To him the strike was synonymous with liberty. "Show me a country where there are no strikes and I'll show you a country where there is no liberty. The state, where it has interfered with industrial affairs, has become the greatest tyrant in the world."

Gompers's biggest battles were with the courts and their use of the injunction as a strike-breaking device. He was twice sentenced to a year in jail for contempt, both convictions being thrown out on technicalities, after seven years of litigation, by a politically-sensitive Supreme Court. Personally friendly but neutral with both William McKinley and Theodore Roosevelt, he was led by his courtroom frustrations to give up the doctrine of political neutrality in 1908. When William Jennings Bryan agreed to include an anti-injunction plank in the Democratic platform, Gompers and other federation leaders campaigned for him against "injunction-judge" William Howard Taft. Although Bryan lost, this was the seed of the long and close association between organized labor and the Democratic party, which blossomed in the New Deal of Franklin D. Roosevelt.

Gompers's original adherence to craft unionism was pragmatic in its day. There were no industries of any consequence to organize. At the end of his half century of involvement, the world had changed. Millions of workers in the steel, automobile, rubber, and other mass-production industries were unorganized because they could only be unionized industrially. Gompers and his lieutenants refused to encourage this type of organization, and his successor, William Green, was the most docile of men.

The labor movement slipped into the background during the prosperity of the twenties. The depression and the New Deal, which it spawned, brought the problems of unemployment and worker representation back into the political forefront, but the AFL was still dominated by the craft unionists, and organized labor's dormancy lasted about a decade.

By 1935 the industrial union leaders were ready to revolt. Their spokesman was the mercurial John L. Lewis, head of the United Mine Workers Union. Lewis's mettle had been forged in that most scattered and disorganized industry, the coal mines. The worst New England mill or New York textile sweatshop was a paradise compared to the working conditions in a typical coal mine.

Lewis had little empathy with the fat-cat, conservative leaders of the skilled and prosperous craft unions. As far as he was concerned they were only a minor annoyance in the labor spectrum.

It was the other 90 percent of the labor force, the skilled and the semiskilled working in a variety of occupations in the major industries, who were important. They could be successfully organized only in vertical, industrywide unions, a concept the craft unionists abhorred. Joined by Sidney Hillman and David Dubinsky of the clothing workers, Lewis led eight of the unions into a new organization named the Committee for Industrial Organization, the CIO. When the AFL expelled several of the unions for taking this action, the CIO formally seceded from it in 1938 and changed its name to the Congress of Industrial Organizations.

The late thirties were turbulent times for organized labor. The government-union alliance blossomed under Roosevelt, with labor winning its cherished right to collective bargaining under the Wagner Labor Relations Act of 1935. Using the new legislation and employing the sit-down strike, the automobile workers succeeded in organizing General Motors, but only after a series of bloody battles in the streets. Once this largest bastion of industrial opposition was breached, it became only a matter of time before all of the major industries were organized. Both the AFL and the CIO prospered in the recovery brought about by the forthcoming European war. The CIO went a little pinko for a while after Hitler invaded Russia, but down deep American organized labor remained substantially more conservative and apolitical than its European counterparts.

The performance of the union organizations in World War II was excellent, with the notable exception of John L. Lewis and his United Mine Workers. Lewis struck for higher wages at the height of the hostilities, forcing the government to take over the mines. This action horrified a nation with 5 million men under arms. Lewis's truculence and a transportation strike in 1946 produced an antilabor backlash in the first postwar Congress. The result was the Taft-Hartley Act, which outlaws the compulsory closed or all-union shop, mandates cooling-off periods before strikes, and prescribes other restrictive covenants.

Labor learned a lesson with Taft-Hartley. There was some movement of individual unions in and out of both the AFL and the CIO, but they gradually patched up their differences and remerged as the AFL-CIO in 1955. George Meany was elected president of the combined organization and proceeded methodically to restore order. As president of the AFL before the merger, Meany had met cries of corruption and Communist influence by expelling the radical Harry Bridges and his International Longshoremen's Association. He faced up to similar allegations in 1957 by expelling Jimmy Hoffa's Teamsters Union, the largest in the country. In 1968 Walter Reuther broke out the United Auto Workers in a policy dispute, but they came back in 1981. With those exceptions, organized labor has presented a coherent and cohesive front for decades under Meany and his successor, Lane Kirkland.

• • •

Unfortunately, coherence and cohesiveness are the enemies of innovation. This dichotomy is expressed in a number of different ways in different disciplines. The physicists say that for every action there is an equal and opposite reaction; the biologists say "You can't just do one thing"; the actuaries speak of "risk-reward ratios"; the economists speak of "zero-sum games"; the street saying is "You can't have it both ways." By quelling discord and uniting into a common political philosophy, the union leaders, particularly the AFL-CIO, block themselves from the change necessary to their own survival.

The big unions have a new enemy and they don't know it. The new enemy is foreign competition. The recompense that workers can receive from their employers is no longer controlled by the customary collective bargaining to determine which adversary deserves which piece of the pie; the pie itself is being taken away. In the developed industries, where big labor competes, wages and fringes account for 85 percent of revenues with profits, at the most, 5 to 6 percent. Where there is foreign competition, wage increases without productivity increases will cause bankruptcy or loss of revenues, either of which results in job losses. It's as simple as that.

This simple truism comes as a wrenching psychological shock to union leadership. For nearly two centuries, since the beginning of the Industrial Revolution, the employer, the capitalist, has been the natural enemy of the worker. Since the New Deal removed the courts as the ally of the businessman, the large unions have had unprecedented power. With monopolistic unions and industrywide bargaining agreements, the wages in the basic smokestack industries have been raised far beyond the wage level of the average American industrial worker. It became easy for the managements of the large corporations, when pushed by the government, to take a shortsighted point of view and pass on wage increases to the American consumer when there was no alternate source of supply. The new world economy has changed all that.

The first reaction for labor and business — and sometimes government — is to exclude the foreign competition. After all, we've had tariffs of one sort or another for centuries. And we still do. We have tariffs to prevent unfair competition like "dumping" product surpluses or in retaliation for international restraints of trade. We have both import and export restraints where the national security is involved, and we have had import restraints, such as the automotive import limitations of the last few years, to give breathing spells to beleaguered industries. But in the new world economy, the days of widespread tariffs are gone forever. International trade is too big for that solution.

Back in the days of Fortress America and its Ming mentality, when international trade was a small part of our economy, we could temporarily afford such shortsighted policies; overdone in the twenties, they led to the worldwide depression of the thirties. Today, they are unthinkable. In 1969 exports and imports together affected about 16 percent of the goods we produced. By 1982 they exceeded 40 percent; by now they probably affect more than half our total output. Any significant restraint-of-trade policy would wreck our economy.

Of course, we don't call these things tariffs or boycotts or restraint-of-trade practices anymore — we call them "industrial policies." The term means that the government, not the free market, will decide which industries to protect and which to leave alone. Naturally, the government would have to protect the weakest industries, and those with the most political clout. The rest of the economy would have to pay the bill, and therein lies the rub. If we protect steel, our automobiles will become less competitive. If we protect machine tools, all our expanding manufacturing industries will be penalized. If we protect television sets or textiles, consumer dissatisfaction will soon be evident at the polls. Some trade restrictions will have to continue, of course, if only in retaliation for similar practices elsewhere, but, as a general policy, it is a losing battle. The only long-term solution is to become more internationally competitive. That's not going to be easy.

All of us are profoundly affected by the changes in the new world economy, but none so profoundly as big labor. Management does have some options. One is automation. Automation has a minor effect on management employment, since management skills are relatively similar, and it is easier for white-collar workers to adapt. Also, administration and overhead constitute less than 10 percent of wage costs in the smokestack industries. Management does not help by paying big bonuses; bonuses don't add much to the total costs, but they sure make contract negotiations more difficult. Management can shift labor costs to other countries, a practice that is going on at an alarming rate. Management can diversify. Some of the diversifications look a little weird, with steel companies buying oil companies and oil companies buying department stores. I can sympathize with management's desire for survival, but many of the diversifications draw resources away from the primary business and exacerbate the union employment problem.

Nonunion labor has options — some very good options. First of all, the people are flexible. They deal in the labor market as individuals, or as small unions closely allied to the businesses they serve. Closely coupled to management and the marketplace, they are much more attuned to the need for competitiveness and productivity. And they are in relatively small businesses. Statistics abound to show that job creation is taking place in the smaller businesses. In the past five years the Fortune 500 companies have lost 3 million jobs, while the overall economy has made them up and generated 25 million new ones. This is an astounding phenomenon, unmatched by any other industrialized country. This country has absorbed the rapid influx of women into the marketplace and has absorbed the products of the baby boom. Neither of these events is likely to be repeated. About 50 percent of our female population is now working and that figure is stabilizing; the passing of the baby boom will leave us with actual labor shortages in the late eighties.

Much as many might like to think so, this job creation is not explicitly in high tech. The numbers show that the vast bulk of the new jobs are in "low tech" or "no tech." I believe that high tech has been the catalyst, with improved transportation, improved communications, and improved information transfer, but the increased numbers show up in services and small manufacturing. There is a spirit of entrepreneurship and innovation in the land which, for all our international adjustment problems, will serve as the basis for a revitalized America in this new world economy.

● ● ●

Some thoughts on the shifts from manufacturing to services. In many ways, it is a delightful delusion. Clearly, the shift is there, from manufacturing as defined to services as defined. There are the traditional two schools of thought on the effects of this shift. One school says let the manufacturing jobs go elsewhere, and let the United States concentrate on the more desirable white-collar service jobs. The other deplores the loss of our industrial might and frets that we cannot remain a formidable nation if we concentrate on selling one another high-technology hamburgers. But beware of statistical definitions. What is happening is a shift in the concepts of manufacturing.

Many of the activities classified as services are basic components of the overall industrial process. We are accustomed to highly centralized production facilities with components and subassemblies and finished goods. At one end of the production line are large quantities of raw materials stored in excess amounts to prevent supply interruptions in the production process. At the other end are large quantities of finished goods, held in inventory so that products will be available to satisfy the uncertainties of distribution and the whims of the marketplace. Modern information technology allows large reductions in inventory without diminishing product availability. The new technology makes communication from the supermarket shelf or the distributor's supply line as rapid as people want to pay for — days, hours, minutes, or even, in the case of information distribution, milliseconds. Inventory control and materials flow systems are often remote from the production floor. They may be in another building or in another city or, in the case of multinational companies, in another country. The same is true of raw materials or finished goods inventories. Statistical dispatching techniques, better communications, and improved weather forecasts will all make distribution more efficient, reducing on-site material storage. The acclaimed Japanese just-in-time inventory systems are simply the application of these readily available modern information-handling techniques. Don't buy it till you have to have it.

The factory itself is becoming more dispersed. A dozen years ago computers were all made in one place. Now, it is not uncommon for chips to be produced in the United States and Japan, subassemblies in Taiwan, housings in India, and final assemblies in South Korea, with the final device, typical of the complex interrelationships of international trade, sold locally as a domestic product. Much of this comes from the ability of new computer-aided design and computer-aided manufacturing (CAD-CAM) techniques to specify designs and manufacturing methods so precisely that products can be produced by workers in many different countries, joined together by a common mathematical language.

The new look of manufacturing and industry must incorporate into the old concept of a factory the new reality that the inventory control and handling systems, as well as the computer-aided design and manufacturing systems, wherever they may be, are part of the whole production process. In computer jargon they are off-line, but as integral a part of the goods-producing process as the banker who supplies financing, the insurance company that spreads risks, or the home office manager who coordinates the complete process from his tower in Manhattan, Los Angeles, or Dallas. Our high-technology and service industries are not entities that stand by themselves, remote from the problems of the factories, but key and closely coupled components of the entire industrial production process. The nation that understands this concept will prosper.

All these trends bode ill for big labor. The market is shrinking for the products manufactured by the basic industries. The ending of the era of cheap energy saw to that. To save the costs of energy, industrial goods will have to be smaller, to use less steel, copper, and rubber. Energy expenditure correlates to a large degree with environmental degradation, a further reason to cut energy use. But the ultimate result will be a substantial reduction in the volume of materials handled and the number of employees needed to handle them.

The classic economic concept of modern industrial society has been the economy of scale. This simply meant that the more units you could produce the lower would be the cost per unit. This is still true in the traditional factory, but not necessarily so in the costs of the final product. Large-scale production facilities are not easily adaptable to change. The rapidly changing nature of the world economy and the high cost of capital have led managers to recognize that they are often better off to trade some manufacturing efficiency for some adaptability. These realities have led to a trend away from the economies of scale to the concepts of "flexible manufacturing" in which lower costs of capital and adaptability to market changes result in a lower-cost product. Right or wrong, there is no question that the freedom to employ nonunion labor is a major contributor to this trend. The success of the minimills in steel production is an obvious example. It is also a factor in loss of union membership.

Another element in the shift away from big labor is in the changing nature of industry, from blue-collar factory manufacturing to white-collar services. Although this shift in jobs is still part of the industrial process, this sector is, by virtue of its diversification and semiprofessionalism, less likely to be unionized.

The overwhelming contributor to the problem is foreign competition. The lower cost of imports is beneficial to the consumer and to society as a whole, but it places a severe burden on the hapless employee whose job is essentially exported. This is going to be a tough nut to crack. It is difficult to perceive how we can bridge the gap between the Korean steel worker at $3.00 per hour and the American steel worker at $25, but it seems almost impossible to make the $8.50-per-hour American textile worker competitive with textile workers in factories now springing up in Uganda, where the going wage is $0.10 per hour. This is a factor of eighty-five.

None of this is helped by the continuation of the basic antagonism between business and labor, which seems to be another of the penalties of bigness, another of those reverse economies of scale that are cropping up everywhere. I think that it comes about because of industrywide and craftwide bargaining. When there is no foreign competition, it becomes very tempting for managements to agree to excessive wage demands when they can be passed on to the consumer. It becomes very tempting for a government to impose excessive settlements favorable to unions in the interests of political peace in a country where an election is never more than two years away. And, quite logically, it becomes very tempting for a union leader, also looking to his reelection, to insist on large settlements. How else could big-union semiskilled labor command a price several times the national industrial average?

But the same situation also prevails in the craft unions. The large construction unions — plumbers, carpenters, electricians — have priced themselves out of the market. Fully half the buildings going up today are nonunion. A large percentage of the craft workers on these jobs are card-carrying union members working for lower wages. Why? Because the individual worker realizes that the building won't be built with union wages and union work rules — the market won't stand the price.

Every job situation is different. I have been involved in a number of wage negotiations where local conditions and specific product markets controlled the narrow gap between what management could afford and the union would accept. Invariably, settlements have been made without rancor and all have prospered as a result. With industrywide and craftwide negotiations, issues are too diffuse and wide-ranging for common-sense settlements. Instead, settlements are made on the basis of power and brute force, with much posturing, fanfare, and political pressure at all levels. No wonder the antagonists hate each other's guts. They almost have to in order to survive the battle. This will change because it will have to, but there will be considerable wrenching psychological readjustment on the part of both big business and big labor before it does. Heads will roll.

• • •

What is the solution to this mess? I wish I felt as confident of straightforward solutions in this area as I do in other sectors of the economy. There are solutions, but they all involve temporary job dislocation and personal anguish, which makes the task very difficult both politically and sociologically.

The problem is obvious. The AFL-CIO is priced out of the world labor market and is going to have to reduce its rates. Price reduction is always a painful task.

The first and simplest thing to do is to revise work rules. Most workers are willing and able to perform more than one type of job. It makes very little sense for a whole crew to sit around waiting for a plumber to show up when a pipefitter could do the job but is prevented from doing it by jurisdictional rules. In the absence of a captive market, this takes money out of everybody's pocket. Paying for idleness is the most wasteful of practices. However obvious that may be, it leads to the employment of fewer plumbers or pipefitters. It's easy to be logical on paper and to prove that everyone will be better off in the long run, but it is awfully difficult for the unemployed plumber or pipefitter to explain to his wife and kids. This one will come hard.

The next solution is to introduce two-tier wage systems, with new hires paid less than existing employees. Not many new employees will come into the beleaguered industries, but if they do, they should be offered jobs only at a wage level the product can support. The problem is to smooth the transition for workers already in jobs, not to add unproductive new employees. This stopgap solution is working well in some industries such as the airlines; it should be extended.

There are already many thousands of unemployed people who will never go back to their old jobs, a problem called structural unemployment. Throughout our history, this country has had migration from one type of job to another, with joblessness in between. The classic in this century was the move from the farm to the factory. There the movement was from a low-paying to a higher-paying job, and the transfer had a potential reward. Now the reverse is true. What are we going to do with a $50,000-per-year steel worker? If he gets a Ph.D. in physics he'll be lucky to start out at half that. But we must be patient and do what we can to help. It is crucial that society understand the difference between these workers and the stereotyped concept of the unemployed. These are solid citizens, able and willing to work, having paid their taxes and carried their load uncomplainingly when employed. They are entitled to special consideration by industry, government, and academia. They must be retrained or relocated, or new industry encouraged to locate near them.

A more realistic approach to plant closings is being worked out. Industry was primarily to blame. The potential for plant closings was always kept a deep secret until the last minute on the theory that employees would malinger on the job if they knew that their time was limited, that customers would stop paying their bills, that banks would withhold credit, and that government and the unions would act to stop the closing. These are all partly true but of minor importance. No employer wants to close a plant, for a jillion reasons. A plant is closed only when the output is perceived to be no longer competitive in the marketplace. The word gets around as activity decreases; everyone knows it's going to happen, but nobody admits it. This is wrong. Oftentimes something can be done to reduce property taxes, lessen oppressive environmental regulations, or sell the operation to the employees, who may be able to produce at lower overhead. The worst cure is to legislate against the plant's closing, as is common in Europe. If a plant is going to close, it is going to close eventually. Prolonging the agony for six months or a year is counterproductive. It will save some jobs for a while, but the long-term result is to send a signal to industry that this is no place to open a new plant. Industry, labor, and government are beginning dialogues, recognizing that plant closings are a fact of life in this new, rapidly changing economy, and that all parties must adapt. I am privileged to have taken part in such a dialogue in the state of Massachusetts. At the governor's urging, the legislature has recently enacted a plant-closing law using the new concepts that we feel will be a model for the nation.

The best tool for restoration of international competitiveness is increased productivity. Americans have always prided themselves on being the most productive people on earth. This was so until the early seventies, when the impending combination of our multifarious national malaises drew our productivity growth down to 2 percent per year. From 1978 to 1982 we were dead in the water, with zero productivity growth. With low inflation, a more encouraging tax structure, and, I hope, some attention to the self-flagellations pointed out in this book, our prospects for renewed productivity growth are encouraging.

There is going to be one sticky element — automation. If we are going to maintain our standard of living in the face of low-cost foreign labor, we are simply going to have to produce more per hour of effort. To do that we must mechanize. In a given economy, if we produce more output per worker, we will have fewer jobs. From the days of the Luddites, who smashed textile machinery in Great Britain in 1811, prophets of doom have denounced automation as socially undesirable because it reduced jobs. Year after year it has been proved that the end result has been a higher standard of living and more jobs. Look at this country now, with 105 million employed.

Robotics is another buzz word of our day. To the pessimist, it brings specters of factories without people, soulless robots grinding out products in the pitch dark twenty-four hours a day, three hundred sixty-five days a year, while the unemployed and their families starve silently in the streets about. To the optimist, it is a new freedom, the elimination of the drudgery of boring, repetitive work, the opportunity for more leisure time, a higher standard of living. Whatever your viewpoint, the competition is there, and we must meet it. James A. Baker, executive vice president of the General Electric Company, puts it most succinctly. In his words, "The robots introduced into our plants are not the biggest threat to our employees. It is the robots in our competitors' plants [abroad]. . . . America's manufacturing industries face three choices: Automate, emigrate, or evaporate."

The action that will bring us most quickly to the road to solution is increased cooperation between business and the labor unions, particularly those represented by the AFL-CIO. This is such a fatuous statement that I hate to make it. There is nothing more irritating than to plow through a chapter of turgid prose delineating a national problem only to have the writer pontifically declare that the adversaries must learn to communicate and cooperate with each other, especially when you know damn well that they have no intention of doing any such thing. But stay. Don't go away. A new ball game is going on in the next lot; they need to join it.

For centuries now unions and management have fought for their pieces of the economic pie. Unions have won their fight for equal partnership. The old battle is over. Workers understand that. It is the reason that AFL-CIO membership has decreased by 3 million while 25 million jobs were being added to the economy. But while the adversaries were battling, someone stole the pie — international competitors.

Nations have no friends in international affairs; they only have common enemies. That is why, for example, the United States could team up with Russia against our common enemies, Germany and Japan, during World War II, while we now team up with Germany and Japan against our common enemy, Russia. The people are the same. The adversarial nature of the battle just shifted. So should it be in commerce.

I am not suggesting that business and the labor unions become friends. God forbid. That would cost too many jobs by itself. Besides, no bureaucracy has ever planned for its own dissolution. I am merely suggesting that they shift their efforts away from battling each other to tackle the new adversary, foreign competition. There is plenty of work for everybody here. Japan has done it. So has West Germany. Even France and Great Britain, for all their labor problems, present a common export front. If we in these United States, backed by our huge domestic market, can work to forge a common business–labor union coalition on international affairs, we have the muscle to restore ourselves to our rightful position as number one in international commerce.

Think it over, National Association of Manufacturers. Think it over, U.S. Chamber of Commerce. Think it over, AFL-CIO.

It will work.

8

Go Directly to Jail— Do Not Pass Go

ALL FORMS of primitive life show some degree of sociability and cooperation, starting at the lowest level with single-celled organisms arranging themselves in tissuelike sheets for mutual convenience in feeding, progressing to viruses, which organize like armies to overwhelm the defenses of a common enemy, and culminating in the millions of microbes that live comfortably and congenially in our own digestive systems, symbiotically assisting us to break down the complex compounds we imbibe into manageable hunks of malleable molecules to be employed in the continuing battle for our mutual survival.

In the social insects we observe mind-boggling complexities of cooperation. A single honeybee, genetically programmed with a read-only memory to defend the hive or to search for food, is as biologically effective as a clipped toenail; but a swarm of bees can tell the time of day, calculate the geometry of the sun's position, forecast the changes of the seasons, or warn of the approach of a potential enemy. A few dozen termites, collected and observed in the laboratory, epitomize disorder as they mill about and touch one another nervously. As insects are added, at some point they form a critical mass; the change is electrifying. Seemingly injected with a shot of negative entropy, they organize into platoons and begin to stack up pellets to exactly the right height, to turn the arches that connect the columns, and to build the cathedral and its chambers in which the colony will live out its life for generation after generation to come, air conditioned and humidity controlled. They become the ultimate in organization — a single organism, a cohesive, collective brain, carried on a zillion legs.

The social insects have built up these ultimate generation-spanning organizations because of a single, ongoing basic objective — collective survival. It is not possible for an individual honeybee or termite to pick up a little venture capital and strike out with a new colony on its own. The genes in the read-only memories won't allow it. So each can do its own specialized task, confident that its fellow worker will not quit for a better job or sleep in with a hangover. But nature is, in many respects, a biological and thermodynamic zero-sum operation. The plant or tree or homeowner who possessed the cellulose from which the insects obtained their energy and their building materials would not be too admiring of the social organization of the termite colony. It is unfortunate, but all sorts of collective behavior can act to the material disadvantage of those who are not included in the system.

Vertebrates exhibit a wide range of collective behavior. Some species of moles build underground passages, divide up work functions, and have a queen mother similar to the social insects'. Birds operate in family units for procreation, but join collectively for migration. The higher animals sometimes hunt in packs, sometimes individually. Most of the associations are loose, being centered around procreation and protection of the young. For most animals, constantly in danger from predators, adolescence is short, so that even family units tend to break up fairly quickly. The differences seem to correlate fairly well with the degree of intelligence and the degree of mobility. A bird or a billy goat not only has a more programmable memory, but the physical mobility to move to the family association of its choice, a luxury not available to the termite or the subterranean mole.

Humans, among all the vertebrates, have set their own course. As human intelligence evolved, the human store of knowledge increased, and with that, the necessity to develop complex mechanisms to retain and manipulate that knowledge. Highly programmable memories developed along with sophisticated software for assembly and retrieval. To lapse into Silicon Valley jargon, we have outgrown the simple read-only memories (ROMs) of the insects; they have become programmable (PROMs), in order to adapt readily to experience, they have random access (RAMs) to react to changing environments, and the random access has become amenable to modification or programming (PRAMs). Humans took advantage of this increased knowledge to gain superiority over all their predators.

As Pogo points out, we have only one enemy, and we know who it is. Unlike the bird, which must learn all the elements of survival in a few days or be gobbled up, the child can be protected and nurtured for years until the accumulated wisdom of the ages can be cycled into its brain. The period of adolescence, primarily to assimilate language, exceeds a decade in most civilized societies. In the developed countries, adolescence extends well beyond the time of physical maturity. Sixteen years is the minimum age for dropping out of school according to the law in this country; twenty-two years is the common age at college graduation, and many people extend their education beyond that to the point where the preparation period for emergence into productive society uses up a third of their expected lifetime.

A society that protects and nurtures its young for decades must be complex, durable, and highly predictable. At the family level, the rules that govern durability and predictability are quite simple and distinct, almost genetic. As the number of individuals in a cooperative organization increases, success is harder to come by. Politically, a tribe or a small isolated village can have the simple objective of mutual survival with little opportunity for members to make alternative choices. Larger combinations like cities and sovereign states are very difficult to coordinate because the associations are primarily geographic, with little other common purpose. Ironically, there is now a common international purpose, the salvation of civilization, but we may blow ourselves to smithereens before the world's leaders are made to understand that simple goal.

The same concepts apply to economic organizations. Simple partnerships can be coordinated fairly easily, while the optimum rules for coordinating multinational corporations for the common good have yet to be devised. In all cooperative combinations, especially where resources are limited, people have made cooperative agreements not only for the betterment of the members, but to confront common adversaries or competitors more efficiently. The net result over time is to promote the common welfare by making the best use of the available talent.

Contracts between humans have existed since our brains developed to the point where it became possible to think about the future and to provide for it beneficially by actions taken in the present. The oldest contract must be the one for marriage. It most likely evolved concurrently with the evolution of the intellect and the concomitant lengthening of adolescence. Those humans who provided best for the care of the young survived preferentially. Before the act of procreation was sanctioned, provision was made for the care of the offspring who would come along months after the original thrill had passed. The marriage contract is certainly restraining. It restrains the parties from other unions, more often than not for a lifetime. It removes two people from the existing pool of available mates and can be a severe constraint on the unmated in small tribes. It is so restrictive that in some cultures the penalties for breaking the marriage contract can be quite severe.

The essence of a contract is that it deals with the future and, in so doing, preordains future conduct. It voluntarily limits the future choices of the parties participating in the agreement, perforce limiting the possibilities of those who wish to associate or compete with those parties. If, in a given tribe or village, a person should choose to spend a lifetime with another who has already entered into a marriage contract, such a choice is not available in the ordinary course of conduct. These contractual restraints have caused considerable turmoil in all societies throughout history, but both ancient and modern experience demonstrate that we remove them at our peril.

In trade, restraints are the very basis for the existence of contracts. If you agree to buy a house from me, I am restrained from selling it to someone else, even though a third party may come along with a better offer. Similarly, unless you want two houses, you are restrained from buying from another seller. Not only do we restrain each other, but we limit the ability of others to do business with either of us.

The concept of cooperation is deeply rooted in our intellectual evolution, but the concept of competition is most fundamental to all living things. Although all organisms are genetically programmed to compete where necessary, and do so for sustenance and preferential procreation, it is a natural tendency to arrange for noncompetitive environments whenever possible. Most forms of life don't go looking for trouble. They may not reason, but they don't make many mistakes. Not only are they noncompetitive in their external environments, they are distinctly noncompetitive within their own societies. Whether honeybee or termite, bird or billy goat, all cooperative organizations divide tasks and assign them to particular individuals or groups. They organize instinctively because that provides the most efficient system; that is, it uses the least amount of energy and provides best for the common welfare. Monopolies, or shared monopolies, are the most natural way of life.

Humans do the same thing. Monopolies abound in all forms of society because, properly monitored, they are the most efficient systems, cause the least amount of wasted effort, and thus act to the betterment of the group. We tend to think of monopolies in terms of public utilities, railroads, or communication systems, but, in fact, they permeate all elements of our society. We have, for example, a common need to be prepared to fight wars and we have a common need to interpret laws. It wouldn't make much sense for everyone to walk around carrying a gun, prepared to fight for his country at the drop of a hat, even though the Constitution provides for it. Nor would it make much sense for each of us to make his or her own interpretation of what the law is.

Therefore, we assign to the military the task of fighting our wars and to the judiciary the task of interpreting our laws. There may be some potentially stalwart warriors on the bench, and there is certainly a plethora of courthouse lawyers in the military, but society does not allow either profession to encroach on the other's territory. Their monopolies are considered so important that they literally wear their badges of monopoly on their sleeves. The military parade around in brass and ribbons to attest to their days of glory, while the judiciary cloak themselves in robes of black to attest to their sobriety and dignified importance. There's no mistaking who's who in those two businesses. From time to time some individuals take improper advantage of their special privilege. Society has mechanisms to deal with those improprieties, but nobody goes around trying to dismantle the Air Force, and even FDR couldn't reorganize the Supreme Court.

Society encourages a multitude of monopolies, but it also looks kindly on an endless number of noncompetitive and price-fixing agreements, particularly in the professions. A group of lawyers who decide to form a partnership can set prices and allocate professional territory on a perfectly legal basis. If one partner prefers to practice antitrust law, all the other partners can refrain from practicing that specialty and refer clients to the specialist without offering the cases to competing law firms. Physicians, physicists, and financial consulting firms have the same privilege. In total, most partnerships act as group monopolies held together by contracts that fix prices, allocate territories, divide markets, and generally act in restraint of trade.

Monopolies were the rule, not the exception, in the earliest organized societies. Not that anybody thought about it very much, but monopolies do eliminate waste and knock out unnecessary duplication of effort. Unfortunately, monopolies have the capacity to restrict output and control prices to the detriment of society as a whole. This dichotomy has plagued civilization from the beginning, but the relative importance of the choices has varied over time.

In primitive societies, and in agrarian societies to this day, the populace was generally self-sufficient, so that the market-controlling aspects of monopolies were not available. If the village blacksmith raised his prices, the farmer shod his own horse. If the general store charged too much for clothing, out came the family sewing machine. Monopolies were not restrictive, because substitutions were available.

The United States was primarily agrarian before the Civil War. After it, the railroads began to bring the concepts of the European Industrial Revolution to the heartland. The railroads themselves were the first of the modern corporations, followed by the consumer goods industries. With specialization and central administration, the new corporations had enormous competitive advantage over the cottage industries and the mom-and-pop distribution systems of the latter half of the century. Smaller companies, unable to compete except in specialized markets, were absorbed or forced into bankruptcy.

Concentration fed on itself until national markets came to be dominated by a relatively few large firms. The concentration permeated the economy in sugar, steel, oil, pipe, utilities, and railroads. Corporations banded together in the form of pools, or trusts, somewhat similar to modern holding companies. The Industrial Revolution moved in faster than society was able to accommodate it. Prices were lower, more goods were available, and in totality, since just about everyone was benefiting from the economic growth, no one wanted to tinker with the mechanism that was producing it.

But along with its benefits to society as a whole, the rapid economic development of the late 1800s brought oppression to the underprivileged and scandal among the privileged. City dwellers, including children, worked long hours in dirty, poorly lit, and unsafe places, far from the plush headquarters of the remote corporate owners. Labor and local businesses both fell under the power of corporations in trusts and other combinations that grew steadily more powerful. City officials who gave out valuable lighting, water, street railway, and other contracts were bribed routinely. Western farmers felt that they were suffering from the growing power of railroads and industries. Stock prices were manipulated in merger schemes as trusts and combinations proliferated. Trust stood for monopoly, and in America this period gave monopoly its bad name.

How to rectify these inequities was not at all obvious, particularly to congressmen who shared private business sympathies and to a public that believed in free enterprise. The public was angry, but the politicians had none of the solutions, such as labor laws and regulatory agencies, which were to come along later. Overall economic benefits may have been real but were not apparent; the people were ready for strong remedies. President Benjamin Harrison won election in 1888 with the promise that the Republicans would find ways to deal with the trusts while raising protective tariffs, a strange combination that was to restrict efficiency at home and prohibit it from abroad. Tariffs were the priority in Washington; the administration sought out cosmetic approaches to the trust question.

Senator John Sherman, an aging but respected senator from Ohio, had vainly sought legislation to promote competition and introduced a vaguely worded bill to that effect. Motives in the Congress were varied as usual. Some didn't want to tackle the problem at all; some wanted to protect the "little man," uncompetitive though he might be; some were against bigness in general; and some sought to restrain the abuses but retain the economic efficiencies of large size. Even looking back from a century of experience, it is difficult to perceive a solution that would have fit the emotions of the times.

The Congress could find none. In frustration, they decided

to forbid everything and the hell with it. The Judiciary Committee kept Sherman's name on the bill but rewrote it completely into a form so all inclusive and unspecific that most members thought it would be unenforceable. The Congress, with no little tongue in cheek, enacted the legislation as reported, and President Harrison signed it into law on July 2, 1890, with the assurance that it was primarily cosmetic. The Sherman Antitrust Act has been the bedrock of American business regulatory policy for the past ninety-five years. A more defective piece of legislation can hardly be found.

The main provisions of the Sherman Act proclaimed:

> Section 1. Every contract, combination in the form of trust or otherwise, or conspiracy, in restraint of trade or commerce among the several States, or with foreign nations, is hereby declared to be illegal . . .
>
> Section 2. Every person who shall monopolize, or attempt to monopolize, or combine or conspire with any other person or persons, or monopolize any part of the trade or commerce among the several States, or with foreign nations, shall be deemed guilty . . .

The act is appalling in its contradiction of natural law. The first section forbids contracts in restraint of trade. All contracts are promises for the future, limiting the degree of choice between the parties themselves and between the parties and others who might want to deal with them. The conscious acts of the human intellect are what distinguish us from the lower forms of life, which cannot make conscious choices for the future. When entered into in trade or commerce, they must constitute some degree of restraint, which is the essence of a contract.

The second section is equally contradictory to human nature. Monopolies abound in human affairs because in most cases where they exist, they are the most efficient and cost-effective mechanisms for maximizing human welfare. When they develop in the conduct of business, they are, by their very definition, restraining trade. The village blacksmith constitutes a monopoly, but it would be asinine to insist on two blacksmiths in a village with one horse. The problem is to distinguish between good, controllable monopolies and bad, predatory monopolies. The Congress, frustrated by its inability to distinguish, threw them all out, flipping the problem to the courts to let the good ones back in.

The courts recognized a hot potato when they were tossed one. They showed none of the arrogance or omniscience characteristic of many of their constitutional interpretations. This was a piece of legislation stating a national policy in vague, poorly defined, but all-inclusive terms. They hadn't the foggiest notion of how to reconcile the contradictions. There was precedent in the common law against certain contracts and against monopolies, but these arose from medieval concepts of business and from the excesses of monarchs who formed monopolies to favor royal sycophants.

A great many renowned legal scholars — William Howard Taft, Oliver Wendell Holmes, Charles Evans Hughes, Louis Brandeis, Learned Hand — struggled with the problem, but none could come up with a good answer to the paradox of how to interpret a piece of legislation which, literally interpreted, forbade everything. Then, as now, learned journals printed turgid analyses, and somber justices handed down convoluted opinions with all the solemnity and exquisite detail of theologians assigning real estate on the heads of pins to the dimensionless bodies of celestial spirits. There was no answer, then or now. The Congress had slipped them a mickey.

Initially the courts ducked, bobbed, and weaved. The first Supreme Court decision, in a sugar trust case, declared that manufacturing was only incidentally and indirectly related to trade, so that the Sherman Act did not apply, and the Court lacked jurisdiction. (We don't see that one quoted much anymore.) Most of the present doctrine for antitrust is taken from those early struggles of the courts; they lasted for a good twenty years. Judge Robert H. Bork, in his 1978 treatise *The Antitrust Paradox: A Policy at War with Itself*, and Professor Dominick T. Armentano, in his 1982 *Antitrust and Monopoly: Anatomy of a Policy Failure*, treat those early decisions in brilliant fashion. The question was whether monopolies were illegal per se or whether they could be judged on the basis of being "reasonable" or "unreasonable," that is, good or bad. Chief Justice Edward Douglass White argued in 1897 that a law striking down all contracts that restrained trade would destroy "all those contracts which are the very essence of trade, and would be equivalent to saying that there should be no trade, and therefore nothing to restrain." Even the great trustbuster, Teddy Roosevelt, did not believe that unrestrained competition was either possible or desirable. He proposed to set up a Bureau of Corporations, which would investigate and distinguish between good trusts and bad ones. He couldn't get the bill passed because he wanted to make the distinction himself. Confusion reigned supreme until the courts were rescued from their dilemma by a secretive, fabulously wealthy old man named John Davison Rockefeller.

•   •   •

John D. Rockefeller was born in Richford, New York, on July 8, 1839. In 1853 the family moved to Cleveland, Ohio, one hundred miles west of Titusville, Pennsylvania, where the first oil well was drilled ten years later. He grew up physically unimposing, with small eyes, high cheeks, and a long masklike face, which graphically portrayed the crucial characteristic of the man: his utter detachment from and dread of emotion-alism. His parents had forged an iron discipline; his mother, a devout Baptist, would tie him to a post and beat him when he was disobedient, while his father, a bogus doctor who sold patent medicines, would trade with his boys and cheat them, to "make 'em sharp." "Doctor" Rockefeller was an extroverted character of doubtful reputation who was once indicted for rape, a background that doubtless encouraged his son to with-draw into himself and into obsessive hard work. As a young bookkeeper, Rockefeller had to promise himself not to work after ten in the evening, so fascinated was he by figures.

At the age of twenty-six, Rockefeller gave up his job as a bookkeeper to go into partnership in a refinery with two easy-going Englishmen, the Clark brothers. Although the business prospered, the brothers' personalities did not fit with that of the sly and secretive John D., so he bought them out for $72,000 within two years. He teamed up with his brother William and the shrewd and wealthy Henry Flagler. At the time, entrepreneurs and fortune seekers were being drawn to the oil-producing fields, where fortunes were made and lost in weeks as the price of oil fluctuated wildly. As the rush to the fields stimulated overproduction, prices soon dropped, from $20 per barrel in 1863 to $0.10 per barrel a year later. At one time a barrel of oil was cheaper than a barrel of water. Demand was growing, but transportation systems and refining capacity were built more slowly than wells were drilled. Rec-ognizing that refining and transportation were the keys to success in the new industry, Rockefeller set about to control both.

With his new partners, Rockefeller systematically began to acquire refineries. In 1870 he owned 4 percent of the refining capacity of the country; a decade later he controlled 90 percent. He accomplished this growth through sharp trading practices, careful attention to costs, and a recognition of the new technologies, which would give the large-scale refiner an enormous advantage. The development of destructive distillation, or "cracking" of the petroleum molecule, put the small, undercapitalized owners out of business. Rockefeller used much of his muscle to obtain large rebates from the railroads by threatening to build his own pipelines. Overproduction by the drillers put them at his mercy; he used every competitive advantage ruthlessly.

He cut prices drastically as his costs came down. The more he cut prices, the more the market developed, and the more money he made. But the more he cut prices, the more competitors he put out of business, and the more social upheaval he caused. The more efficient he became, the more disorganized his opponents became. As his control of the industry increased, he became the most hated man in American business, the personification of the robber baron. But the secrecy of his methods, as much as his ruthlessness, made Rockefeller such a special figure of hatred. As his business expanded, his opponents never quite knew what was hitting them. When he bought out his Cleveland refinery competitors, he kept the fact secret; they pretended to be still competing, acting like partners in a rigged poker game. His dealings with the railroads were conducted with a compartmentalized, undercover network that would have rivaled a modern national espionage system. He frightened people.

His actions might not have been considered more cruel than those of many another man who looked forward cleverly to the dominance of a maturing and consolidating industry were it not for the secrecy and the suddenness of the consolidation. It was all over in a decade. By 1890, when Rockefeller controlled refineries and transportation, he expanded into pipelines and oilfields, shipping and exporting. In another five years, 70 percent of Standard Oil's business was overseas; Rockefeller had his own network of international spies and agents, ready to take on rivals or rulers throughout the world.

From his New York headquarters at 26 Broadway Rockefeller controlled a unique organization, untouchable by state governments, which seemed small beside it, or by the federal government in Washington, which had few regulatory powers to cope with it. Standard Oil used bribery and legal manipulation to evade local control of its many trusts and corporations. Its income was greater than that of most states, and its profits were big enough to finance its own expansion, independent of the big bankers, who hated it with a fervor equal to that of the smallest displaced businessman. Something had to be done to control this octopus.

It was Rockefeller and Standard Oil, as much as anything, which goaded an impotent Congress to pass the all-inclusive Sherman Act in 1890, but it took a long time to bring them to heel — twenty-one years. By that time, John D., who had retired in 1897, was innocuously setting up charitable foundations and passing out shiny new dimes to strangers he met on the street. Henry Flagler had moved to Florida, where he amassed another huge fortune in railroads and luxurious resort hotels. Purged of his Standard Oil connections, he became a revered legend in southern Florida.

By that time the government also had in place regulatory agencies to curb corporate excesses, real or imagined. State agencies regulated utility monopolies, and the Interstate Commerce Commission had matured into an effective agency to control the railroads. Labor unions were becoming a potent force under the leadership of Samuel Gompers. And the great Standard Oil was feeling the effects of free market competition. New, well-managed companies appeared on the scene. Tidewater Oil, Gulf, Sun Oil, Texaco, Union Oil, and Shell challenged Standard's monopoly and reduced its market share from 90 percent in 1890 to 64 percent in 1911. The free market was working in its most classic sense.

But in the minds of the public and the politicians, 1911 was a great year for the Sherman Antitrust Act. The Supreme Court upheld the conviction of the Standard Oil Company for violation of the act and ordered it dissolved back into its independent component parts. There was no question that the company was in literal violation of the act; all agreements in trade were. The Court recognized that and tried diligently to go beyond the all-inclusive aspects of the act to a "rule of reason," to the elusive target of distinguishing between good and bad combinations. A bad combination was one which practiced predatory pricing, that is, it lowered prices to exclude competitors, then restricted output to raise prices again and reap monopoly profits. John S. McGee, in a now classic article,* pointed out that Standard Oil did not employ predatory practices because it would have been economically foolish to do so. It didn't make sense. Rockefeller had captured the market by reducing costs and pricing accordingly. There was nothing to gain by further reductions, which would have lost money. Not that he would have had any compunctions about it, but as McGee states after sifting through eleven thousand pages of the trial record, "I am convinced that Standard did not use local price cutting in retailing, or anywhere

*John S. McGee, "Predatory Price Cutting: The Standard Oil Case," *Journal of Law and Economics*, October 1958.

else, to reduce competition. To do so would have been foolish; and whatever else has been said about them, the old Standard organization was seldom criticized for making less money when it could readily have made more."

The Court was in a jam. It either had to exclude everything or find some reason to differentiate between the good and the bad. Bad corporations used predatory tactics to reap monopoly profits. But there was no evidence of any such action on the part of Standard Oil. In fact, if the Court could look around it, which courts can't do, it would have found all sorts of evidence to the contrary. Competition abounded and prices were still falling. So the Court settled the matter on the basis of intent; it concluded that the company's actions had been carried out with "the intent to do wrong to the general public and to limit the rights of individuals."

Intent is tough to determine. It's tough enough when an act has been committed; it is almost impossible when the event has not occurred. Who is to know what is in the minds of men and women? Who is to predict the future, especially in the rough and tumble of the free market? Who is to proscribe intent when the supposedly intended event did not occur? The Supreme Court in desperation embraced the Tar Baby of intent when it enunciated its convoluted rule of reason; the efficiency of our economy has been the worse ever since for that badly flawed decision. Some seventy-odd years later, the Tar Baby is as sticky as ever.

Never mind that the price of oil went up after the decision; never mind that it plunged the government into a regulation of the energy industry that haunts us still; never mind that generations of businessmen have looked over their shoulders at that decision in every legitimate effort to improve market share, puzzled as to how "intent" will subsequently be construed; the people and the politicians were delighted. Any law that had busted up Standard Oil must be a good law. It followed that if one law was good, two laws must be better.

• • •

Before descending Dante-like to the next level of the maw of antitrust policy, let us look a little at the goals and economic theory of antitrust. The basic goal of economic policy in a free society must be that of the common welfare. Fleeing primarily from a European continent where controlled economies and economic suppression prevailed, our Victorian forefathers were as convinced as most Americans are today that the free market optimized the common welfare. The common welfare usually meant the welfare of the consumer, not always because we are all both producers and consumers, but generally because producers usually have the resources to take care of themselves.

But there is a basic dilemma in the choice of appropriate policies to maximize the common welfare. At the extremes, it is the choice between monopoly and unrestricted competition. Monopolies, properly administered, are very efficient and therefore desirable. Some industries, like electric power companies and railroads, are so capital and land intensive that regulated monopolies are mandated in all societies. But monopolies grow old and lazy and greedy, so that the door must always be open to competition when they are not regulated. At the other extreme, unrestricted competition has its own set of problems; a blacksmith shop or gasoline station on every corner benefits no one. Profit margins reduce to the bare minimum above current marginal costs; such prudent provisions for the future as product development and warranty reserves are squeezed out; and the wastes of duplication are obvious.

Theoretically, the free market handles the latter problem

in an efficient manner. The consumer, by choosing the better products, forces the uncompetitive producer to go out of business. But therein lies the sociological and political glitch. Uncompetitive producers do not like to go out of business. They — and sometimes thee and me — seek protection from the law. If they don't get it, they vote in lawmakers who will give it to them, and theories of the common welfare be damned. Our political system is the best there is, but it is not perfect; it handles this problem poorly. On the one side, wearing the black hat, is the large, powerful, efficient producer; on the other side, in the white hat, is the aggrieved loser, the little guy forced by the laws of economics and the preferences of the consumer to retire from the contest. We all have a natural, instinctive aversion to bigness and a natural inclination to sympathize with the underdog, the loser — a natural suspicion that maybe he got a bum deal. The sociological and political problem of our economy is how to find a balance between the large, efficient producer, with its concomitant contribution to the common welfare, and the small, uncompetitive producer who needs special protection to survive.

The problem needs addressing, but the antitrust laws are the wrong place to address it. It can be alleviated by tax breaks, small business set-asides, education and training, tariffs, or what have you, if society is prepared to pay the price of inefficiency, but not in the antitrust laws. They are too blunt an instrument.

• • •

We have been looking at the extremes of the business spectrum, monopolies versus unrestricted competition. There are identifiable gradations. One is the distinction between cartels and mergers. Cartels are agreements between independent organizations to restrict output, reduce competition, and maintain prices. Clearly, they should be illegal per se. There are no efficiencies to enhance the public welfare; they merely enrich the members at the expense of the consumer.

Mergers are entirely different; the parties to a merger expect to achieve the efficiencies of consolidation and to prosper by passing on some of the fruits of these efficiencies to the customer and retaining some for themselves. They reduce the number of competitors in the market, but they do not reduce competition, because their competitors must strive to meet their price reductions. Except in rare cases of extreme market concentration, mergers are, if anything, socially desirable.

Then there is the distinction between mergers and internal growth. Mergers can be questionable, but market supremacy through internal growth presumably means superior efficiency and should be applauded.

These simple distinctions group only a few of the infinite gradations of market concentration realities. To deal with them and eliminate the socially undesirable requires the skill of a neurosurgeon. The Sherman Act is a sledgehammer. But no matter. For the people and the politicians of 1911 it had served its purpose. It had broken up the dreaded Standard Oil.

Now that there is a mechanism for breaking up the big guys, how about some further protection for the little guy, went the reasoning of the times. Let's nip those monopolists in the bud and prevent them from making the first price cut or the first consolidation that will threaten us competitors and maybe put us out of business. Let's knock 'em off before they get too far down the road. Thus was born, in 1914, the Clayton Act, and its watchdog agency, the Federal Trade Commission (FTC). The Clayton Act ostensibly prevents price discrimination, whatever that means. For the past seventy years it has been interpreted to prevent price reduction.

What happens is this. It's okay to cut prices, merge vertically, horizontally, or catty-cornered, consolidate dealerships, tie in with other firms, or whatever, when your market share is small, but when your market share becomes large enough to threaten your competitors, whammo! — all these things become illegal. Where that crossover point comes and what you are trying to accomplish is difficult to determine. The Congress realized the complexity of such determinations, and so set up that predecessor of Big Brother, the Federal Trade Commission, to look into your head, figure out what you intend to do, and stop you before you get started.

Most harassed businessmen feel that the Clayton Act and its progeny were set up by do-gooders opposed to the democratic capitalistic system. No such thing. It was set up by associations of pragmatic, hardheaded small businessmen who could see that the development of the modern industrial economy was going to threaten their livelihood. The most nefarious of the progeny, the Robinson-Patman Act of 1936, was actually drafted by the United States Wholesale Grocers' Association, with the express purpose of stopping the spread of supermarkets. Fortunately, the act failed in its original purpose, but it has caused untold economic mischief ever since, because it makes vigorous price competition very difficult. It forbids price reduction except when justified by costs; accurate cost allocation is an art even with today's sophisticated accounting systems; any such system is open to challenge. It is looked upon in business as an anticompetition, not an antitrust, act.

I have sympathy for the small grocers who were forced to sell out or close by the spread of supermarkets; such businesses, then and now, deserve assistance in their economic transition. But looking back from the vantage point of almost fifty years, it would have been a terrible travesty of justice to forbid American society access to the most effective and efficient food distribution system ever developed. Think of it the next time you go to a supermarket. The mom-and-pop grocery stores are long gone, but the Robinson-Patman Act is still with us.

The whole current antitrust ball of wax, or if you prefer not to mix metaphors, the antitrust Tar Baby, is founded on a false economic premise, long preached at Chamber of Commerce meetings, that social welfare is best served by maximizing competition. Not so. The essence of the free market system is not the existence of competition but the *opportunity* to compete. As long as the opportunity to compete is available in nonregulated industries, the market will and does adjust to the optimum competitive situation, or if it isn't optimum, it will be a hell of a lot better than the FTC can predict in advance.

It is the false premise of the virtue of competition as an end in itself that not only stifles our economy but now permeates all of our society, in education, civil rights, and equal opportunity legislation. The sequel is that there should be equality of result, not equality of opportunity. If there is no governmentally ordained barrier to entry, competition will take care of itself. We see it every day. Most large firms are quite diversified and have the ability to enter many markets. If one firm captures leadership in a market and exploits it by excessive rates of return, others will jump in faster than you can say Jack Robinson.

The market is self-policing; even if there were no antitrust laws, no large firm would dare to overly exploit a market for fear of providing a price umbrella under which competitors would move in. I'd love to see an exploitive monopolist show up in our industry. We'd be at his throat in five minutes.

The same is true for small businesses. The healthiest part of our economy comprises the small businesses that find a niche, a chink in the large company's armor, where they can move in and provide a better service. That's where all the new jobs are, as we saw in the last chapter. Small businesses are thriving; they don't need protection in today's economy. Don't take it from me; look at the figures.

I doubt that antitrust laws were ever protective of the common welfare, but they certainly aren't now. They are not only archaic, they are obsolete. They are not only obsolete, they are downright embarrassing in a modern economy. Judge Bork puts it more courteously in *The Antitrust Paradox*.

> The thesis of this book has been that modern antitrust has so decayed that the policy is no longer intellectually respectable. Some of it is not respectable as law; more of it is not respectable as economics; and now I wish to suggest that, because it pretends to one objective while frequently accomplishing its opposite, and because it too often forwards trends dangerous to our form of government and society, a great deal of antitrust is not even respectable as politics.

Let us look at two modern antitrust cases — *The United States of America* vs. *The International Business Machines Company* and *The United States of America* vs. *The American Telephone and Telegraph Company* — to bring out this thesis.

• • •

The IBM case started out on the wrong foot. The Antitrust Division of the Department of Justice began its investigation of IBM in 1967, after noting that the trade press had reported that IBM's share of the computer market was around 70 percent. It wasn't a very careful investigation. The decision to proceed was made by an acting assistant attorney general who wrote a memorandum alleging that IBM refused to price its hardware boxes separately and would offer only an entire system at a single price. This allegation was completely false, showing a lack of knowledge of the distinction between hardware and software, the first thing anyone has to know about the computer business. It was true at the time that IBM bundled its software into the price of the hardware, but a glance at any IBM price list or a discussion with any customer would have shown that hardware was offered on a box-by-box basis. No two systems were exactly alike; the price of a "system" was simply the sum of the prices of the boxes included in it. Thus, the decision to bring this major, costly antitrust suit began with a mistake.

The complaint threw the book at the company. It claimed that IBM had excessive market share, that it erected barriers to market entry by its competitors, that it reaped excessive profits, that it priced below costs to establish monopoly positions after competitors had been driven from the field, that it stifled innovative competition, and that it "granted exceptional discriminatory discounts to universities and other educational institutions."

The company proceeded painstakingly to refute and demolish each of these allegations. IBM was certainly dominant in the computer field, as it had been in the mechanical tabulating business, but its share of the market had decreased from 80 percent in 1952 to 37 percent in 1967, hardly the record of an incipient monopolist. Regarding barriers to entry, if it had tried to erect them, it certainly hadn't been very successful, because the company introduced into the trial record a list of 136 competitive vendors of electronic data processing equipment.

The charge of excessive profits and pricing below costs were mutually contradictory. The stream of technological improvements in the years before the complaint and during the suit was overwhelming. Processor speed increased fourteen hundred times from 1952 to 1977. The cost per hundred thousand multiplications decreased during that period from $1.26 to $0.01. The price of main memory decreased five hundred times. The fact that the company had reduced prices by factors of hundreds while still making money made any claim of pricing below cost ridiculous, while the record of competitor entry belied any claim of excessive profits. There were plenty of competitors to choose from if customers did not like IBM's prices.

The charge that the company granted exceptional discounts to universities and other educational institutions is an example of what I mean when I say that antitrust enforcement is downright embarrassing. It is common practice for any special interest group to give preferential treatment to educational systems that will emphasize its point of view. Religious organizations support entire school systems. Philanthropists endow chairs at universities whose faculties think as they do. Others give seminars; I lecture for free at six universities; many groups raise money; the list is endless. Computer companies today fall all over themselves to make students computer literate, hoping, of course, that their equipment will be preferred. Is it possible to believe that such actions should be the basis for civil and criminal prosecution by the United States government?

The charge that IBM stifled innovative competition sticks in the throat. The industry has been the most innovative and the most competitive that this country has ever seen. The evidence is all around us, not in the depositions in a court of law. On what planet did these prosecutors live while making these allegations? Did they read newspapers, watch television, wear digital watches, use hand-held computers? If IBM had a monopoly, were they saying that it had a monopoly on innovation? In this day of high technology?

A monopolist is one who enriches himself at the expense of his competitors. Look at the list of the richest people in the country. Only one is from IBM, and he inherited his money. The others in the computer industry are from Wang, Bell & Howell, Computervision, Hewlett-Packard, Digital Equipment, Intel, Scientific Data Systems, Prime Computer, Xerox, Data General, Texas Instruments, Control Data, Cray, and a company with the silly name Apple. Don't you feel sorry for these poor downtrodden competitors?

IBM is a rough, tough, aggressive, driving competitor, over-all the best in the business. I know. We buy from them, we sell to them, we compete with them. A lot of people work for the company, and I'm sure that many walk close to the fine line of proper competition, but in thirteen years of litigation the government never laid a glove on one of them.

The statistics of the suit stagger the imagination. The case lasted thirteen years, with the industry changing dramatically each year; the industry they ended up with was far different from the one they started to analyze. There were 387 witnesses; imagine sifting through the testimony of all those witnesses. The total verbiage has never been calculated, but the official trial record alone ran to over one hundred thousand pages, or 40 million words.

This book may run to one hundred thousand words, less if you're lucky; 40 million words will produce the equivalent of four hundred books the length of this one. You realize that trial records are not usually easy reading and that a diligent investigator would be hard put to read more than one such book a week. At that rate, it would take over eight years merely to read the trial record. In addition, thousands of ancillary documents were accepted into the record. A reading of the entire official content would be beyond the lifespan of any presiding judge, even one appointed to the bench directly on graduation from kindergarten.

IBM spent over a billion dollars on its defense; God knows what it cost the taxpayer. It was ridiculous. As a people, we should be ashamed of this spectacle, and we should be grateful to the assistant attorney general who wiped out 40 million words with two when he withdrew from the entire case because he considered it "without merit."

•   •   •

As a layman, I have never understood why the suit was brought against the telephone company in the first place. It was, and still is, an operating monopoly. As all monopolies should be when there are barriers to competition, it was placed under government regulation many years ago. One dominant federal regulator, the Federal Communications Commission (FCC), and fifty others, one for each state, regulate the subsidiaries and affiliates. Telephone service was reliable, efficient, and comparatively inexpensive. We all complain about utility bills, but anyone who has traveled abroad can attest to the superiority of our system compared to the nationalized monopolies of other nations.

If the regulators wanted the companies to alter their practices, they had all the power in the world to force that change through the rate structure, as anyone associated with a public utility knows full well. Yet on November 20, 1974, the U.S. Department of Justice filed an antitrust suit against the American Telephone and Telegraph Company (AT & T). They charged that AT & T had used its dominant position in the telecommunications market to suppress competition and enhance its monopoly power. They sought the divestiture from AT & T of the Bell operating companies and the divestiture and dissolution of Western Electric, AT & T's manufacturing facility.

The pretrial skirmishing on this one took seven years. The trial itself started in 1981, sputtering along for about a year, and was stopped by a settlement in 1982, at about the same time as the IBM case. I can take you through the same dreary statistics on man-hours, words, and wasted dollars, but you can figure them out for yourself. Since the trial never really got up to speed, I'm going to explain this one on common-sense, not antitrust, grounds, which are very different. Also, since the basic issue has not yet been addressed, the problem is going to be around for a long time, to the irritation and inconvenience of all of us. You won't be any richer, but you may feel better if you understand what is happening.

The early days of telephony were more hectic than the textbooks indicate. Like most inventions, the telephone drew heavily on previous work and had scarcely appeared before notable improvements were made. The development of alternating electric current in Europe in the early 1800s gave hope to the idea that the undulatory currents of speech waves could be duplicated electrically, and several inventors devised methods employing the make-and-break principle of the telegraph to the transmission of the pitch of sounds. Alexander Graham Bell, a teacher of the deaf in Boston, was quite knowledgeable about the nature of sound. He developed a variable-resistance method of transmitting electric currents from a sound-actuated membrane, and he filed a patent application on February 14, 1876. The famous "Mr. Watson, come here. I want you" was the first intelligible speech transmission, but others were not far behind. Elisha Gray, a Chicago inventor, filed patent applications on the same day, only hours after Bell's. Gray's invention was backed by the telegraph giant, the Western Union Company, and improved on by the genius of Thomas A. Edison. The inevitable suit was settled by Bell's agreement to stay out of the telegraph business and to pay Western Union a 20 percent royalty on all Bell telephones for a specified period of time.

After that shaky start, it was not unusual for telephone companies to start up all over the country. When Bell's basic patents expired in 1893 and 1894, entrepreneurs surged into the telephone industry. Eighty-seven independent telephone systems were established in 1894, and by 1902 the number had grown to four thousand. The complications of interconnections between systems and the capital intensiveness of the exchanges proved too much for the small entrepreneurs. Because they lacked capital, the original Bell backers in Boston lost out to the J. P. Morgan interests in New York. Morgan supplied the capital to consolidate the companies, and the telephone system was recognized as a natural monopoly, one in which competing organizations were too expensive to be in the public interest. During the twenties, state and federal regulatory bodies were set up to control this natural monopoly, and there the industry sat until recently.

To simplify the explanation of the next development, I will divide the industry into two segments, local and long-distance. Originally, both local and long-distance service were capital intensive, with local service requiring expensive exchanges, and long-distance requiring thousands of miles of wires on wooden poles with very few channels per wire. In recent years local service costs per customer have gone up substantially. Exchanges are complex and versatile, cables must be run underground, and the use of the telephone for local communication has become universal. It is no longer a luxury, it is a necessity, especially for the young and the old. Teenagers never hang up the phone unless forced to; for the elderly and the shut-in, it is the prime source of communication with the outside world; for the poor and the indigent, it is the substitute for the automobile. Those who need it most can afford it least.

Long-distance service has gone in the opposite direction. With microwaves, satellites, multiplexing, and optical transmission systems, long-distance service has become much cheaper and is no longer as capital intensive as it used to be. It is no longer a natural monopoly and should be open to competition. Competing companies have petitioned for and won the right to enter the long-distance market. Technologically, economically, and sociologically, this makes a lot of sense. Politically, it does not.

As the cost of local service has gone up, there has been considerable political pressure on regulatory agencies to keep rates from rising to meet true costs. The telephone companies, like most utilities, are allowed a certain rate of return on total capital, so they have been relatively indifferent to the source of that return. Regulators then have skewed rates to favor the local customer and to overcharge the long-distance customer as a matter of public policy. The result is that long-distance services are charged at rates that subsidize local customers. Potential competitors seek only to provide long-distance, never local, services. This is known in the trade as cream-skimming, and it has given rise to the typical gobbledegook verb, "to cream-skim."

For years, naturally, cream-skimming competitors have sought to break out long-distance services from the AT & T monopoly, since they can compete easily under the umbrella of the local service subsidy. The 1982 agreement substantially does this. Long-distance services will be competitive, but local services will remain monopolies managed by the operating companies.

But who is going to pay the local subsidies? The cost of

local service in a large metropolitan area is typically $20 a month. The customer is charged $10 of this, a 50 percent subsidy. Three dollars of the subsidy is borne by special services like Princess phones. The other $7 per month is charged against the long-distance customer. Who is now going to pay the seven bucks? The local regulators and politicians say "Not us." Legislation charging rip-off and making it illegal to transfer the charges has been introduced. The new long-distance competitors want no part of it, while AT & T can't continue the subsidy and compete. As of now, there is no decision, nor is it clear who is to decide.

It is incomprehensible to me that after seven years of pretrial negotiation, the company, the courts, and the Justice Department did not settle this question, the fundamental issue of the litigation. The reason is that the regulators, the source of the problem, were not made parties to the action, and nobody else wanted to bell that cat, not even Bell itself. The question is still wide open, and the result is chaos. You see it in your service and in the complicated local and long-distance billings you receive every month. What's the answer? I don't know. Seven years of antitrust controversy did not even address the question.

●　●　●

So much for domestic antitrust problems. Let us now look at the international situation.

As we have seen, from the end of the Civil War until the turn of the century, the United States was transformed from an agrarian nation to the emerging industrial giant of the world. The transformation was rapid and uncontrolled, leading to much economic abuse or perceived abuse. Many were enriched beyond their ability to utilize their riches sensibly; others were impoverished by the violent twists and turns of

a buccaneering economy. Society had no unemployment insurance, no health care programs, no pensions, no "safety
nets" to cushion the shocks and smooth the readjustments.
With the memories of European persecution and the background of an independent, agrarian society, the citizenry had
a suspicion of and an aversion to the concentrated economic
power of a Standard Oil or a U.S. Steel. In frustration as much
as anything else, the nation turned to the antitrust laws as a
means to strike out at bigness and to protect the "small dealers
and worthy men" who were taking the brunt of the economic
transformation. Unfortunately, those laws survive today to
bedevil a completely different economic society.

Other nations had very dissimilar histories. In England and
on the European continent, economic concentration and even
the divine right of kings was still the order of the day. Japan
was just emerging from its feudal past and forming the first
alliances between the new emperor, Hirohito, and the controlling families of the Japanese economy, the *zaibatsu*, the
"money dealers." While we were vigorously enforcing the
Sherman and Clayton acts, other nations, unable to afford the
inefficiencies of enforced competition, were turning to nationalized industries and government-business cooperation.
Japan, in particular, has a culture based on cooperation and
conformity; our history of competition and adversarial litigation was and is abhorrent to the very nature of their society.
This is not to say that theirs is better, merely that it is different.

Under the MacArthur occupation, Japan set up an industrial
society modeled on that of the United States. The zaibatsu
were disbanded, the emperor became a figurehead, and the
country embraced most of the concepts of our industrial economy, including even a monopoly law. Most of these concepts
endure today, but their culture has not been able to absorb
some of them. It couldn't stand confrontation, so it had to be

based on conformity and cooperation. The last airplane of the MacArthur occupation had hardly left the ground in 1952 when the modifications began. A new, good-faith, or shinko-zaibatsu, group was formed with all the old players, and a coordinating government agency, the Ministry of International Trade and Industry (MITI), was established. Free trade was impossible against the competition of the powerful United States, so MITI established rigorous import barriers to protect their rebuilding industrial base. Export was vital to an impoverished nation, so exemptions to the monopoly law were enacted to permit cartels in international trade. The MITI formula has proved very powerful indeed: protect and encourage emerging industries, parcel out the domestic market as a base, price predatorially for market share internationally, provide long-term, no-interest loans to take the pressure off short-term profit performance, then sit back and wait for the competition to go broke. It works beautifully.

Nowhere does the Japanese system work better than in research and development (R and D). There is a striking example in semiconductors today. A key component of all computer systems is the semiconductor memory. The basic memory is a grid of tiny transistors, each containing one "bit," or binary element of memory, packed by the thousands onto a quarter-inch square of silicon. The grid configuration allows reading access in random fashion compared to a reel of magnetic tape, which must be read serially. These memories, therefore, are called random access memories, or RAMs. The trick is to pack the largest number of bits onto one chip. Early memory designs, which packed 1000 bits, were known as 1K RAMs, K being the symbol for kilo or 1000. American technology later produced 4K RAMs, then 16K RAMs, then 32K RAMs.

When the Americans developed chips with 64,000 transistors, or 64K RAMs, the Japanese decided that they had better get into the business. The government appropriated several hundreds of million dollars in subsidies and granted cartel exemptions under their monopoly law to six companies, Nippon Telephone and Telegraph, their communications monopoly, Nippon Electric Company, Hitachi, Toshiba, Fujitsu, and Mitsubishi. All other companies were politely told to stay out of the business.

The six were told to play catch-up with the Americans on 64K RAMs; they were handed the domestic market on a silver platter and told to price for world market share. They did just that. Pooling R and D has several enormous advantages. It takes out the largest risk element in product development, eliminates duplication of effort, and, most important, allows concentration of a critical mass of talent, which speeds up progress exponentially. With no development risk, a guaranteed domestic market, and loans repayable only after the companies earned a profit, the Japanese started with the American technology base and captured the bulk of the world market for this critical component within two years. These practices, of course, would be illegal to the nth power in the United States.

Contrast that with a typical example in this country. In the late sixties, automobile air pollution had become a major insult to the environment of our larger cities. The Environmental Protection Agency was established and immediately mandated a timetable for the reduction of noxious gases from the exhausts of automobiles. The timetable was short, and the development was expensive, but the public was aroused and no relief was politically achievable. The automobile and oil companies began R and D on antipollution devices independently, since joint action was forbidden by the antitrust laws.

At the time, I was a member of the Department of Commerce Technical Advisory Board, an unpaid nonpartisan group of academics, businessmen, and technical professionals who advise the department on matters of technological policy. The board recognized that the pollution issue was common to the industry, a matter of national concern, and, by the statute, a problem that must be solved quickly. We reasoned then that a common R and D program would not only be quicker and cheaper, but would give none of the firms a competitive advantage since the information would be available to all. We recommended to the Justice Department an R and D antitrust exemption to be monitored by the Environmental Protection Agency. The Justice Department reacted with such horror that I feared we would be indicted just for making the suggestion. The suggestion was turned down; at least a dozen separate R and D programs were initiated, all eventually ending up with the same answer, the catalytic converter. The Japanese, of course, pooled their resources and came up with less expensive, better converters in a shorter period of time. I believe that this is one of the factors which led to their rapid inroads into the American automobile market in the next decade.

After the electronics fiasco, there has been some movement to grant relief on R and D to American industry. One group has thumbed its nose at the Justice Department and gone ahead on its own, but that is risky business. The Congress has passed one bill granting relief, but it is pretty weak. It reduces the triple-damage penalty to single damages and makes for more equitable compensation of attorneys' fees. Big deal.

Research and development is only one piece of the antitrust problem, albeit the most crucial one at the moment. And the domestic market is only one piece of the total market. In the long run, it is the position of the United States in the international market that counts. When half our industry is subject to foreign competition, it no longer makes sense to separate the two. We can make laws to regulate our own industry, but we cannot make laws to regulate the industries of our foreign competitors. There are international agreements, to be sure, but they have been proved to be blunt instruments indeed. We may call for our competitors to be fair and sportsmanlike, but they don't play by Marquis of Queensberry rules. They can't. We're too big for them. They reason that a quick punch to the solar plexus when the referee isn't looking is their best defense and in their national interest. We are not going to change that feeling.

There is great debate in the land about industrial policy. If we have had an explicit industrial policy for the last century, it has been the policy of antitrust. More than a policy, it has been an act of faith that if the marketplace were kept open and unobstructed, the resulting competition among numerous proprietors, those "small dealers and worthy men" of the last century, would satisfy consumer desires and assure the fulfillment of the national welfare. In the words of Judge Learned Hand (and you can't find a more imposing legal monicker than his), "Great industrial concentrations are inherently undesirable regardless of their economic consequences." That article of faith comes from a different age, was wrong to begin with, and has certainly not stood the test of time. It should be renounced.

The antitrust posture has assumed that America is essentially a closed economy, now a completely untenable concept. As an industrial policy, antitrust has discouraged cooperation, consolidation, and combination, with complete disregard of the necessity of these responses in order for American firms to compete against the nationalized and nationally supported industries of the rest of the world. Examples abound. It is common knowledge that the Federal Trade Commission was considering antitrust action against General Motors well into the seventies, well into the period when everyone else on this earth was aware that GM was getting clobbered by foreign competition. In fact, it was a hot item right up to the year General Motors lost money.

Putting aside even the intellectual and sociological depravity of antitrust, the idea is no longer manageable. As society becomes more complex and incomes rise, it is not easy to define a market to determine whether or not a firm has a monopolistic position. Definitions of markets drag along in the courts for decades, with the markets themselves changing all the while. Most goods we buy are not physiological necessities, but luxuries that could be replaced by other goods to produce just as high a real standard of living. Rolls-Royce has a virtual monopoly in the top level of the automobile market. But so what? Nobody has to buy it. The same is true of swimming pools or summer homes or sirloin steaks. At the other end of the economic spectrum, choices abound in supermarkets or discount department stores. No one *has* to buy any specific product anymore. Can you think of one? I can't. If a company prices a product too high, people will shift to different products. The very idea is archaic and intellectually barren.

We should rid ourselves of the century-old Sherman Antitrust Act and all its progeny. Only two concepts of the antitrust industrial policy should be retained.

Laws against predatory pricing should be kept on the books. Predatory pricing is the practice in which a supplier with superior resources cuts prices and keeps them low until his competitors' resources are exhausted. Such practices do not work in a modern free economy, but they do work in international trade, where the deep pockets belong to a government and the scruples against the practices do not exist. For our national protection, predatory pricing should be outlawed.

The formation of cartels for price-fixing purposes should still be forbidden. Mergers, vertical, horizontal, or what have you, tie-ins, distribution agreements, and so forth, have at their base a desire to compete by better efficiency and potentially serve the public welfare. Price-fixing cartels promise no efficiencies of production and serve only to enrich the participants against the good of society. They serve no useful public purpose.

As for the rest of antitrust, out with it — sweep it away. Rid us of the cobwebs of a century of economic obfuscation.

9

Export, Emigrate, or Evaporate

THE YEAR 1776 marked the publication of two historic documents, the Declaration of Independence, written by Thomas Jefferson, and *The Wealth of Nations* by Adam Smith. They were curiously complementary, the one a resounding, emotional call to freedom, the other a rational, careful analysis of the benefits freedom could bring.

Jefferson's clarion cry was terse, succinct, goading: "We hold these Truths to be self-evident, that all Men are created equal, that they are endowed by their Creator with certain unalienable Rights, that among these are Life, Liberty, and the Pursuit of Happiness."

The lines sprang from the page in their clarity — they were the battle cry of a great revolution.

Smith's sentences were rambling and prolix.

Every individual necessarily labours to render the annual revenue of the society as great as he can. He generally, indeed, neither intends to promote the public interest, nor knows how much he is promoting it. . . . He intends only his own gain, and he is in this, as in many other cases, led by an invisible hand to promote an end which was no part of his intention. . . . By pursuing his own interest he frequently promotes that of the society more effectually than when he really intends to promote it.

These words sparked no revolution. They were words to savor and to chew, to be read and reread.

But the thoughts go together. Jefferson's were political, to set up a great nation. Smith's were economic, to set up a philosophy by which nations could prosper. The acts of the invisible hand in its pursuit of happiness provide the economic and political foundation for our society's successful system of democratic capitalism.

Among other things, Adam Smith was a free trader. The doctrine of free trade is easy to understand. If the other fellow makes something more cheaply or better than you can, you should buy it from him. If, however, the other fellow is in another country, the problem gets a little more complicated. If someone in your own country makes a similar, but a little more expensive product, he will appeal to your patriotism and your good fellowship to buy from him. But, knowing that you will act in your own interest, which in this case would also be in the interest of the society, he seeks to put impediments in the way of your purchase of the foreign product. In the eighteenth century, the impediment usually took the form of an import tax or tariff.

The tariff was very appealing. It protected the clean-living, virtuous domestic producer from the foreign devil — who usually had webbed feet, or smelled funny, or had a different colored skin, or worshiped a strange god — and it was an excellent source of revenue for the government. It fulfilled the most ancient axiom of taxation, "Don't tax him and don't tax me; tax that feller behind the tree." By putting the tax on an import, it made it look as though the feller behind the tree, the foreigner, was paying the tax. He wasn't, of course; like all taxes, it was paid by the consumer, but it was well hidden. The tariff was such a popular means of raising revenue that it remained the primary source of federal revenue until the unlucky year of 1913, when the federal income tax law was first enacted.

There is another complication with international trade — the question of currency exchange. If you buy something from another country, you generally pay for it in the currency of your own realm. If you don't have something to sell in return, that country will gradually build up a horde of your currency, which is no good domestically. Gradually, the seller realizes that he has traded material goods with true value for some symbols of value that are of little use to him at home; sensibly, he stops selling or raises prices to prohibitive heights. Then everybody loses. The same situation applies in reverse, so the best of all worlds occurs when each nation has something to export to the other, roughly in equal value. Although from time to time it is desirable for a country to be primarily an exporter or an importer, or an exporter to one country and an importer from another, in the long run there is no such thing as a favorable balance of trade among the community of nations. That leads only to a net exchange of real goods for paper or metallic symbols of value. Until recently, unfavorable balances of trade were brought into line by fluctuations in the relative value of currencies, called the exchange rate. All these things seem obvious to us, but they were not so obvious in Adam Smith's day, or in the centuries before.

Ptolemy (A.D. 100–165) was one of the greatest astronomers and geographers of ancient times. During the Middle Ages his works were discredited and lay dormant, but with the Renaissance curiosity for things unknown, the concepts of Ptolemy were dusted off and revitalized. Ptolemy believed that the earth was round and that gravity is directed toward the center of the earth. He also believed that the earth was motionless and that the moon, sun, and the planets revolved about it at various rates of speed. (It wasn't until Copernicus came along in 1543 that the concept of the earth as a moving planet was brought out, but that didn't make much difference to the early navigators, who were a long way from doing any space travel anyhow.) Ptolemy's big contribution was in cartography, the science of making maps. His system of assigning coordinates of longitude and latitude made possible the coordination of the map-making capabilities of the seafaring nations and led to the great voyages of exploration, beginning about the year 1400. His maps were magnificent, considering that they were a millennium and a half old, but they weren't perfect. He exaggerated the land mass from Spain to China and underestimated the size of the ocean. This mistake encouraged Columbus to make his famous voyage in 1492.

The great adventurers of the sea in those days were the Chinese, the Spaniards, and particularly the Portuguese. China, as we have seen, dropped out of the running for internal reasons, but Spain and Portugal continued exploration for centuries. As outposts were set up and new territories annexed, international trade as we now know it began to build up. Unfortunately, the new territories, especially in the Americas, had little agricultural or manufactured goods to trade, tobacco being an isolated exception. The adventurers thus primarily sought treasure, with an emphasis on precious metals.

These early traders made a big mistake. They did not recognize that precious metals could not be eaten, worn, or slept in, and therefore did not constitute real wealth, but only the symbols of wealth. Spain was the worst offender. The country was turned inside out providing goods and services to be sent to the New World in exchange for gold and silver. An undeveloped country, Spain built up a naval fleet of the first order and standing armies beyond its means, all the while beggaring its agrarian economy. The treasure became currency, but there was nothing to buy. The result was a classic, colossal inflation, with too much money chasing too few goods. The Spanish economy collapsed, the empire was dissipated, and Spain ceased to be a world power. It has never recovered.

Notwithstanding the example of Spain or the legend of Midas, the concept of exporting goods for money appealed to the governments of the most advanced countries. To assure a predominance of exports, these governments perforce placed curbs on imports. There developed then the first organized system of economic beliefs of modern times, the concept of mercantilism.

Mercantilists believed that money, or precious metals, was the most desirable form of wealth, and that where the precious metals were found in abundance there would also be found opulence and prosperity. Therefore, as nations without mines could not obtain the precious metals without foreign trade, and even then only when trade was conducted as to cause a so-called favorable balance, imports were to be discouraged and exports encouraged.

It was this concept of mercantilism that Adam Smith opposed. He came along at the right time. The Industrial Revolution in England had begun about the time he was born, and was in full flower by 1776. The mercantilists were then in command of trade policy. Their concepts were in tune with those of the landowners who wanted to keep out cheap agricultural goods. The agriculture of the day was primarily produced by hand labor with no economies of scale. The landowners saw no particular advantage in expanding production; they were content to continue the feudal practice of keeping food scarce and expensive.

The industrialists were a more practical lot. The name of their game was machinery; the more they produced, the cheaper their goods became. They favored a strong export policy; they realized that if import duties were lowered on wheat and other grains the populace would have more to spend on their cotton and woolen goods. The concept of free trade was right down their alley. It took about fifty years to come about, but Adam Smith's ideas gradually took hold, and England became the leader of the free-trade movement and the leading industrial nation of the nineteenth century, but not soon enough to prevent the loss of her prime colony.

On the other side of the Atlantic, trade, taxes, and tariffs were touchy subjects indeed, so touchy that they became the prime factors leading to the American revolution. For a good many years the early settlers in British North America had little say in their government's economic and trade policies. While this did not particularly disturb many colonial citizens, a number of individuals became increasingly restive after 1763, at the end of the Seven Years War. They began openly objecting to many acts of Parliament that they felt unduly restricted or interfered with their trade, including the imposition of taxes.

The British government, never having heard of Adam Smith and completely unable to fathom the clamor over taxation without representation, was particularly obtuse. Desperate for revenue to pay for what we called the French and Indian War, the Parliament in 1765 imposed on the colonies a Stamp Act, which specified that stamps must be purchased to be affixed to such documents as deeds, mortgages, liquor licenses, playing cards, and newspapers. This caused such a commotion that the act was repealed a year later.

Still not understanding the problem, the Parliament tried to sneak in an indirect tax in the form of tariffs on specified imports. This was even worse. The Townshend Acts of 1767 placed custom duties on goods — paper, glass, tea, paint, lead pigments — that the colonists were incapable of producing themselves. The colonists were furious; radicals staged public protests, fomenting the Boston Massacre of 1770. Three years later many of the same radicals pitched East India Company tea chests off British ships into Boston Harbor to prevent any colonist from paying the import duty on tea. The tariff was the single biggest factor triggering the American revolution.

This pre-Revolutionary experience with taxation without representation, even when that taxation came disguised in the form of tariffs, meant that Americans would be very suspicious of all taxation schemes once they had declared their independence in 1776. Consequently, throughout the Revolutionary War, the Continental Congress was denied the power to levy taxes of any sort. Even after the war the individual states practiced a sort of tariff anarchy, imposing discriminatory and arbitrary duties upon one another and presenting foreign traders with a bewildering array of tariff rates.

The adoption of the Constitution brought order. Indeed, the very first function listed in the document was a clause granting the House of Representatives the "Power to lay and collect Taxes, Duties, Imposts, and Excises." The first tariff bill was a revenue raiser, taxing imports across the board at 5 percent of their value. For many years this was enough to cover the federal government's quite modest expenditures.

With a free-trade orientation about in the land, not much would have happened to affect tariffs in the early years had not a series of European wars disrupted U.S. export and freight trade. At first it was France trying to break up U.S.-British trade, but later the principal offender was Britain, trying to cut off our trade with Europe. Responding to real and imaginary maritime insults and injuries, Presidents Thomas Jefferson and James Madison first raised tariffs, then imposed an embargo, and finally promulgated a strict no-trade policy against Great Britain that culminated in a full-fledged war in 1812.

At the conclusion of that undecisive war, tariffs were doubled to raise revenue and to protect our war-nurtured infant industries from British competition. Doubling wasn't enough. Cut off from their normal markets, British factories had produced an enormous surplus of goods during the War of 1812. After the war much of this surplus was dumped on the United States at prices far below original cost. The influx of these extraordinarily cheap goods ruined a number of domestic manufacturers and drove down price levels on all goods, plunging the nation into a serious financial and economic crisis, the Panic of 1819. So much for the free traders.

The clamor for protection became politically irresistible. Up to this point the free-trade consensus had come from a coalition of Southern cotton growers and New England shipbuilding interests. After the Panic of 1819, the northern financiers and manufacturers demanded a seat at the table, crying for protection for infant industries. The issue came to a head in 1828 when a political ploy backfired, resulting in the enactment by Congress of a most grotesque bill, which came to be known as the Tariff of Abominations.

Democrat Andrew Jackson needed the support of high-tariff advocates to win the presidential election in 1828. Jackson's supporters proposed a bill to raise tariff levels, deliberately making some of the rates exorbitantly high. Politicians re-

sponsive to the special interests of their home districts amended
the bill to include equally high rates on other commodities.
The higher the average rate grew, the more certain Jackson's
supporters were that the coalition of strict low-tariff southerners and free-trade New Englanders would vote it down.
But Daniel Webster, the most persuasive orator in the Senate,
switched his support to the manufacturing protectionists, and
the bill passed. Average tariffs were quintupled under the act;
it took a decade to get them down again.

These actions shook up the southern states badly. Prospering with their one-crop cotton economy, southerners began
seriously questioning the advantages of remaining united with
those northerners who seemed totally uninterested in southern economic desires. Slavery was ultimately the issue that
split the nation, but the roots were economic, with free trade
and tariffs forming the opening wedge. The underlying issue
was whether the northern free-labor, protectionist system or
the southern slave-labor, free-trade system would ultimately
prevail.

Andrew Jackson survived the fiasco of the Tariff of Abominations, as did his vice president, John C. Calhoun, a free
trader from South Carolina. But when Jackson failed to support tariff reform, Calhoun resigned the vice presidency. Next,
South Carolina declared the act unconstitutional and threatened to secede from the Union. Jackson prepared to go to
war if necessary. The Union was temporarily saved when Ken-
tucky Senator Henry Clay worked out an acceptable compromise. Such was the importance of tariffs in those days.

The Clay compromise worked for about twenty years. Then
the rise in the power of the northern manufacturers tipped
the balance back to the protectionists, and tariffs started to
go back up. Meanwhile, the issue of slavery became dominant,
straining the bonds of the Union to their eventual rupture.

After the Civil War, the Republican Party, with the support of the victorious northerners, kept tariffs for the most part relatively high.

The break finally came in 1913, when a constitutional amendment legalizing direct income taxes was passed after several previous attempts had been declared unconstitutional. With pressure off tariffs as revenue raisers, Woodrow Wilson was able to make some significant tariff reductions, and the country entered World War I with the tariff in the background as a political issue.

With war's end, the battle started all over again. The third of President Wilson's Fourteen Points, his proposal for the postwar world, called for "the removal, so far as possible, of all economic barriers and the establishment of an equality of trade conditions among all nations." When the Senate failed to approve the Versailles Treaty, out went the whole Wilsonian concept of foreign policy, including free trade. The American public seemed to ratify the Senate's rejection when in 1920 they awarded an impressive mandate to Republican Warren G. Harding and his promise to lead the country back to "normalcy."

Back went the high tariffs. A series of ever more protectionist bills raised tariff rates under Harding and Calvin Coolidge. President Herbert Hoover made the biggest mistake of all. Attempting to improve the depressed condition of U.S. agriculture, he proposed to raise agricultural rates significantly; he made the same mistake that Andrew Jackson had made a century before. His proposal opened the gates for every special interest lobby and the bill got away from him. The result was the infamous Smoot-Hawley Act of 1930, which set up the highest general tariff rate structure that the United States had ever enacted. It triggered an angry reaction overseas. One nation after another retaliated by raising its own trade barriers against U.S. exports. Under the impact of higher tariffs, competitive devaluations, and heavy-handed financial controls throughout the world, international trade slowed to a standstill in 1931 and 1932, and the U.S. economy staggered toward total paralysis. The Great Depression had begun.

When Franklin D. Roosevelt came into the presidency in the midst of the depression, he had little difficulty convincing the Congress that the Smoot-Hawley tariff had been a colossal debacle; it was also clear, with a century of experience from Andrew Jackson to Herbert Hoover, that wholesale rewriting of the tariff laws by Congress was not an efficient way to regulate business; and, finally, it was clear that lower trade barriers between nations were in their general interest if the special interests of the individual nations could be reconciled. International trade was an area not for all-encompassing legislation, but for specific negotiation.

A new element was added to international trade in 1934; the basic approach was to promise lower U.S. trade barriers in return for similar concessions by other countries. The Reciprocal Trade Agreements Act totally altered the process of changing domestic tariffs by authorizing the president to negotiate reciprocal trade agreements with other countries.

The United States immediately opened negotiations with several countries; within two years bilateral agreements had been completed with six nations, and by the middle of the Second World War, a total of thirty bilateral agreements was in place. It was a good start for the massive changes to come.

The United States entered the postwar period as the colossus of international trade. Militarily and economically, its former foes lay in ruins, its future enemy exhausted and helpless before its awesome nuclear potential. Economically, it had no challenger. Its factories and growing fields were unscathed by war and in full production, ready to feed and rebuild the world. The mills and the foundries of all the great nations, friend and foe alike, were in complete disarray, unable to meet the needs of their own populations, much less to compete in the international arena. Even more than Rome in the ancient West and China in the medieval East, the United States was the center of the universe. It could make its own rules, dictate its own terms.

Never in history was a nation as magnanimous in victory as the United States of America in the late forties and early fifties. It could literally have colonized the free world by doling out its resources to its friends. It could have kept its former enemies under complete dominance by maintaining military control and insisting on reparations. It could have stopped Soviet expansion by threat of the use of nuclear weapons. (That would be an unthinkable thought today, but what would Stalin have done had the situation been reversed?) The United States chose to do none of these things. It rebuilt the free world through the Marshall Plan. It supervised free elections in West Germany and Japan and kept only those troops requested by the new governments. It turned the other cheek to Soviet mischief throughout the world, never once seriously flexing its nuclear muscle.

It was a heady time in America. Its youth came back from the wars confident that they had saved the world from tyranny. There were no doubts in those days. Domestically, the economy boomed. The world's demand for steel and copper and rubber seemed insatiable; automobiles and appliances poured from the factories by the tens of millions; suburban housing and shopping centers sprang up around the cities in ever widening circles; newly mechanized farms could not keep up with the world's great appetite. Internationally, our former enemies could not believe their good fortune or express their gratitude more strongly; a new and independent Israel was nurtured proudly from the turmoil of the Middle East; the expansionist ambitions of Soviet Russia were contained.

As in the days of the Ming emperors, delegations flocked from all the world to the new Middle Country, to seek our largess, to plead for protection, to pick our brains, to ask for guidance. Our business conduct and our management techniques were studied assiduously and copied reverently. We taught and lectured loftily with a confidence and a cockiness that bordered on narcissism. We never stopped to think of the reason for our superiority. We couldn't lose. We had a monopoly on everything.

We were equally magnanimous in our approach to international tariffs and trade. The General Agreement on Tariffs and Trade (GATT) was set up in 1947 to become the major framework for international trade among the non-Communist nations. We approached the GATT negotiations as an equal partner to all the other nations; we flexed no muscles; we drove no bargains. I believe that our intentions were noble, but down deep we had to be conscious of our overwhelming superiority. We strove, insofar as possible, to reduce all tariffs and quotas to zero. We made concessions that we didn't have to make in an effort to tear down all barriers.

The name of the game was free trade. We approached the ideal of free trade with a religious fervor close to fanaticism. Anyone who wanted to retain even one teeny-weeny tariff was guilty of mortal sin; cynics who questioned the true faith were forced to wash out their mouths with soap. No one looked back at the two centuries of turmoil over tariffs and trade, turmoil that had literally led to wars and revolutions, to panics and depressions, turmoil over which administrations were banished from office. North was set against South, East against West, farmer against financier, manufacturer against mariner. If opposition to free trade was a sin, there had been many sinners in our history, people like Washington and Jefferson and Jackson and Lincoln, to name a few. Why, all of a sudden, was everyone in the country in complete agreement on this complex subject?

The answer was monopoly. Because of a war-ravaged world, we had a virtual monopoly on excess agricultural products, a surplus of minerals and other raw materials, and we were already supplying the world with most of its manufactured goods as the need for armaments had decreased. We were the market leaders, in business school terminology. It is a first principle of business planning that the market leader wants no restraints on its ability to compete. It needs no protection because of its superior hold on the market. And it struggles as hard as possible to deny protection to its competitors. We had a monopoly; naturally, we developed a monopoly mentality.

Free trade is not a religion from which heretics must be cast out. It is an ideal, a goal, which can be approached asymptotically but never achieved, like reaching the speed of light, or batting 1.000, or mixing the perfect martini. A completely free market is the most efficient market, the most desirable market, and, in a perfect world, the most productive market for all mankind, but it is not achievable in an imperfect world, and we should so realize.

From the magnanimous mentality of the early postwar years, we metamorphosed rapidly but smoothly to the monopoly mentality of the fifties and then to the Ming mentality of the sixties and seventies. We were economically supreme in those early years, and we were militarily the bastion of the free world. We felt a duty to be the policeman to the planet, to constrain the Stalins of the present and to prevent the re-emergence of the Hitlers of the past. Our economy was strong; we could afford a large military budget. The economies of

Western Europe and Japan were weak; they could not afford military establishments, and we did not feel it prudent to rearm them. When we saw fit to halt the spread of communism, as in Korea and Vietnam, we had the only military force to meet the enemy. It was our economy that paid the price, our guns that were fired, our blood that was spilled, not the economies or the guns or the blood of our trading partners. We had to protect our ideals, but we also had to protect our customers.

Since our system and our culture seemed so obviously superior and our monopoly so secure, we began to feel it appropriate to export our culture and our concepts and our mores along with our goods and services. It was a package deal. Take it or leave it. Live by our rules or go without.

We didn't worry very much about imports. There weren't very many of them anyhow, only a few scarce minerals and a trickle of manufactured goods. We used exports as carrots and sticks, to be doled out to the good guys and held back from the bad guys. We didn't have to encourage or stimulate exports because we could sell everything we could make. Even when we were rebuilding the free world, exports and imports together totaled less than 10 percent of our gross national product.

There was a great deal of concern in this country about how nations treated their citizens and how they related to other nations. We were concerned for human rights all over the world. Why not use this nation's economic might to improve the lot of the oppressed in other countries? A good question, and a noble thought indeed. Unfortunately, noble thoughts do not always achieve noble ends, especially when out from under our jurisdiction.

Human rights concerns are not new, nor are they exclusively the domain of Americans. The endowment of all with certain inalienable rights was written into our Declaration of Independence, but it is also in similar documents in all the non-Communist countries, in the charter of the United Nations, and even in the constitutions of some of today's most repressive states.

The U.S. campaign for human rights around the world has been institutionalized in a number of pieces of legislation. The Harkin amendments to U.S. economic aid legislation and to military aid legislation make human rights a consideration in the allocation of assistance, and human rights provisos are now attached to loans from the Export-Import Bank, to investment guarantees from the Overseas Private Investment Corporation, to agricultural sales, and even to the services of the Peace Corps.

The score card on the effectiveness of U.S. human rights policies is not very good, and most foreign observers see our human rights policies as politically naive and fundamentally unworkable. Charles Frankel, a former assistant secretary of state, claims that the policies imply that "a government can insert itself between another government and its citizens," and that this is contrary "to international law and reasonably peaceful relations between nations."

Economic sanctions have been painfully unproductive; if there ever was an area where we have obviously been shooting ourselves in the foot, it is this one. The continuing sanctions against South Africa have been an enormous impediment to the moderates who have been trying to effect change in that beautiful but ill-starred country. I believe that the country will have a bloody revolution if progress toward racial equality is not speeded up, but we can't make it happen. Progress is slow, too slow, but our actions are only making the problem worse.

During the detente years with the Soviet Union, the number of dissidents allowed to emigrate was increasing — slowly, but it was increasing. The U.S. Congress, impatient with the progress, passed the Jackson-Vanik amendment, placing economic sanctions on the Soviet Union unless emigration was speeded up. The Soviets reacted typically. They got their backs up and stiffened emigration procedures. Result: emigration of dissidents has decreased practically to zero.

At the time of the Afghanistan invasion, President Jimmy Carter cut off grain supplies to the Soviet Union, hoping to advance the cause of world peace, as he put it. The action had not the slightest effect on the Russian policies in Afghanistan, but it did cause considerable economic hardship in the American farm belt. The Soviets turned to Argentina, also on our list, who sold them enough grain to finance their own invasion of the Falkland Islands. Some peace move that was! We have now lifted the restrictions on the Soviets, but they are wary and have not increased their purchases to their former level. We have also lent the Argentines money to finance their recovery. At present, the Russians are still in Afghanistan, the Argentines are threatening to repudiate their debts, and the farmers in Iowa are still bankrupt.

In 1981 President Ronald Reagan made a similar mistake. Persuaded that the Russian gas pipeline to Europe would make Western Europe too dependent on Soviet energy, he cut off the supply of American earth-moving equipment to the project. The principal loser was the Caterpillar Company, the U.S. blue-chip manufacturer of earth-moving equipment. At the time, Caterpillar was suffering a great deal of competition from its Japanese counterpart, the Komatsu Corporation. Reagan's action handed the business to Komatsu and almost bankrupted Caterpillar. Our European friends refused to go along with our embargo; they wanted the gas and they wanted the business. The result was that the pipeline went rolling merrily along; we lost the export business and the jobs that went with it, but most of all, we have been branded as an unreliable supplier. The embargo has now been rescinded, but the Japanese are well established, and people are still unemployed in Peoria, Caterpillar's hometown. It's not playing well in Peoria, believe me.

During the seventies a number of scandals that exposed bribery in high places in Europe and Japan broke out. American exporters were accused of bribing a Japanese prime minister and a European monarch, as well as procurement officials in the Middle East. There seems no question that laws were broken, since there were a number of convictions under existing legislation. There is also no question that bribery is immoral, unethical, and strictly in conflict with the conduct of an orderly society. The laws that were on the books at the time spoke to those concepts and provided adequate remedy for the offenses. However, in its zeal and outrage, the U.S. Congress passed the Foreign Corrupt Practices Act, going far beyond what was necessary or desirable to prevent similar abuses.

The first thing the act did was to impose stringent internal accounting controls on all public corporations, whether or not they did business overseas and regardless of whether they were otherwise regulated. I am on the board of directors of a Massachusetts electric public utility that does no business beyond state borders and is strictly regulated by both state and federal agencies. The company, and all similar companies, was required to install expensive accounting systems under the act, the cost of which would have to be borne by ratepayers.

For companies doing business abroad, no facilitating payments other than simple sales commissions were allowed. This was a typical Ugly American reaction, completely oblivious of the customs and laws of other sovereign nations. In some South American countries, it is customary to pay $50 to get a telephone installed. No fifty, no phone, simple as that. In many countries, it is customary to tip a customs agent, otherwise your box goes to the bottom of the pile. Both actions were illegal under the act. In each case the employees are very poorly paid and expect these tips as part of their meager compensation. It is no different from tipping a waiter or a taxi driver in this country. (In Tahiti it is illegal to tip waiters or taxi drivers. I pity the poor Tahitians who may come to this country and try to eat or travel.)

It is completely impossible to export this kind of morality. Furthermore, the penalties under the act are quite severe; in many cases the business executive is criminally liable even if the practice is forbidden by company policy, and whether or not there was knowledge of the violation. The upshot is that the prudent company turns down export business in certain countries where there is any possibility of vulnerability to the penalties of the legislation.

I treated the domestic inefficiencies of our antitrust laws extensively in the last chapter. It's tough enough to compete efficiently under bad legislation when your competitors have to live by the same rules. When they don't, there's no horse race. No other government restricts enterprises nearly so much in setting up joint ventures abroad, in engaging in consortium bidding, in licensing foreigners to produce patented goods abroad, in dealing with centralized state trading countries, or in negotiating with cartels like OPEC. No other government offers so few guidelines as to acceptable behavior abroad; no other government is so eager to apply its antitrust laws extraterritorially.

It is true that there are amendments to the Sherman and Clayton acts allowing companies to combine to promote their exports, and recent legislation allows consortia for joint marketing, but the rules are so uncertain and the penalties for breaking them are so severe that corporations have been leery and unwilling to take chances with breaking the law. Overall, it is difficult to see how restrictions on U.S. firms that are not paralleled by restrictions on their foreign competitors can really improve competitive conditions around the world, or fail to hamper our exports in general.

A number of other impediments to exports are tied to the questions of human rights, morality, treatment of ethnic groups, differences in cultures and customs, or unfair practices, as we see them. There are embargoes and boycotts for countries whose practices we don't like. There are requirements for environmental impact statements in other countries. Opinions on the practicality and desirability of these impediments ebb and flow. But there is another major class of international trade problems that spark strong debate in our society and are far from being settled. These problems relate to secrecy.

The practice of secrecy in connection with the industrial arts is persistent through history. Dyeing was an extremely secret process; in fact, at one time during the Middle Ages it was so carefully guarded that it was felt to be one of the magic black arts. The working of iron, and metallurgy in general, were secrets confined in the past to a few nations, and in those nations to a few families. The nation or the family that possessed these secrets had a great advantage, both for wealth and for war. The smith in early times was regarded as a magician, or one who understood all the secrets of nature; he was an aristocrat.

According to Venetian law, the relatives of artisans who emigrated were imprisoned if they were unsuccessful in inducing the emigrants to return home; and the emigrant, if apprehended, was put to death. The laws of Florence threatened with death any who carried the secrets of the silk or brocade industries into foreign countries. In Nuremberg braziers were prohibited from showing their furnaces to strangers. In Belgium enticing manufacturers of bone lace to emigrate was punishable. In the eighteenth century the elector of Saxony established a pottery manufactury that was virtually a prison for the workers. On the walls was inscribed "Be secret until death."

When England spurted out to lead the Industrial Revolution in the early eighteenth century, the other industrially developing nations made frantic efforts to learn the secrets of her success, and Great Britain made equally determined efforts to keep them hidden. Foreign manufacturers resorted to expedients beyond number to secure knowledge of English improvements in iron smelting, pottery making, and cotton spinning. They induced artisans and master manufacturers to seek their fortunes in other countries. They sent agents to England with letters of introduction by means of which they tried to secure access to industrial plants; when this failed, they sent spies, under various disguises, to secure drawings and firsthand knowledge.

England retaliated in kind; there was a law prohibiting the export of the stocking frame, and another protecting silk machinery, which had previously been stolen from the Italians. Up to 1825, skilled artisans were prohibited from emigrating; Josiah Wedgwood even suggested a secret arrangement with the government for opening letters of workmen who might want to emigrate.

The Americans, by virtue of their common language and heritage, were the most successful in such espionage and in stealing British secrets. Samuel Slater was born in Derbyshire and apprenticed at the age of fourteen to Sir Richard Arkwright, an inventor of cotton-spinning machinery. Soon skilled in improved textile machinery, Slater was induced to emigrate by Americans from Rhode Island. In 1789, though forbidden by law to leave the country, he was disguised as a farm boy and spirited to Pawtucket, Rhode Island, where he designed and built the first successful spinning mill in the United States and founded the American textile industry.

In 1810 Francis Cabot Lowell, of Boston, went to England and managed to gain access to the Lancashire cotton mills. Absorbing the English technology completely, he returned home and was able to design looms that were ultimately superior to the best English models. The Americans built on Slater's and Lowell's foundation and, protected domestically by high tariffs, proceeded to dominate the industry by the end of the century. That's not how the history of the United States textile industry is generally written, but that's how it happened.

As the pace of invention and international travel picked up, it was no longer practicable to hide trade secrets completely. Most governments recognized that excessive secrecy was detrimental to society and moved to legal systems for the protection of inventors. Authority for the grant of patents was specified in the Constitution, but this country didn't get its act together until 1836, when the first modern patent system was set up. By 1883 a patent treaty signed by seventy-nine nations granted international reciprocity. For the past century the patent system has worked well internationally, with few economic or trade problems.

Protection of secrets for international security is another matter. Instead of getting better over the years, it has been getting worse. There wasn't much to it prior to World War II. There were military secrets, but they applied primarily to military matters, like the size and distribution of forces, not inventions or production processes. The first big scientific secret was the development of radar by the British, and its importance in the Battle of Britain early in the Second World War was crucial. The secret was well hidden, and even the later transfer of the technology to the United States for further development went on without international incident.

The current controversy over military secrecy began with the discovery of nuclear fission by Otto Hahn and Fritz Strassman in Berlin in December 1938. They checked their hypotheses with Lise Meitner, a former colleague exiled to Sweden. She talked it over with her nephew, Otto Frisch, another Jewish exile working with Neils Bohr in Denmark, just before Bohr went to Washington to speak at an international theoretical physics conference at George Washington University.

Joined by Enrico Fermi, an Italian, Bohr broke the news in January 1939 to an international group that included conferees from Germany, Russia, Japan, Italy, and France. Within a few weeks of the discovery, and within days of the announcement, fission experiments were conducted in Washington, New York, Paris, Copenhagen, Tokyo, and Leningrad. Igor Tamm, the Soviet Union's premier nuclear physicist, stated to his students in Leningrad, "This means that a weapon can be built which will destroy a city out to ten kilometers."

There never was any secret to nuclear fission. Countries had to make their own decisions as to whether to press on to a weapon. France was occupied and had no choice. Germany and Japan were counting on a short war; they gave the program no priority. Russia started but curtailed the effort when Germany invaded. England made the most early progress but transferred its efforts to the United States when the drain on its industry became excessive. Only the United States could spare the resources to do the job. When the United States succeeded, there was no question that others would follow. As in most technological developments, the only secret was that the task was actually being accomplished.

There lingers to this day a feeling that we could have kept the secret if it had not been for Russian espionage. Nonsense. Klaus Fuchs and others saved them time and money, but they would have succeeded anyhow. Espionage is a legitimate part of foreign policy in the Soviet Union, as it is in most nations. In modern industrial societies, technological secrets cannot be kept indefinitely. One can hope only to keep ahead of the potential enemy until the next invention comes along.

It should be possible to keep military secrets by using appropriate classification techniques, but it is impossible to keep unclassified developments under wraps. Once an item such as a robot or a microprocessor or a personal computer gets into the public domain, there is no way that item can be kept out of unfriendly hands. If we don't sell it, our trading partners will. This does not mean that we should spill our guts or give away the store, but it does say that we should use some common sense in export restrictions. The great strength of this country is not in its military secrets, but in its economic strength. If an item or a service capability is available for another country, we not only lose sales and jobs by denying its export, we brand ourselves as unreliable suppliers, hurting our economy across the board. American exporters are good citizens; when they apply for an export license, they are putting themselves on record that the export will not adversely affect our nation's security. I have searched the records in great detail, as have officials from the U.S. Department of Commerce; neither they nor I can find a single case where an export license denial has enhanced our national security or our foreign policy objectives, but we can find countless examples to the contrary. Let us discard our Ming mentality; we are not the only people who can do anything. Let us stop shooting ourselves in the foot. Let us bring some common sense to export policy.

•   •   •

So much for exports. Now take a look at imports.

At the close of World War II, we had everything to sell to a war-ravaged world — and in those days we sold it pretty much on our own terms, with our own definitions of secrecy, security, proper ideology, and morality. As a corollary to that condition, there wasn't very much to buy. Imports did not concern us. They didn't amount to much; they were not important. But to the people on the other side of the deal, they were very important indeed. Our imports were their exports. Their economies were weak; their infrastructures and their productive capacities had to be rebuilt; they needed foreign exchange. For them, it was export or die.

It was quite obvious to all our potential postwar trading partners, former friends and former foes alike, that they could not compete in industrial goods with the formidable productive capacity of the United States. We were preaching free trade. Why not? We had the capacity, we had the monopoly, we were the market leaders. We practically made it into a religion. What could they do? Nothing. Until they were rebuilt, they had to join the true church, go along with the gag.

The reactions of the various countries were diverse. Most of them felt that they needed import barriers to protect their rebuilding industries, but they had to move carefully lest they offend the American colossus. They all joined the GATT in 1947 and labored diligently to reduce one another's tariff barriers; to the United States these negotiations were a small part of the world rebuilding process, but to other nations they were crucial to economic survival. In the United States, not one person in ten thousand, even businessmen, has heard of the GATT, but throughout the rest of the free world, GATT negotiations are followed like baseball scores. And they play hardball.

The Canadians, unscathed by war and closely tied to the American economy, were enthusiastic free traders. The Europeans moved quickly. As soon as the war was over, Jean Monnet, the French minister of finance, promoted the idea of gradually uniting the economic interests of democratic European nations. By 1951 Belgium, France, Italy, Luxembourg, the Netherlands, and West Germany had formed the European Community to abolish all tariffs affecting trade among themselves, but they also set up a common tariff on goods imported from other countries. Great Britain went it alone for years, but finally joined the European Economic Community in 1973. The tariffs are high enough that U.S. companies have had to set up European subsidiaries to compete.

The Latin American countries first set up the Organization of American States to provide for the common defense, regional cooperation, and the peaceful settlement of controversies. Out of that grew the Andes Pact, entered into by most of the Central American and South American countries, including Argentina, Brazil, and Mexico. The Andes pact was set up not so much to exclude imports but to encourage corporations in developed countries to build factories in the member nations. Once a factory is established, barriers are set up against imports. This practice is now being followed in the Pacific basin. Generally speaking, foreign ownership in these new industries is limited to less than 50 percent. Such industrial policies will be even more prevalent in the future, particularly in China and India.

In the Middle East, Israel is a special case. Since it has no oil and few other natural resources, it exists practically as an economic ward of the United States. There is a story in Israel that if Moses had turned left instead of right when he came down from the mountain, that country would have struck oil and would have no economic woes. The oil-producing states, mostly Moslem, have long felt exploited by the United States and Europe. In 1960, joined by Ecuador and Venezuela, they formed the Organization of Petroleum Exporting Countries (OPEC). They didn't have much muscle until American oil consumption built up to the point where the United States, the petroleum giant, became a net oil importer in 1968. In 1973 King Faisal of Saudi Arabia imposed the infamous oil embargo in reprisal against the supporters of Israel during the Arab-Israeli war. The OPEC cartel became the strongest in history, literally controlling the world's economy for more than a decade. Its power is beginning to wane now because of market forces, but the experience shows that when sovereign nations choose to set industrial policies that upset free markets, it can take a mighty long time before free market forces can prevail.

Japan went it alone. It had no choice. A defeated nation, which had never had a chance to win a war, it was occupied by an enormously powerful enemy. It had no natural resources, it had inadequate geography for its population, its primitive industry was completely demolished, it had a strange culture, it was a pariah in the modern industrial world, it had a complex language not widely understood beyond its borders, it was surrounded by enemies whom it had ruthlessly tried to exploit, and it had nothing. No one needed it for anything.

The Japanese gave lip service to the concept of free trade. They had no culture of free trade; they had been until recently a collection of fiefdoms with strong local traditions and many barriers to commerce even within the individual islands. They had been ruled economically by the zaibatsu, the financial persons, who had teamed with the military on a foolish quest for economic lebensraum by force. But they also had a tradition of strong, bureaucratic discipline, and when the ruler said the name of the game was democratic capitalism at home and free trade abroad, democratic capitalism and free trade it was. They pushed the emperor aside, broke up the zaibatsu, set up a democratic capitalistic system modeled on the United States, and proceeded to hold free elections. They even passed a monopoly law and joined the GATT.

But they knew they had no chance to compete head to head with the United States; MacArthur knew it too. His orders were to get the Japanese economy going, and that he did. Before leaving in 1952, MacArthur's administrators allowed the Japanese to set up provisions for the protection of emerging industries; they allowed and encouraged exceptions to the monopoly law; they fostered cooperation between government, labor, and industry. They did their job well.

The Japanese had some things going for them. They were a homogeneous society; all spoke the same language and had the same cultural traditions. Their society was based on cooperation and discipline. Living on remote islands barren of natural resources, they were accustomed to hard work and sacrifice for sheer survival. As a defeated nation, they were occupied and ruled by a bewilderingly different army of white giants with a strange language and strange ideas. But the occupation was essentially benevolent and though they had to work hard and bear sacrifice for the sake of their children, they could still maintain their traditions and achieve their cultural independence.

Labor had a tradition of loyalty, cooperation, and subservience to employers; there was no adversary relationship and strikes were unheard of. Business and government got along well; it was sometimes difficult to tell which was which, so closely were they entwined. All had a common objective, the rebuilding of a nation. The Americans were happy to give them the tools with which to do it.

The Japanese set about rebuilding their country with diligence and vigor. They sent delegation after delegation to the United States, the new center of the universe, as centuries before they had sent delegations to China to learn the language, skills, and techniques. They protected their emerging industries, identifying and allocating home markets. They pooled research and development to maximize the use of their meager technological skills. They made exceptions to their monopoly law in the name of efficient markets; they couldn't afford competition or duplication.

They worked hard, and still do. They work six days a week to our five, a great competitive advantage. They set up a system of maximum savings: defer consumption; save for the future. They were delighted to have the American military umbrella, which allowed the weak nation protection from its enemies at no cost to itself, an enormous competitive advantage not available to her trading partners. Think of the efficiency possible in our economy if we had had no military expenditures and no shattering wars for the last forty years. Insofar as possible, they imported nothing but knowledge.

Out of all this grew the Japanese model. It is quite simple. They work hard and save their money. They have no military expenditures. They fight no wars, leaving that expense and disruption to others. They maximize cooperation among industry, government, and labor. They set common economic objectives. They identify high-volume markets. They set aside their antitrust laws and pool research and development. They protect their domestic markets by tariffs, subterfuge, and cultural tradition. They build up their production facilities, confident of their domestic markets. They arrange low-cost loans for their export industries; the loans do not come due until the business makes a profit, eliminating the requirement for short-term earnings. They close this low-cost capital market to foreigners. They price low for world market share. They spew out product at high volume and low price, then sit back and wait for the competition to go broke. Nothing to it. With closed capital and consumer markets, high financial leverage with no pressure for repayment of loans, and industries targeted for special consideration, the Japanese export markets are practically without risk.

All these restrictive practices go on all over the world while the United States goes blithely on, crippling our exports and scolding other nations about unfair policies without doing anything to combat them. We are still playing by Marquis of Queensberry rules while the other guys are swinging billy clubs.

The result of these badly conceived export and import policies is a creeping disaster. The starkest measure of the impending crisis is the balance of trade deficit. This measure is the amount by which exports exceed imports, or vice versa. The long-run ideal is for the two to be equal, although that never happens in the real world. In most of the postwar years, the United States ran a trade balance surplus as this nation exported to rebuild the world. Throughout history, imbalances were self-adjusting as the value of currencies varied to close the gap. If the trade balance ran a consistent surplus, the value of the currency increased, so that anyone who bought dollars to purchase American goods had to pay more for them, making exports more expensive and imports cheaper. That is why there were so many bargains in Europe in the fifties and sixties and right now, too. The dollar was strong and the European currencies were weak. In engineering, it is known as negative feedback, or self-correction. It is what keeps the volume in your automobile radio constant as the signal strength varies with distance.

In the last few years the whole system has gotten out of whack. As we continue to shoot ourselves in the foot with inefficient policies, we have become less competitive internationally; our exports have decreased and our imports have increased. But the currency no longer self-adjusts. Our low inflation and large budget deficits have led to high real interest rates that have attracted oodles of foreign capital to the United States, masking the feedback effect of the trade imbalance. The dollar has gotten even stronger, exports have continued to decrease, and imports have gotten cheaper. This is what the engineers call positive feedback. It's what causes the ear-shattering squeal in a public address system when a microphone is held too close to a loudspeaker.

A few years ago the trade balance turned negative. In 1981 it was $8 billion, in 1982 it was $30 billion, in 1983 it was $60 billion, in 1984 it was over $100 billion. Do you know what a $100 billion deficit means in terms of jobs? There is a rule of thumb that says $1 billion in sales provides thirty thousand jobs. If we import $1 billion worth of goods from another country, the jobs are created there and not here. While we are importing the goods, we are exporting the jobs. A $100 billion deficit means that we are exporting over 3 million jobs.

But, you say, we have low unemployment, and more people are working in the United States than ever before. True. Unfortunately, the jobs being created are in low-paying service jobs, while the high-paying jobs are disappearing. Well, you say, perhaps we are in a postindustrial phase and are developing into a high-technology and service economy. Academic poppycock! We cannot maintain a prosperous economy by selling each other high-technology hamburgers. We have to have goods to sell abroad, if only to get the foreign exchange to buy the imports, neglecting such crucial items as standard of living and national defense. They already know how to make hamburgers in Tokyo. We taught them.

The balance of payments deficit is a ticking time bomb. The obvious corrective first step is to reduce the deficit. But there are a number of trade policies we can improve very quickly, and simultaneously.

We can amend the Foreign Corrupt Practices Act to recognize the customs and the business realities of other countries. We can beef up the Export-Import Bank to counter subsidized foreign competition. We can stop requiring environmental impact statements for exports; we are a rich country, but many underdeveloped countries have higher priorities, such as food and shelter, than the environment. They should make their own choices. We can take a hard look at our secrecy policies, both military and industrial. They don't work.

We can stop trying to export our morality. We use economic sanctions to the point where we are encroaching on the sovereignty of other states and getting our exporters branded as unreliable suppliers.

Above all, we must realize that the free-trade emperor has no clothes. It's a wonderful, desirable long-term goal, but we can't force it on other nations. Japan, OPEC, and the European Economic Community don't believe in it, and never have. Look at the record.

This does not mean that we have to have a national industrial policy, which the academics call for. We have too many already. Nor should we try to emulate Japan. Our society can't do what its people do. Besides, Japan is a lame-duck nation, her supremacy already challenged by the hordes in the rest of the Pacific basin. But we should come out in the open and admit that we are protecting industries like steel and automobiles and textiles. We should hold these industries' feet to the fire and demand productivity for protection. As it is, we surreptitiously provide protection while sanctimoniously preaching free trade.

There is nothing politically, morally, or practically inconsistent with calling for deregulation at home and realistically competitive trade policies overseas. There is no contradiction in businessmen calling for the government to get off our backs at home and by our sides abroad. We are no longer King of the Hill. We are just another country out there fighting to make a living in a new international arena. Let us discard our Ming mentality. Let us not go into the battle limping, with a hole in our foot.

10

Commencement, Not Conclusion

WHEN I LAST LOOKED at China, the shining star of the magnificent Mings had darkened through the centuries into the malevolent maw of Mao Tsetung's Cultural Revolution, when radical Red Guards patrolled the streets, pillaging and vandalizing at will, closing the universities for four years and reducing the economy to chaos. It seemed that that great nation, like a common alcoholic or drug addict, must sink into the pits of despair before it could reach for the rungs of the ladder of renaissance. As Mao and his premier, Chou En-lai, approached the end of their natural lives in 1976, China suffered its final indignity under the rule of Mao's vindictive wife, Chiang Ch'ing, and her infamous Gang of Four, whose further degradations caused a bitter power struggle between the forces of radicalism and the forces of moderation. Fortunately for civilization, the forces of moderation were victorious. When the two rulers died in the same year, the moderates imprisoned the Gang of Four and began the rapid road to recovery.

Consistent with the modern compression of time, the degradation of centuries was reversed in less than a decade. The architect of this bloodless renaissance was an incongruous-looking little septuagenarian named Teng Hsiao-p'ing. His nickname is the Little Bottle, a play on the word *teng*. No movie star he. Teng is barely five feet tall, slim, his youthful features weather-beaten from the rigors of multiple imprisonments, his round eyes and slightly puffed cheeks making him vaguely reminiscent of a Cabbage Patch doll. Now without an official title, he took over in 1977 and promptly opened China to the world. The Ming mentality is long gone in China. Teng wants to assimilate our technology, absorb our management techniques, attract our capital. He has already had visits from premiers and presidents and ex-presidents, captivated the American public on his own visit to the United States, and proceeded to base his backward economy on the model of American democratic capitalism. The major accomplishment of his octogenarian year was to renounce the doctrines of Marx and Lenin as "no longer appropriate to solve our modern-day questions."

Think of it. Only forty years ago we "lost" China to the Communists. Thirty-five years ago we fought a sad war in Korea to stop the progress of the Red tide, actually goading the Chinese military into direct combat after the landing at Inchon. Thirty years ago we developed an antiballistic missile system, later abandoned, to defend our homeland against the perceived Chinese nuclear threat. Twenty-five years ago the fate of the offshore islands of Quemoy and Matsu was the central topic in a debate between John Kennedy and Richard Nixon, the debate that catapulted Kennedy into the presidency. Who remembers Quemoy and Matsu? Today they wouldn't make it into a game of Trivial Pursuit. Twenty years ago we were mired in the senseless war to stop the spread of communism into the hapless nation of Vietnam. Fifteen years ago we had no official diplomatic relations. Ten years ago we were still wrangling over which of the "two Chinas" to support.

Today the low tiled-roof houses that once lined Peking's network of residential alleys are being bulldozed. In their stead are Western-style high-rise buildings that tower over the city. A recent addition is the twenty-two-story, thousand-room Great Wall Hotel, by day its glass curtain walls incredulously reflecting the squalor of the old neighborhoods that remain, by night its glowing electric lights a beacon to attract the French, Japanese, German, and American barbarians called to aid this emerging nation in its quest to join the prosperity of Western capitalism.

Why did this transformation occur? It was not by force of arms, certainly. Every attempt we have made to force our will upon the nations of the Asian mainland has failed ignominiously. It was not by threat of nuclear annihilation or massive retaliation. Teng has not paid the slightest bit of attention to our nuclear posturings, our testing in the Pacific, or our aborted antiballistic missile program; nor has he rattled his own nuclear sabers. It was not by our policy of Communist containment; God knows, that has been a sad and bloody failure in the Far East. It was not by our preachings of morality or exhortations to human rights; China has a harsh and cruel history, but the metamorphosis is from within, not without. It was not by our trade policies, our boycotts, our embargoes, our Export Authorization Act, our Foreign Corrupt Practices Act; no, it was in spite of them. The change has come about for one simple, pragmatic reason, a recognition by China of the superiority of the democratic capitalistic system, a superiority that offers potential for prosperity to all, from the party potentate to the penniless peasant, from the warrior to the coolie, from the mandarin to the merchant. It is as simple as that — the most populous nation on earth converted to capitalism by example.

So can it be with the Russians. The Soviet economy is in tatters. Nothing works. Machinery breaks down; there are no spare parts. The very hotels erected as fancy façades for foreigners are falling apart from poor construction. This vast and fertile nation is incapable of feeding itself; it must import much of its grain. Fifty percent of its agricultural produce comes from the 10 percent of the farmland that the peasants are allowed to cultivate for their own use and sell on the open market. The official excuse is bad weather; if that is so, the Soviets are now in their sixty-sixth consecutive season of bad weather, a song that won't sing forever. Their military power is impressive, but in every comparative test in the Middle Eastern wars their equipment has proved vastly inferior, so inferior that the Egyptians sent them packing after their own last debacle, and the Syrians are having second thoughts after their ignominious performance against Western-built Israeli missiles.

The Soviet socialist philosophy is incapable of competition in modern industrial society. The central planning, the lack of market feedback, the absence of incentives, the unavailability of choice, the suppression of suggestion, the oppressive military burden are all insurmountable impediments to competition with the "invisible hand," with all its warts and pimples. The apparachniks who govern the Soviet society know this, and admit it privately, but the moderates who would effect change are held helpless under the hand of the aging leadership of the Politburo, a leadership that is nearing the end of its natural life, as were Mao Tse-tung and Chou En-lai in 1976. We should be ready when the time comes.

A healthy Soviet economy is not only in our economic interest, it is in our national security interest. It won't affect
their military particularly; they cream-skim theirs right off the
top. It can help world peace if the citizens of the Soviet Union
can free some time from the dull, dreary pursuit of basic
survival to broader concepts of cooperation. We should want
them to be fat, dumb, and happy, like us; then they won't
want to fight with anybody.

We and Russia are nuclear hostages to each other. There
is no military solution to the impasse between us — not build-
downs or freezes or Star Wars or SALT or START. Arms
control talks are almost peripheral issues. At the very best,
over this decade, we can hope to cut arms by 20 percent,
from fifty thousand nuclear warheads to forty thousand. So
what difference does that make? None. The Soviets don't care
biddledy-boo whether we have two aircraft carriers or twenty.
They know we are not going to start a war, and they certainly
know that they are not. They know better than we do that
they can't win. It was Nikita Khrushchev who said, "The
history of a social system will be decided not by rockets, not
by atomic and hydrogen bombs, but by the fact of which
system ensures greater material and spiritual benefits to man."

Their system is a loser, and they know it. The Soviet Union,
like China, is most impressed with the strength and versatility
of the American economy. To the extent that we hurt that
economy, by excessive military expenditures or by regressive
internal policies, we detract from our national security.

Somewhere in the Soviet Union there is a Russian Teng
Hsiao-p'ing. He will emerge slowly, inexorably, and, I think,
peacefully, forced to the forefront by the shrinking of the
world and the changing world economy. The Soviet Union
cannot continue to exist in isolation. We don't have to find

this person; better we should keep our hands off. But we should prepare ourselves for the coming by discarding our own prejudices and policies. Instead of making further preparations to blow up the world, we should do what we can to prepare for economic cooperation. We should ease up our restrictions on Soviet trade. It's worth the gamble.

Wouldn't it be nice to be preparing to deliver McDonald hamburger stands to Russia instead of MX's, skyscrapers instead of Star Wars, merchandise instead of missiles. It has happened in China. It can happen again.

But while we bust our britches with pride over the superiority of our system, we are in danger of losing our preeminence because others have started to use it better than we do. Starting with Japan, the Asian countries have adopted our system, while in the United States we are allowing it to deteriorate. The examples of Asian emergence are both spectacular and frightening. Singapore, Sri Lanka, Hong Kong, Malaysia, Thailand, Taiwan, Korea. All are booming, eclipsing even Japan, embracing capitalism, forming economy-oriented governments, building schools, training labor, while, on the other side of the world, Europe slips into a cyclical pseudo-socialism. The balance of economic power is changing, and changing rapidly.

Let me emphasize what we are competing with. Capable factory workers are available in Malaysia for $0.59 an hour, no fringes. In Bangkok, hard-working females come from the paddies into the city each day for $70 a month, a bowl of rice for lunch, and a bus ride each way. The products are just as good and just as available as anything made in the United States. In fact, you are using them now in great quantities and can't tell the difference. You are using $150 billion more of these products each year than foreign countries are using of American products, a trade reversal that has taken place in less than five years. When a billion Chinese get up to speed, the competition will be fierce.

● ● ●

The road to restoration of our international economic competitiveness will be long and difficult. The necessary short-term fixes — elimination of the budget deficit and adjustment of dollar exchange rates — will be tough enough; tackling the long-term problems will be even tougher. I am going to mention only a few of the new directions needed, and then sketchily, for they should be the subjects of another treatise.

In our government policies, particularly taxes, we shall have to emphasize work, savings, and investment, not consumption and redistribution of income. We shall have to reassess our self-appointed position as policeman to the world. The developing nations spend practically nothing on defense; why should we be their protector? We shall have to increase our productivity; this means automation and at least temporary loss of jobs. We shall have to strive for innovation, trodding upon sacred cows in education, tax policy, patents, and antitrust. We shall have to take a more realistic approach to trade policies, particularly export subsidies and trade concessions; this means more funding for the Export-Import Bank and a hard-nosed approach to negotiations under the General Agreement on Tariffs and Trade. We shall have to continue a degree of protectionism, but the protected segments of the economy must be held to strict programs of competitive reform.

The race will be arduous indeed, but it makes no sense to join it with holes in our arches. Before we can begin to do some new things right, we should correct some of the old things that we are doing wrong.

We should not be wasting hundreds of millions of dollars

on protection of such creatures as the snail darter and the striped bass. The snail darter exists in abundance and needs no protection. It is now recognized as being so abundant that it has been taken off the endangered species list; the whole Tellico Dam fiasco served no purpose whatever. The first environmental studies report that the effect of the Westway Project on the habitat of the striped bass cannot be determined. Any sensible person knows instinctively that in the vast ecosystem of the bass, the effect of one small landfill is negligible. Never mind that this legislation was misused to halt major construction projects, and that the opponents of Tellico and Westway never gave a tinker's damn about the fish. Legislation that encourages such mischief should not remain on the books.

Women should receive equal treatment with men in the marketplace; they still have a long way to go. But correction of past injustices does not excuse ignoring biological differences. De Toqueville stated that democracy will fail when minority groups insist on special treatment from society. We might as well throw in the towel if we insist on special treatment for a minority group that consists of a majority of the population.

The men who wrote the Constitution set up a marvelous system of checks and balances when they created the executive, the legislative, and the judicial branches of our government. Judicial activists are upsetting that balance as self-appointed interpreters of the Constitution. We cannot be internationally competitive with inexperienced judges running our schools, our public housing, our sewer systems, our elections, our power plants, and our mental health systems. The judges have become so aggressive that they are being mousetrapped; lackluster legislators are writing statutes so vaguely that affected parties are being forced into the courts, allowing

legislators to evade responsibility. The solution is not to turn
the judges into inevitably ineffective administrators, but for
the executive branch to veto legislation that does not meet
minimum standards of clarity and specificity.

Education is the key to competition. If we don't want to
work with our backs, we have to work with our brains. If we
are going to compete with coolie wages, we'll have to work
smarter. We can insist on equality of opportunity, but we
cannot realistically hope for equality of result. We need good
teachers and we need special attention for good students. We
need a thorough overhaul of bilingual education programs.
The cruelist handicap we can inflict on children in these United
States is not to teach them English.

Energy is the lifeblood of production. Our abundance of it
fueled this society from the turn of the century until 1968,
when we became a net importer of petroleum. Since then,
we have been going downhill competitively. Fossil energy is
in abundance now, but that won't last long. The energy of the
nucleus, fission or fusion, is intrinsically the cheapest and
safest form available to us and will certainly be the fuel of the
next century, as fossil fuels are used up. We have foolishly
priced it out of the market in the United States and are already
feeling the competitive pressure from Canada, Japan, and
France. Those of us who have worked with nuclear power
plants have always known that they are inherently safe, but
have never been able to prove it to the populace. Data from
Three Mile Island now show conclusively that the chance of
radioactivity escaping to the atmosphere is a thousand times
less than the design basis, and that there is absolutely no need
to evacuate the area in the event of a nuclear accident. I realize
that no one is going to accept these conclusions and that no
additional nuclear power plants will be built in this century,
but think of our children competing with those billion

Chinese. We can't afford to give away all our competitive advantages.

In the postwar period of our production monopoly, we built up, with our Ming mentality, an exaggerated sense of our own managing ability. There is a concept in manufacturing economics known as the economy of scale. It simply says that the more widgets you turn out on the same piece of equipment, the cheaper each one will be. This may seem pretty obvious to you, but you'd be surprised at how many Ph.D. theses were written in esoteric proof. Naturally, in order to realize the economies of scale, the widget makers became more and more specialized, and less and less adaptable to change. Woe to the engineer who tried to redesign the widget or substitute a gidget; the financial men would be on his back, complaining about the capital cost. Nobody worried about the competitive cost because there was no competition.

If one widget-making machine went out of whack or if there was a work stoppage, the whole system broke down. Managers soon came to feel that they could not afford redesigns or work stoppages and built up large inventories in case one part of the machinery went out of whack.

Lo and behold! Along came some people who built more flexible machines that could be redesigned and didn't require such large inventories; they also inspired their employees so that there wouldn't be work stoppages. They didn't have the economies of scale, but they had the business. Now our managers are trying to learn from them. Let's face it. We have good managers, but we're not perfect. We make mistakes. Let's learn from them.

Labor has similar problems. Back when we were the only producer, gains from productivity grew rapidly. Labor naturally deserved a piece of the action and got it. When labor and management fought about how to slice up the pie, their relations became atrocious, and the pie began to get smaller instead of bigger. The wage-price spiral continued after productivity increases stopped; inflation was the result. Inflation was fought with the worst possible fuel, cost-of-living adjustments, known as COLAs. Fortunately, in recent negotiations, cost-of-living adjustments have been cut way back. These agreements are known in the trade as Diet COLAs. We are beginning to learn.

I am reasonably optimistic that if we work hard and do sensible things, we can recover many of our international advantages. I am not at all sanguine about wage differentials. I think that big labor unions are priced out of the international market, which now means the domestic market also. Try as we may, I don't see how we can produce our way out of the differential between $50,000 per year and $0.59 per hour. That's a factor of over fifty. Something's going to have to give.

I hate to admit it, but the American public has always been suspicious of big business; it probably comes from our agrarian origins. One hundred years ago, people had good reason to be. Capitalism, raucous and swashbuckling, was in its early stages; there were few government regulations, and few choices for the consumer. The public and the politicians were frustrated in their inability to control abuses. In their frustration, they passed one of the most senseless pieces of legislation ever conceived, the Sherman Antitrust Act. Almost a century later, that misguided statute is still with us, outlawing all contracts, good or bad. Now we have government regulations galore, labor unions, foreign competition, and a plethora of products to choose from. It is virtually impossible for a predatory monopolist to emerge and survive. But the law is still on the books, with bevies of bureaucrats, public and private, dependent on its continuation, persistently instilling suspicion of the lurking predator waiting to devour us all. Some concepts in our society need modification; this one needs expurgation. Throw it all out; perhaps we should bring back some pieces, like forbidding cartels, but it is best to start from scratch.

The days of Fortress America with its insulating oceans are gone. Full 50 percent of our goods produced is subject to some kind of foreign competition. The American public insists on low-priced, high-quality goods; as consumers, it doesn't care where they come from. We are in an enormous trade imbalance. We cannot continue to enjoy these low-priced goods without exporting other goods with which to pay for them. If nothing else, we will need the foreign exchange. There are no ifs, ands, or buts about it. We must export, emigrate, or evaporate.

The external solutions to the problems of international competitiveness are not clearly in sight, but even the internal ones require major modifications to our societal values and our way of living. Are we up to the task? I say yes because I am encouraged by the adaptations I already see.

Life was onerous for the generation that grew up during the Great Depression; for a period, it was a time without hope. In contrast, the hardships of World War II were wrenching for its generation, but they were soul-satisfying because they brought a sense of sacrifice and common purpose. The postwar generation was like a bunch of little rich kids. Everything was there on a silver platter. They were King of the Hill and the United States was Chung-kuo, the center of the universe. The Ming mentality evolved, but something went wrong on the way to the palace. They set out to mold the world in their image, but it didn't happen according to the script. In frustration, the Ming mentality metamorphosed into the malaise of the Me Generation, a spiritual low point for America.

Each generation is a secret society; it has its own incommunicable enthusiasms, tastes, and interests, which are a mystery both to its predecessors and to posterity. The generation that is coming of age is no exception. It has grown up observing the failure of the promise of the Great Society; it has matured in the ignominy of Vietnam and Watergate; it has wept in the agony of the assassinations; it has writhed under the contumely of the Ayatollah; it has watched with horror the panorama of starvation in Africa; it lives under the threat of instant annihilation. It is a generation mature beyond its age.

This generation has already learned that we cannot be all things to all people, that we cannot instantly solve the world's problems, that we cannot force change by throwing either money or missiles at those who do not share our views. If there is a word to characterize it, that word is *pragmatism*.

I have talked to my children and to my children's children and to their friends. I have held seminars at high schools and at universities. I have listened on airplanes and in cocktail lounges. These young people realize that more weapons do not provide more safety or stability; they recognize that we are depriving them of their patrimony by excessive budget deficits and by unearned Social Security benefits that they cannot hope to receive; they understand that there are no free lunches; they travel and watch television and instinctively comprehend the problems of international competitiveness. That's why they are so conservative. That's why they voted so overwhelmingly for conservatism in the last elections. They go to school to get jobs, not to evade the draft. Smokestacks to them, as to me, represent employment, not pollution. To them, the economy is important, not something for derision. They have no intention of performing hysterectomies on the geese that lay the golden eggs. That instinctive recognition is a lesson that the rest of us must relearn. The health of our economy is fundamental to our material well-being, to our national security, and to the inner spirit of our society.

The very foundation of a civilized society is that it gives sustenance and support from its economic surplus to those who do not produce food or clothing or other economically useful goods themselves, but give society other contributions such as military protection or succor or beauty or spiritual satisfaction in return. It makes no difference what you call the output — wages, profits, dividends, savings, capital investment, or a child's allowance — it must come from the surplus of the economic system. It must come first from the efforts and impulses of those who make shoes or provide capital or produce power or collect scrap iron. It remains also true that there is a limit that can be paid out of that economic surplus, for whatever noble purpose, without society suffering from that burden. We can ill afford to endanger the existence of that surplus by the continuation of economically destructive practices.

As we focus our attention more sharply on the changing world economy in this penultimate decade of the millennium, we must ever keep in mind that what we consider the hallmarks of civilization — charity, art, learning, law, government — subsist primarily from the surplus of those who till or spin or trade the wares of those who do. In the final analysis, only a strong and healthy economy can bear a civilized international fruit.